SpringerBriefs in Business

For other titles published in this series, go to
http://www.springer.com/series/8860

Roland Benedikter

Social Banking and Social Finance

Answers to the Economic Crisis

Springer

Roland Benedikter
Stanford University
The Europe Center
Stanford, CA, USA
rben@stanford.edu

ISBN 978-1-4419-7773-1 e-ISBN 978-1-4419-7774-8
DOI 10.1007/978-1-4419-7774-8
Springer New York Dordrecht Heidelberg London

Printed on acid-free paper

Springer is part of Springer Science+Business Media (www.springer.com)

For Ariane and Judith

Foreword

In this intellectually provocative volume, Roland Benedikter provides a lucid, cutting-edge treatment of the present-day process of banking and financing in the global economy. The description of the anatomy of the crisis of 2007–2010 is followed by a disquieting analysis of the many pathologies involved, which, if not cured, might jeopardize the stability of our model of Western democratic social order. The sense of omnipotence, fostered over the last three decades by an ambivalent economic theory that insisted on the self-referential nature of finance, came to dominate the mental habitus not only of traders and financial institutions, but also of political authorities and educational agencies.

Against such a picture, Benedikter advances the proposal of social banking and social finance as new, progressive approaches to money and finance, capable of reorienting the present situation. The author not only provides a most useful array of information about social banks, but successfully endeavors to make explicit the philosophical background underneath this specific mode of exercising the banking and finance activity.

All the great economists, from Adam Smith onward, have recognized that economic institutions – such as the banking and finance system – do not emerge in a cultural vacuum, as if they were given by nature. They have also recognized that market institutions generate and induce desirable as well as undesirable social traits. It follows that we cannot simply exonerate ourselves from the duty of considering the feedbacks of specific economic arrangements on human character. The main point advanced by the author of this volume is that there is not a unique route to economic progress. On the contrary, there is a variety of models of market economy, each one of them in tune with a particular cultural matrix.

According to Roland Benedikter, finance can once again become a humane – and humanistic – activity in the form of social banking and social finance, where interpersonal relations (not to be confused with mere social interactions) and ethical values occupy the center of the stage.

In this sense, this volume represents an important addition to the literature groping for a new "financial humanism" in our time. Benedikter has rendered us a great service by contributing so much to this urgently needed area of inquiry. The closely knit narrative tells a fascinating story, so much so that the reader feels that one cannot leave it aside too lightly.

I would strongly recommend the reading of this volume.

Cambridge, Massachusetts
December 2010

Stefano Zamagni, PhD
Professor of Economics
Johns Hopkins University
Member of the Academic Committee
of the Human Development,
Capability and Poverty International
Research Center (HDCPRC)
Harvard University

Introduction

The global financial and economic crisis, which began in 2007 and is still having repercussions in 2010, instigated the re-evaluation of the way we do business in many parts of the world. Coming under renewed scrutiny are particularly our financial institutions and the political will to regulate them in ways that will protect the assets of those who have trusted their fiduciary commitments, perhaps too easily.

The emerging fields of social banking and social finance represent fairly recent attempts to include broader considerations of fairness, social value, and justice in our models of economic well-being. They are approaches to the financial industry that have surfaced and gained public attention mainly during the most recent economic crisis. In the wake of this crisis, they may provide useful lessons concerning how to improve local and global financial systems by serving as "best practice" examples.

Why, how, and where?

Social banks were among the most successful economic endeavors worldwide during the 2007–2010 period with annual growth rates of up to 30%, whereas most mainstream banks suffered during the global crisis. Social banking is not about fundamentally changing the capitalistic system, but rather about improving some of its core features by putting into practical use the *triple bottom line* principle which identifies *three areas of focus*: profit, people, and the planet – instead of profit alone. To be useful for the greater task of improving the global financial system, a comparison between social banks in Europe and the United States, such as the one contained in this volume, proves to be particularly fertile – because most of the existing social banks are currently found on the two sides of the Atlantic, and because their differences and similarities are instructive.

While this brief volume is not restricted to the most recent economic crisis, it uses it as the starting point to explore the general approach of social banking and social finance now being practiced in Europe and in the United States. It has been written in cooperation and exchange with some of the most important leaders of social banks of the world.

The main audience for this volume are students and teachers in colleges and universities, members of the civil society as well as "average" citizens who want to know more about how to concretely improve the current management of money and finance. Thus, the primary goal of this volume is to enhance the "financial literacy" of the general population, among them first and foremost the future generations of "world citizens." It attempts to explain some perspectives of the unprecedented global financial crisis of 2007–2010 in an easily accessible way in the hope that new approaches can be developed to ensure innovation as a feasible alternative to our past focus.

I hope this volume succeeds in its task.

Stanford, California
December 2010

Karen S. Cook, PhD
Ray Lyman Wilbur Professor of Sociology
Chair of the Department of Sociology
Director of the Institute for Research
in the Social Sciences
Stanford University

Acknowledgments

My thanks belong to The Europe Center of Stanford University, to the Stanford Program on International and Cross-Cultural Education (SPICE), and to the Orfalea Center for Global and International Studies of the University of California at Santa Barbara, which have encouraged and generously supported the writing of this volume. I particularly thank Amir Eshel, Roland Hsu, and Laura Seaman (Stanford) and Mark Juergensmeyer and Victor Faessel (Santa Barbara).

This text has been written in cooperation with Julian Kühn, director of the Institute for Social Banking Bochum, Germany, and executive board member of the GLS Treuhand Foundation. Julian has been a chief executive and board member in the international social banking sector for more than two decades. His direct experience in the field was of inestimable value for this text.

I further thank David K. Korslund, PhD, Global Alliance for Banking on Values London; Sven Remer, PhD, Institute for Social Banking Bochum; and Jack Ucciferri, Orfalea Center for Global and International Studies, University of California at Santa Barbara, for carefully reviewing the manuscript and giving advice.

Last but not least, I thank Nick Philipson, Charlotte Cusumano, and Elizabeth Aseritis for lectoring and editing this volume.

Stanford University
December 2010

Roland Benedikter

Contents

Social Banking and Social Finance

Abstract This small volume provides a concise introduction to contemporary social banking and social finance. Written in a short and easily understandable manner, it explains the history, the philosophy, the current state, and the perspectives of social banking and social finance. It describes their place within the global economy and the visions of their "global alliances" for the years to come. The focus is on the basic mindset that gave birth to social banks about a century ago, and that still constitutes their main driving force in the age of globalization, and on the comparison of the current state of social banking in the United States and Europe. Since most social banks are found on both sides of the Atlantic, their interplay can be considered as instructive also regarding the worldwide development of social finance.

This volume consists of three parts. Part 1: Social banks have been among the most successful financial institutions worldwide during the economic crisis of 2007–2010 and have emerged strengthened by it. Therefore, the volume provides a short analysis of this crisis from the viewpoint of social banking and social finance. Part 2: It then describes the main ideas and methods of social banking as new approaches to money and finance, capable of re-orienting the financial system in order to avoid further crises. Part 3: Finally, it draws the perspective of how social banking and social finance – as integral parts of the growing global civil society and the broader international movement toward sustainability – may work together with the mainstream banking and finance industry by serving as "best practice" examples in selected fields.

Keywords Financial and economic crisis of 2007–2010 · Globalization · Capitalism · Civil society · Financepeace · Financial humanism · Liberation finance · Microfinance · Social banking · Social finance · Sustainability · Triple bottom line

1 Preface by the author: Recommendations on the Didactical Use of This Volume

Social banking and social finance are relatively new developments within the international banking and finance industry. While their "basic mindset" dates back about

R. Benedikter, *Social Banking and Social Finance*, SpringerBriefs in Business,
DOI 10.1007/978-1-4419-7774-8_1, © Roland Benedikter 2011

100 years, their establishment as modern institutions has been only a recent process since the 1970s. While most social banks developed *locally* in competition with the mainstream banking and finance business, their rise was closely interwoven with the spread of *national* and *international* civil society movements in the 1980s and 1990s. And while early social finance movements brought together social activists and innovators already since the financial and economic crises of the first half of the 20th century, their surfacing to the attention of the broader public of our days, as well as their affirmation as serious actors in an increasingly multifaceted concert of global financial players, occurred only with the most recent financial and economic crisis.

Indeed, there is some evidence that the definitive consecration and recognition of social banking and social finance institutions as parts of the global financial and economic system occurred not before the crisis years of 2007–2010, when they celebrated an overwhelming success by factually doubling their assets within less than 3 years. In doing so, they benefited from a broad spectrum of customers who were disappointed with mainstream finance and who started to shift remarkable amounts of money to social banks – some of them in protest, but most in search of a better perspective: of transparency and reliability, a down-to-earth approach of investment, a focus in the "real economy" with practical local ties (instead of abstract international speculation), a new "financial humanism" in the form of a heightened responsibility for sustainable development both in the social and in the environmental spheres (instead of maximum short-term gains at any cost, which proved to be socially and environmentally unhealthy). This shift toward social finance was, in its essence, part of a basic mindset shift under the influence of the crisis. It increased the potentials and the outreach of social banks noticeably.

Today, in the aftermath of the peak of the crisis, social banks find themselves in a situation so far unprecedented in their history. Although it would be premature to speak of a "breakthrough" toward becoming actors of equal importance to the international mainstream financial players, social banks have stably established themselves on a worldwide scale. They have become realities that can no longer be ignored. Their viewpoints on economic and social development, in the past often considered as "alternative" or "exotic", have become part of the ratio of public discourse.

Strengthened by this new visibility, social banks have forged worldwide alliances that aspire to provide "best practice" examples of how to run banking and finance in a less speculative, more reality-oriented manner in order to avoid further crises. While social banks do no pretend to change the basic pillars of current capitalism, they conceive themselves as progressive, i.e., more community- and environmental-friendly approaches to capital and money: as more sustainable forms of finance. They envision themselves as parts of the global trend toward a new "human ecology," connected with a vast array of innovative fields which comprise, among others, green technologies and renewable energies, free software and open knowledge, civil society community participation, and grass roots democracy. All of these developments foster a new combination of global and local (sometimes branded "glocal"), as well as a new, conscious intertwinement between private and public. And all of them believe in the slogan "All different – all equal" propagated years ago by the

United Nations. Indeed, social banking is about fostering radical individual creativity through the creation of greater social fairness. Since money stands in the midst of the capitalistic society of our days, social banking is an approach to finance that is relevant to all these developments.

In short, what becomes visible today is that although social banks – as well as the social finance sector, which comprises not only banks but also foundations and social enterprises – are numerically and quantitatively still relatively small factors within the international financial business, their importance is growing. This momentum creates a side effect which in the long run may be of greater importance than the sheer numbers of assets: it starts to create a cultural influence.

Social banks are becoming cultural powers or, to better put it, timely expressions of the contemporary cultural innovation. To put it with the director of the Birkbeck Institute for the Humanities of the University of London, Slavoj Zizek, social banking starts to function as an "agent of economical subjectivation": by addressing a *specific* and *confined* field of the current societal system (i.e. the financial dimension), it starts to influence and thus to change the system as a whole.

This situation is, from my viewpoint, similar to the momentum which progressive civil society organizations dedicated to the environment, like for example "Greenpeace" dedicated to the rescue of nature, represented in the 1980s and 1990s. One single whale saved by Greenpeace was factually only one single whale, but the action was about *whales* and, by extension, *whale catching* as such, and even more – about our relationship with animals and the planet. Like Greenpeace in its best days (and they are certainly not over yet!), social banks today are competing for a "symbolic worldview supremacy" in their field. Like Greenpeace in the days of the worst environmental pollution (and the damaging mindset behind it), social banks after the worst financial crisis in decades are increasingly recognized by the broader public as actors that may contribute to correct things – i.e., as constituent parts of a new culture of finance.

As we will see, the affinities reach out also into the terminological field, but with changed presuppositions. As "Greenpeace" was regarded as "rebellious" by the institutionalized political spheres of the 1980s and 1990s, today there is a broad political call for a new "Financepeace" to be co-inspired by alternative institutions like social banks – a call issued officially by nobody less than a group of members of the European Parliament in Brussels, which represents 27 nations with more than 490 million European citizens.

Without doubt, this positive reputation may be only temporary, or reveal itself as marginal. In any case, the current situation puts a lot of new responsibility on the social finance sector, now in a much broader and internationally received dimension than ever before.

In this situation of transition, the present volume provides an introduction to the philosophy, methods, current organization, and perspectives of social banking and social finance. To tie this information to the current state of affairs, it uses the crisis of 2007–2010 as a point of departure.

Nevertheless, it has no pretension to explain the full array of origins and causes of this crisis, since the latter was of very, maybe even exceptionally, complex origins. Thus, the following pages are about sketching only some main motives that triggered the crisis, in order to see to which extent social banking and social finance may provide answers to the shortfalls of the mainstream system. One "main motive" of the crisis of 2007–2010 consists, in the view of most social bankers, of what we will call the "Sandglass principle" of "neoliberal" mainstream capitalism between 1989 and 2007 (including its surviving remnants until today).

The text is structured in three parts as follows:

1. A short and simplifying analysis of the crisis of 2007–2010 (Sections 2 and 3);
2. An introduction to social banking and social finance as answers to the crisis in selected fields (Sections 4–9);
3. Perspectives resulting from the dialogue between the mainstream financial industry and social banking for the future (Sections 10–14).

In addressing these points, this volume has a didactical stance. Its main purpose is to serve students and teachers, the civil society, and the broader public.

The volume focuses on the comparison between the United States and Europe. The two primary reasons are

- *first*, that the large majority of social banking and social finance institutions are still found on both sides of the Atlantic;
- *second*, that by analyzing their interaction and relationship, an introductory overview of the basic issues connected with the topic on an international dimension can be achieved.

While the center of attention of this volume lies on social banking and social finance as innovative models to improve the existing capitalistic system, it also tries to introduce some basic critical understanding of how the current system of money and finance works. This is another reason why I depart from the economic and financial crisis of 2007–2010.

In order to serve its didactical purposes, I have structured the text as a *dialogue between the main text and the footnotes*. The main text gives the essence, while the footnotes comment on it, question it, or complement it – and thus differentiate it to the extent that is necessary to create a "living" and open picture. I hope that with this "two-dimensional" method, an inner dialogue within the reader is stimulated that may open up questions (which in my view are of greater importance than "answers,") and that may serve as a basis for further discussions.

I suggest the 12 sections to be used as 12 single lessons. In my experience, the procedure that has proven to be most effective for students and teachers is to read through the whole volume and then review each section, with two groups giving presentations on each of the parts: one or more students giving their personal account of the *main text* and others commenting on it with the help of the *footnotes*. Another idea to make the sometimes complex content appealing to "beginners" includes the option to designate individual students and/or civil society members to "play" the persons that are cited in the text, by reading (or reciting) their statements or by acting in their place. I encourage the reader to "use" the text actively in a "Brechtian" sense: that is, the text wants to be "used" rather than to be studied and then simply "repeated." Such an approach is, in my view, appropriate to the spirit of the topic.

I hope that the material provided in the footnotes and in the "further reading" list that includes easily accessible videos, acoustic statements, images, and texts from the Internet may stimulate independent inquisitiveness and research by the reader.[1]

2 The Financial and Economic Crisis of 2007–2010: A View from the Standpoint of Social Banking and Social Finance

> "Sometimes it's a crisis that forces change. The world that emerges out of the economic and financial crisis of 2007–2010 won't be the same. The banking and finance system will be based on sounder principles. There's a huge opportunity over the next 10 or 20 years (to improve things)."
>
> Gordon Brown, Prime Minister of the United Kingdom 2007–2010, longest serving Chancellor of the Exchequer (that is, minister responsible for all economic and financial matters) of the United Kingdom in history (1997–2007), April 6, 2009

From 2007 to 2010, the U.S. *mortgage crisis* first turned into an international *banking and financial crisis* (in its beginnings often called *credit crunch*). Then, it expanded into a global *economic crisis*.

What happened? How can we understand the basics of this most important financial and economic crisis of our times, one of the most influential international crises after World War II? [2,3]

---

[1] In addition to peer reviewed articles, books and media productions by experts and practicioners, this material consciously includes, even though to a minor extent, civil society cooperative information and shared knowledge, a.o. from Wikipedia, green economy activist sites, Youtube, alternative news and commentary blogs like the Huffington Post, and similar sources. The reason is that these in their majority open and democratic collaborative efforts "from below", i.e. through public participation of the civil society, are in principle and as such (though not in all their realizations for sure, and obviously with all the pros and cons involved) congenial with the creative – e.g. community oriented, participatory and basis democratic – approach of social banking and social finance. In the specific case of this booklet and its scope, I don't think that these sources should and can any longer be excluded from a serious, i.e. rational, experimental and progressive discourse about finance and economics, although I know that some colleagues may see this elsewise (and certainly with well founded reasons whose validity I wouldn't deny). Regarding the debate about the pros and cons as well as the potentials and limits of such an approach see the more accurate discussion in footnote 243.

[2] There are two main points that we have to keep in mind when attempting to understand the financial and economic crisis of 2007–2010.

First, there are multiple ways to look at the complex interweavement of causes and factors that led to this crisis, as well as to its effects and outcomes. We can discern at least seven different ways to analyze the crisis that have surfaced through the public and academic discussions of the last years; in essence, they correspond to the seven types of answers to the crisis discussed in this

If we abridge things a bit, simplify them to an acceptable extent, and try to start with what happened first (that is, with the so-called "phenomenology", or with

volume in part 10. Sure enough, the multifacetedness of viewpoints, which are often "incommensurable" (J.-F. Lyotard) with each other, but which at the same time all seem to catch in some way important aspects that have their own legitimacy and plausibility (and have therefore to be included in the attempt toward a balanced and integrative view), is certainly sometimes confusing and discouraging. But we have to get used to the current situation of "interpretational pluralism," because it applies to basically every important social development in today's age of "ripe modernity" (J. Habermas). This is because the democratic Western societies have reached a level of complexity where many different positions can – and shall – coexist aside of each other in order to catch the greater picture. Thus, the historical moment of our culture is characterized by the principle of "deep ambivalence" (Z. Bauman) as a creative moment. "Deep ambivalence" means that everything observed, including traumatic global events like the crisis, presents features that are often contradictory and dialectic in nature, and can thus be "read" in different ways.

What we can learn from this situation in my view is that we should be open to appreciate and to recognize a vast array of different approaches of understanding, without excluding anyone in the first place, and – as far as possible – without biases against none of them. Only later on, we may decide which one makes most sense to us, and which one not. So the first rational step would be to stay openminded to many approaches. That includes "alternative" hypotheses about – and understandings of – the crisis like the one presented on the following pages, inspired by the viewpoint of social banking and social finance. The point in the first place is not if this viewpoint is "right" or "wrong", but if it can open new views within the pluralistic concert of timely interpretations. The following is – and certainly wants to be – an "alternative," non-mainstream approach of "reading" the crisis. Nevertheless, this approach does not conceive itself as being opposed to other viewpoints, but rather as complementary to them, as far as possible. I hope that it will be received in this sense.

Second, the way we look at the crisis and how we observe and understand its basic features, besides all open-mindedness depends *also* unavoidably on the ideological, philosophical, and methodological standpoint we (consciously and unconsciously) hold. That seems to be a paradox, but seems how our mind works. Our mind is open, on the one hand, but it is also bound to certain previously made experiences *at the same time*. So, for example, a Marxist, even if she or he sincerely tries her or his best to be openminded, may read the crisis in a very different way than a neoconservative, and both may argue that the viewpoint of the other is not correct. The dispute that is taking place today – and that will most probably continue over the years to come, as long as there is no consensually accepted interpretation of the crisis, its origins, and its effects, not to mention how to prevent further crises – is due to the fact that there are many ideological factions, who besides sharing certain basic judgments, are often battling each other for "interpretation supremacy."

They are not seldomly accusing each other to not understand things properly – because, for example, of allegedly not being "scientific enough", not having the "right mindset", of not being "empirical enough" or (on the contrary) of being too tied to specific empirical findings, or because of accusing each other simply of "not being a (good) economist" (which usually means not to be a *mainstream* economist of this or that affiliation).

I will go into this problem of "interpretation power plays" with regard to the crisis more in-depth at the end of this publication. In order to make things not too complicated right from the start, let me preventively just say this here: there is in the contemporary scientific discussion the question of whether we can overcome our unconscious fixations at all, in order to be open-minded. According to the findings of some important social thinkers of the past three centuries like Immanuel Kant, John Dewey, Jacques Derrida, Jürgen Habermas, Helene Cixous, Colin McGinn, or Judith Butler, we construct our own realities by our convictions: that is, we always understand

"what became visible" at first glance), we would say that the crisis first surfaced in 2007. A critical mass of the US middle class was not able to repay the mortgage loans they had taken over to finance the purchase of their houses. Some therefore

---

what we already know, and we see what we project into those things and events that we have decided to observe. Our (conscious and unconscious) convictions influence our judgments. That means that our judgments are subjective, and unconsciously bound to prejudices (according to the theory of modern "hermeneutics," which is the art of interpreting things according to German philosopher Hans Georg Gadamer). But in contrast, we in most cases believe that our judgments are "objective." That is due to the fact that our mind does not tend to observe itself when it is working, but rather "loses" itself in the things observed, and thus in most cases it is not conscious of its own act of "constructing" its own world. Thus, the result is that in judging things we are open to make new experiences by observing things, and at the same time we are bound to what we know, and believe.

If this paradoxical situation is the case: that we always try to be open-minded because we feel that it helps us to understand things from different viewpoints, and thus in a more realistic way, and that *at the same time* we are always unavoidably bound to our (conscious and unconscious) convictions and expectations, which bind us to certain restricted positions – then it is important to note right from the start that social banking and social finance in principle, and as such belong to a mindset that by its very basic aspiration is trying to become conscious of this inner dualism, and to work with it to let open-mindedness prevail.

As we will see in the "philosophical" subdivisions dedicated to the origins and basic concepts of social banking and social finance, social banking and social finance belong to a mindset that is the mindset of the contemporary civil society: a mindset that we will call an "idealistic pragmatism," because it tries not to be ideological, but pragmatic, while conceding at the same time that its own attempt is already a "construct" and nothing given by nature; that is, idealistic in its essence, while based on a conscious and unconscious decision. Accordingly, social banking and social finance are in principle not about confrontation and division by applying prejudices against (or in defense of) something or somebody, but about a sober, down-to-earth and realistic attempt to recognize what are the needs of the time. Applied to economy and finance as co-social endeavors: they are *not* about a "speculative economy," which is anonymous and based on abstract numbers; on the contrary, they are about the "real economy," tied to concrete, evolving realities and to "living people" who are connected with ambiguous life realities that are as vulnerable as they are beautiful.

Throughout the pages of this volume, we will approach this "different" and at the same time "integrative" mindset, get to know the basics of its inner and outer dimensions, and see how they fit. At the end of all this, I will come back to the point how social banking and social finance are more about a mindset with which to look at financial and economic issues in a more inclusive way, than about any solution in particular that may rapidly change according to the contexts and to history (solutions that have to be found, according to social banking and social finance, in every single case anew by individual and collective moral intuition).

[3] From what said previously, it follows that any attempt to understand the crisis is of course not the only way to look at it. This is a. o. due to the fact that the two "bubbles" that we are going to discuss as two main (and interacting) pillars of the crisis: the "real estate bubble" and the "derivative bubble" are just two *leitmotifs* in a certainly much more complex overall puzzle. I don't even exclude that it could eventually turn out that per se they have not been the most important factors. Therefore, the explanation presented here should neither be taken as the "whole truth," nor should it be reduced to the notion of being an all too reductionistic, too simplifying, or "only marginal" viewpoint. It is one reading option of what happened among others – not more, and not less.

called this *first stage* of the crisis "the unraveling of a housing bubble."[4] What does that mean? It means this:

In the two decades before the crisis (i.e. since the mid-1980s) many families and average citizens mainly in the United States (less in Europe, even if some European countries, particularly Ireland and the UK, followed similar paths) had taken on increasingly large mortgages, because the housing market was greatly overpriced.

One reason contributing to this situation was the fact that, among other factors, banks were used to give easy credit to all kinds of customers active in – and to all kinds of businesses related to – the real estate market. The more money banks pumped into the housing market in the form of millions of loans, the more the prices went up, and this created a spiral of ever-increasing housing prices that needed always more loans (i.e., bank debts by average customers) to be financed.

The main intent of banks in this "game" was obviously to make gains by lending ever-more money to house buyers, and thus by getting more returns through the interest rates charged to home buyers. The housing market became a big core segment of profit for most mainstream banks of the period, and thus an important factor for the national economy. As a "cash cow" for the financial industry it grew even more important than the "real economy" (i.e., those productive activities that concretely "create" something). The real estate market in large part does not create anything new, but trades and re-trades what is already there (the houses); therefore, it seemed less risky for banks and investors to handle than to fund "open" productive activities with their many inherent risks.

Between the early 1990s and the outbreak of the crisis in 2007, the increasing indebtedness of large portions of the US, Irish, English and other populations as a result of the seemingly never-ending "real estate upward spiral" was generally accepted as the norm.

It was accepted by the debtors because first of all they needed a house, and second, because their strategy in most cases consisted of buying a house using (in great part) borrowed money, keeping it for a certain period – for example, 5 years – and then selling it, hoping that during these 5 years the prices would go up faster than the sum of their debts. If this was the case, the house would not only bring back the borrowed capital, but also generate a profit bigger than the sum of the interests. So the borrowed sum including interests could have been repaid by the debtor to the bank, and a surplus would have been made, on the basis of which a new house could be bought – in order to start the game again. In the course of the years, this game would lead – as many hoped – to an always better and bigger, more expensive house for the debtor.

Obviously this game could only continue if the housing prices would increase continuously, and to a noticeable extent. In the hope that this would happen, many average house buyers took mortgages that were far beyond their possibilities of

---

[4]G. Assenza and A. Martynau: The Financial Crisis: A Brief History of the Future. In: E. Fein (ed.): Economy in The Times of Change. Ideas and Impulses for an Integral Economy of the Future (Wirtschaft in der Zeitenwende. Ideen und Impulse für eine integrale Ökonomie der Zukunft). The Institute for Integral Studies IFIS, Freiburg im Breisgau 2010, p. 10.

repayment and bought overpriced houses that they could not afford with their income. And the banks, taking profit of the overall game, gave them mortgages that they in many cases knew could not be repaid by the income and the assets of the debtor. It was a high risk game for everybody, fed by the increase of the housing prices which thus had to be kept going up at any price.

This in many ways artificial "upspiraling" of the housing prices was also in the interest of the various advertising and selling partners of the banking and finance industry, such as brokers and intermediary traders.

Last but not least, this overall development seemed to be also in the interest of the "neoliberal" Western governments of the period. First, because of their conviction that markets regulate themselves, and that money goes from alone where it works best and produces the greatest good, no particular regulation needed; second, because the "housing price spiral" seemed to present the chance for a better house for everybody over time, most notably without governmental support; and third, because of the effect of the overall mechanism to increase inflation, seen by the prevailing financial and economic theory of the times as something positive for reducing the national debt not by repaying it, but by factually devaluing the owed amounts.[5]

Thus, the continuous rise in housing prices seemed to be in everybody's interest: of the banks, the home owners, the traders and brokers, and the nation.[6]

Again, the whole mechanism could only function if prices continued to increase in principle indefinitely, helped by such factors as inflation. That under certain circumstances it could also be creating negative effects and thus was exposed to a potentially dangerous setback – for example, if money liquidity were to be low, or if there would be a lack of trust in the overall mechanism such that customers were not buying overpriced houses anymore because of a low inflation rate, or simply because the disproportion between prices and incomes would become too big for the average customer to find the requested mortgages. As it seems, none of these factors ever entered the minds of those who favored that system. And to be honest, that was basically everybody – with banks sitting in the first row of the supporters.

---

[5]I will examine that last aspect later (see footnote 47). In my view it is important at this point to understand right from the start the overall "silent agreement" between different societal groups – coming from different social classes! – which contributed to the mechanisms that created the preconditions for the crisis. What we can say already here is that the mechanisms of the interweavment of interests that gave origin to the crisis were of no "class origin." They were due to an implicit consensus of basically all the social classes, at least in the United States and (with some restrictions) also in the rest of the Western world. That is one main reason why I regard most "Marxist" and classically "leftist" approaches to understand the crisis as inappropriate, or at least as one-sided.

[6]Cf. the exemplary case study in: R. Benders: Cleveland against Deutsche Bank (Cleveland gegen Deutsche Bank). In: Handelsblatt Düsseldorf, August 26, 2010. Sure enough, the case here is not about Deutsche Bank in particular, but about the business practices of mainstream banks in the "neoliberal" period between 1989 and 2007 in general, as well as about the overall systemic mechanisms (including expectations and hopes of large parts of the population) they created.

This mechanism of a (necessarily) ever-increasing artificial overpricing of the housing market with the active participation of the lending policies of banks and financial institutions was one main outcome of the "neoliberal" triumph of a "laissez-faire" capitalism that drew its ideological strength and conviction from the triumph over communism (the so-called "concretely existing socialism") with the fall of the Berlin Wall in 1989 and the collapse of communism in 1991. It was one effect of the alleged "end of history,"[7] with a radically deregulated capitalistic lifestyle emphatically propagated by leading thinkers like Francis Fukuyama[8] as the only one left for humanity on earth: Speculative capitalism was not the question, speculative capitalism was the answer. Money, *more* money for sure – or in other words the endless multiplication of money became the basic, all-encompassing cure for the individual, the community, and the nation. That was not only the economic, but also the leading political and – maybe most important – the implicit cultural *mantra* of the past two decades.

The effect was that overpricing rapidly heated up the real estate market to unsustainable levels. In the United States for example, home prices increased up to 90% in 1997–2006. Large amounts of the money available in the financial industry were dedicated to quick profits on the fees generated by the mortgage-lending explosion. This development was encouraged by the drive for high returns for bank shareholders, which were often pushed by institutional investors, including pension funds responsible for the investments of many of the people who were subsequently damaged by the economic fallout of the crisis.[9]

The outcome of this practice – which was in fact a strategy that bet on the self-increasing effect of the spiral and that could function only if the system would endlessly re-affirm itself in the form of a "self-fulfilling prophecy" – has been rightly called the U.S., Irish and English, to a much less extent also the Continental European "real estate bubble".

By the end of 2006, real estate was especially in the anglophone countries so strongly overpriced that the mortgages needed to buy a house, and in many cases also to rent one, were no longer in any reasonable relationship with the wages and

---

[7]See for example F. Fukuyama: The End of History and the Last Man, Free Press New York 1992. "In this book, Fukuyama argues that the victory of Western liberal democracy on a global dimension in 1989–91 may signal a kind of final point of humanity's sociocultural evolution and the definite form of human government." Cf.: http://en.wikipedia.org/wiki/The_End_of_History_and_the_Last_Man (retrieved August 02, 2010).

[8]To be precise though, Fukuyama was (and is) no "neoliberal" theorist in the strict sense; his book is not as narrow as his critics depict it; and he did not support many of the subsequent developments, but opposed them (for example, most of the financial and economic policies of G. W. Bush, Jr.). It is perhaps part of the personal *life drama* of many theorists of capitalism of the time that because of their books, they became symbolic figureheads of a radically speculative interpretation of capitalism (often branded "neoliberalism"), without fully belonging to it.

[9]Cf. J. F. Foster and F. Magdoff: The Great Financial Crisis: Causes and Consequences, Monthly Review Press, New York, NY 2009.

incomes of the "real economy."[10] They were the effects of an abstract "fantasy economy"[11] rather than mirror the real economic productivity and the (individual and collective) development of a country.

Therefore, when a critical threshold was passed in 2006, at one point an increasing portion of mortgage customers could not pay back their debts to the banks anymore, because they were simply too high with regard to their income. Once this "breaking point" was reached by a sufficient mass of debtors, repayments of debts to banks were omitted in a critical amount. Consequently, the banks that had given the loans ran short of money themselves. As an effect, dozens of banks collapsed because they could no longer repay their own debts to other banks and shareholders.

But what was worse, most of the banks that were able to survive in the first instance did not have enough money left to lend to small and middle-sized enterprises. Thus, many of these enterprises ran out of money too and thus had to lower their production and employment, and in many cases they could not pay the full wages anymore. Thus, people had less money to spend, causing consumption to go down. That in turn damaged enterprises and banks even more. These factors combined led to a downward spiral in economic activities and to the collapse of many firms, weakening the national and international economies as a whole.[12]

Additionally, a second important banking-related factor contributed to the crisis: the so-called "derivative bubble". Its unraveling marked the *second stage* of the crisis. What exactly is a "derivative"?

The word derivative denotes "a broad class of financial instruments that *derive* their value from other financial instruments (known as the "underlying"), events or conditions. A derivative is essentially a contract between two parties where the value of the contract is linked to the price of another financial instrument or by a specified event or condition."[13]

Already this description shows that to explain what derivative means in a simple and clear way is not easy. Derivatives are a complex, often intransparent, and widely ramified type of financial instruments and products such that even many experts on Wall Street and many professional economists at leading universities did not understand their nature and mechanisms anymore after they got always more

---

[10]Some would argue though that the increased mortgage debt was not only due to higher house prices, but also due to individuals re-financing existing houses to raise cash to support consumption. I suspect the mortgage crisis was a combination of both these factors.

[11]The Washington Post: It's Fantasy Economy! Some Expert Views on What Should Happen Next. In: The Washington Post, October 19, 2008, http://www.washingtonpost.com/wp-dyn/content/article/2008/10/17/AR2008101702148.html.

[12]Cf. N. Roubini and S. Mihm: Crisis Economics: A Crash Course in the Future of Finance, Penguin Press, London, 2010.

[13]"Derivative (finance)": In: Wikipedia (English), http://en.wikipedia.org/wiki/Derivative_%28finance%29 (retrieved March 12, 2010). Cf. similarly the Stock Market Encyclopaedia of the Frankfurter Allgemeine Zeitung (Börsenlexikon FAZ): http://boersenlexikon.faz.net/derivate.htm (retrieved June 22, 2010).

complex over time – that being one of the main reasons of the crisis, as most experts admitted in retrospect.

But again, simplifying things a bit, we could describe a derivative as a secondary, "parasite" financial contract. It is a contract that speculates on the outcome of a primary, real economic development (the so-called underlying). Thus, derivatives are about betting within an "abstract economy" on what will happen in the future with the enterprises of others that are active in the "real economy" – that is, before "real things" in the "real economy" have happened. In other words, "derivatives" are not about the real world where real people live and work, but about speculating on a possible world that still does not exist.

Indeed, derivatives are to a large extent not about reality, but about imagination and psychology. And since the economy at its core is a very down-to-earth, all too realistic process of handling natural resources, labor, people, capital, and time, as well as (equally important!) of balancing them with each other, derivatives could be described as an imaginary "superstructure" or "fantasy economy." This "superstructure" feeds itself and makes a business out of betting upon "real economy" developments.

Strangely, this "parasite world" or "beyondworld" of the real economy has been the place where most big banks and financial institutions have invested great amounts of their money in the past decade – in the hope of fast, easy and huge profits.[14]

To make all this more clear, let us take an easy example. To a certain extent,

> "derivatives can be considered (as) a form of insurance (with regard not to the present, but to the future). Derivatives allow risk about the price of (an) underlying asset to be transferred from one party to another.
>
> For example, a wheat farmer and a miller could sign a 'futures contract' to exchange a specified amount of cash for a specified amount of wheat in the future. Both parties have reduced a 'future risk': for the wheat farmer, the uncertainty of the price, and for the miller, the availability of wheat.
>
> However, there is still the risk that no wheat will be available because of events unspecified by the contract, such as the weather, or that one party will renege on the contract. Although a third party, called a 'clearing house,' *insures* a futures contract, not all derivatives are insured against counterparty risk.
>
> From another perspective, the farmer and the miller both *reduce* a risk and *acquire* a risk when they sign the futures contract: The farmer *reduces* the risk that the price of wheat will

---

[14]We have to make the constriction here that not all derivatives are purely speculative – such as "exchange traded futures." For example, insurance policies where an individual (or an enterprise) buys fire insurance or health insurance to prevent major financial losses in the future are to a certain extent derivatives too. But they are more or less "down to earth," and transparent. Therefore, what is said here about the (in principle) speculative and intransparent character of derivatives as "abstract" financial instruments "betting about the future of others" is valid predominantly for the more complex and structured derivatives, where it is difficult to determine the "insurance" purchased by whom at which conditions. This is the case where they are constructs of "insurance of insurance of insurance," which were created by speculators (with the help of borrowed money by banks). These constructs were so complex in the end, that nobody could understand them anymore. It is this sort of derivatives that decisively co-caused the crisis – *not* the daily life derivatives that the "real economy" needs to be practically functional.

> fall below the price specified in the contract. And he *acquires* the risk that the price of wheat will rise above the price specified in the contract (thereby losing additional income that he could have earned). The miller, on the other hand, *acquires* the risk that the price of wheat will fall below the price specified in the contract (thereby paying more in the future than he otherwise would). And (he) *reduces* the risk that the price of wheat will rise above the price specified in the contract. In this sense, one party is the insurer (risk taker) for one type of risk, and the counterparty is the insurer (risk taker) for another type of risk.[15]"

It is exactly at this point where the notion of "hedging" comes into play – a third and last difficult term that we have to get acquainted with in order to understand things properly. Have you ever heard of the – equally famous or infamous – word hedge fund?[16,17]

This word was lately used often in news reports, and it has been considered a key word to explain the crisis. Some say a hedge fund is something positive, if not even the embodiment of contemporary finance and wealth; others judge it to be "the negative itself," that is, an instrument of exploitation and speculation, useless for moving real things forward. However you want to see it, there has rarely been a word so disputed and ambivalent in the economic and social history of the past 200 years. But what does "hedging" really mean?

> "Hedging occurs when an individual or institution buys an asset (like a commodity, a bond that has coupon payments, a stock that pays dividends, and so on) and sells it using a 'futures contract' [as described above]. The individual or institution has access to the asset for a specified amount of time, and then can sell it at a specified price according to the contract. Of course, this allows the individual or institution the benefit of holding the asset, while reducing the risk that the future selling price will deviate unexpectedly from the market's current assessment of the predicted future value of the asset."[18]

In the form of hedging,

> "derivatives serve a legitimate business purpose. For example, a corporation borrows a large sum of money at a specific interest rate. The rate of interest on the loan resets every 6 months. The corporation is concerned that the rate of interest may be much higher in 6 months. (In this case), the corporation could buy a forward rate agreement (FRA). A 'forward rate agreement' is a contract to pay a fixed rate of interest 6 months after purchases on a notional sum of money. If the interest rate after 6 months is above the contract rate, the seller pays the difference to the corporation, or FRA buyer. If the rate is lower, the corporation would pay the difference to the seller. The purchase of the FRA would serve to reduce the uncertainty concerning the rate increase and (to) stabilize earnings."[19]

---

[15]Derivative (finance): loc cit.

[16]"Hedge fund": In: Investorwords, http://www.investorwords.com/2296/hedge_fund.html (retrieved August 15, 2010).

[17]Some would challenge the assumption that "hedging" and "hedge fund" are directly related. I believe "hedge funds" as they currently exist (i.e., based on their legal forms of constitution) claim to "hedge" positions. Nevertheless, there is some evidence that they use the term as a way to maximize their ability to charge fees to investors. In my view, this does not change the overall argument presented here in its essence.

[18]"Derivative (finance)": loc cit.

[19]"Derivative (finance)": loc cit.

In summation, that means that "derivatives can be used to acquire risk, rather than to insure – or 'hedge' – against risk. Thus, some individuals and institutions will enter into a derivative contract to speculate on the value of the underlying asset – betting that the party seeking insurance will be wrong about the future value of the underlying asset."[20] Indeed, between the 1990s and 2007, a whole "betting economy" grew where speculators put rapidly increasing amounts of money into bets upon the potential outcome of derivative contracts – in many cases with money lent by banks.

"Speculative trading in derivatives gained a great deal of notoriety (already) in 1995 when Nick Leeson, a trader at Barings Bank, made unauthorized investments in futures contracts. Through a combination of poor judgment, lack of oversight by the bank's management and by regulators, and unfortunate events like the Kobe earthquake, Leeson incurred a $1.3 billion loss that bankrupted the centuries-old institution."[21]

The decisive aspect that makes this – already highly complicated – financial instrument even more complicated is that banks not only invested hugely exaggerated amounts of money into these "bets" upon the future, but also traded with bets upon derivatives to the point that in the end there were literally bets upon bets upon bets upon real economic developments (i.e., products, growth of firms, development of prices, availability of resources, efficiency of services, and so forth).

In fact, the practice was that most mainstream banks put tremendous amounts of money not only into *secondary* derivative contracts (or relatively "simple" future contracts as described initially), but into contracts that speculated *on the tenth or fifteenth level of abstraction* of derivatives "above" and "beyond" what happened in the real economy. They put huge amounts of money into derivatives on derivatives on derivatives – often even into bets that derivatives they themselves had sold to their clients would fail!

The result was an enormous "derivative bubble" that was based on financial products that not only were "derivative" of the concrete achievements of the real economy, but that were speculations on derivatives, i.e. highly intransparent derivatives on derivatives. Thus, a big (and rapidly increasing) part of the pre-crisis economy was in reality a derived economy that functioned above or even better beyond the real economy, feeding itself by it.

One effect of this constellation was that by increasingly trading derivatives (not least with the help of so-called global hedge funds, which increased their financial volumes dramatically in the relatively short time frame between 1990 and 2005[22]),

---

[20]"Derivative (finance)": loc cit.

[21]"Derivative (finance)": loc cit.

[22]My personal hypothesis, however, is that the real problem was not with the hedge funds, but with trading activities in large financial institutions (such as AIG Financial Products) that leveraged the capital into large trading positions that distorted the market. When these positions collapsed, they brought down the institutions. Although they were buried inside extremely large financial conglomerates, these derivative-trading activities frequently were poorly regulated and escaped normal risk control processes, due to the "neoliberal" political and economic approach of the period. This was

the *relationship of trust* resulting from direct mutual interaction between banks and their customers was gradually lost.

This loss was due to the circumstance that in the vast majority of cases, the customers did not know what their money was doing while in the bank (or in the financial institution to which they entrusted their money). In fact, most customers did not know that their money was *not* made available to the real economy in order to function as the driving force and "medium" of concrete relationships between investment (capital), people, production, product, price, and consumption. Most bank customers did not know that their money was instead in large parts put into the "fantasy futures market" (i.e. into secondary bets on what the future of the real economy would bring).

Fact is that the "neoliberal" system of putting large amounts of capital into artificially "betting" on outcomes of the "real economy" (through the means of an ever-increasing "parasite economy") reached, at the end of 2006, a point of complexity that not even many bank leaders knew what was happening; they did not oversee anymore the overall system of "bets on bets on bets" was construed, how it was (if at all) still tied to the real economy, and how it concretely worked.

Secondly, the traditionally well-established mutual trust among banks was also gradually lost because banks increasingly noted that the trade of derivatives between them was not any longer oriented toward constructing something positive together for the overall society. Rather it was – by its secondary nature – inclined to take advantage of the problems and failures of each other in a (more or less) Machiavellian[23] manner.

---

exacerbated by the apparent profits being made, which made senior management less likely to support conservative risk managers.

[23]Niccolò Machiavelli (1469–1527) was an Italian politician, philosopher, historian, and poet. He held that for every endeavor to be successful, cunning and duplicity in statecraft or in general conduct must be employed. Machiavelli was convinced that to mislead one's (political, trade, or business) partner in order to gain the maximum personal advantage is by far preferable to moral, interpersonal, or community oriented conducts. This is because Machiavelli did not believe in the basic humanistic doctrine that the more people are allowed to participate in the common wealth, the more society will benefit from it and evolve. Rather, Machiavelli believed that life is "everybody against everybody, and the winner takes it all." The resulting ideology implicit in his worldview was that in the end, there must be necessarily one winner at the expense of many who must lose everything. As it seems from our current viewpoint, Machiavelli was not that far off from the "neoliberal" interpretation of how a "good finance industry" must work, especially in the period between 1989 and 2007. But while important parts of the traditional, mainstream financial system were de facto based on similar assumptions, the crisis has questioned that view. Would it not be better for an open and democratic society that everybody had in principle the same economic and financial opportunities based on concrete work and truly individual performance in the real economy, rather that in the cunning of manipulations within a speculative, imaginary, and parasite secondary economy of the real estate and derivative bubbles (which in the end, taken as they are, are not real business, but rather bets on business)?

The resulting double *lack of trust* between *customers and banks* on the one hand and *between banks and banks* on the other hand (the latter mainly over reliability in lending politics, asset quality, and liquidity[24]) was one of the main reasons for the unusually rapid spread of panic among banks, customers and governments that ultimately expanded the financial and economic crisis to a worldwide level – with catastrophic effects.[25]

This panic consisted in the psychologically induced behavior that, once the crisis was spotted in its early beginnings, everybody involved wanted to take out his or her investments of the "derivative bubble" as fast as possible by selling huge amounts of assets in a short time – thus devaluating these assets dramatically because of oversupply of secondary financial products that turned out to be useless.[26] Something similar happened with the investments in the "real estate" bubble.[27]

Overall, there were two "bubbles" that led to the economic crisis of 2007–2010: The *first* was the real estate bubble and the *second* was the derivative bubble. By mutually influencing and aggravating each other, they created *first* a financial and *then* an economic crisis on a global level. The result of these two bubbles combined was a "downward spiral" that devaluated not only houses but also many other goods. Because banks and financial services are closely interconnected in our globalized age (not only by borrowing money from each other, but also by cooperating in big investments), the resulting crisis ultimately led to a worldwide recession, increasing poverty and unemployment across countries and continents. Approximately

---

[24]There are two related but separate issues that banks constantly face. One is asset quality and the other is liquidity. There has yet to be a proper in-depth review of how these two issues interacted in the recent crisis.

[25]As D. N. Chorafas has correctly pointed out, the lack of trust was probably the main reason for the second stage of the crisis. The importance of the "trust factor" is a still undervalued element in many analyses of the happenings of 2007–2010. Chorafas writes: "At the tail-end of 2008, (the) central theme would have been that credit is what the crisis is all about. In the year 2009 the keyword became trust. While confidence was at a very low point, capitalism was left without capital and this was impacting upon the real economy like a sledgehammer." D. N. Chorafas: Capitalism Without Capital. Palgrave MacMillan Studies in Banking and Financial Institutions, Palgrave McMillan, New York 2009.

[26]Trying to liquidate derivative positions was one part of an overall liquidity crisis built on the lack of trust. A similar liquidity issue was faced in the economic crisis (often called the "Great Depression") of 1929 (the famous "Black Tuesday"), but with far more drastic results because there was insufficient intervention to restore liquidity. For a comparative perspective, see: The Great Depression, http://en.wikipedia.org/wiki/Great_Depression (retrieved March 10, 2010); and L. Ahamed: Lords of Finance: The Bankers Who Broke the World, Penguin Press, London, 2009.

[27]Or as D. N. Chorafas resumes, "It transpire(d) that many complex financial instruments (were) actually backed by assets that are nearly or fully worthless. These include(d):

- housing loans that may never be paid back;
- corporate loans, with rising default rates;
- a great amount of poorly understood and incorrectly valued structured (financial) products." D. N. Chorafas: loc cit.

7 million Americans and 5 million Europeans lost their jobs, 10 million Americans and 2 million Europeans were pushed below the poverty line, thousands of families (foremost in the United States and the United Kingdom) lost their savings. In the United States and in the United Kingdom in particular, where the deregulation of the financial markets was strongest and where the speculative bubbles of the real estate and the derivatives' "side economies" not only had their (quantitative) main centers (New York and London), but were also intertwined strongest with the economy, the crisis hit the population harder than in Continental Europe. According to numbers published by the US government at the end of August 2010 when the worst days of the crisis had seemingly passed,

> US Government anti-poverty programs that have grown to meet the needs of recession victims now serve a record one in six Americans and are continuing to expand. Close to 10 million receive unemployment insurance, nearly four times the number from 2007. More than 40 million people get food stamps, an increase of nearly 50% during the economic downturn. More than 4.4 million people are on welfare, an 18% increase during the recession. More than 50 million Americans are on Medicaid, the federal-state program aimed principally at the poor. That's up at least 17% since the recession began in December 2007. The federal price tag for Medicaid has jumped 36% in two years, to $273 billion. Jobless benefits have soared from $43 billion to $160 billion. The food stamps program has risen 80%, to $70 billion. Welfare is up 24%, to $22 billion. Taken together, they cost more than Medicare.[28]

Additionally, more than 180 banks in the United States and dozens in Europe broke down only in the timeframe between January 2009 and March 2010.[29] As the US Congressional Oversight Panel and the US Federal Deposit Insurance Corporation (FDIC) reported in February 2010, up to one-third of the remaining 8100 US banks may still be threatened indefinitely.[30,31] Something similar is true for European banks, where at least 25 bigger banks of strategic importance for the overall economy will have to be monitored in the years to come.[32,33]

---

[28] R. Wolf: Record number in government anti-poverty programs. In: USAToday, August 30, 2010, http://www.usatoday.com/news/washington/2010-08-30-1Asafetynet30_ST_N.htm?csp=hf (retrieved August 30, 2010).

[29] Handelsblatt Düsseldorf: Small United States Banks collapse one after another (Kleine US-Banken kollabieren eine nach der anderen). In: Handelsblatt Düsseldorf, 28 March 2010.

[30] The US Congressional Oversight Panel: February Oversight Report: Commercial Real Estate Losses and the Risk to Financial Stability, February 10, 2010, http://cop.senate.gov/documents/cop-021110-report.pdf. (retrieved February 11, 2010)

[31] The US Federal Deposit Insurance Corporation (FDIC): Quarterly Banking Profile, Fourth Quarter 2009, February 23, 2010, http://www2.fdic.gov/qbp/2009dec/qbp.pdf.

[32] Wirtschaftsblatt Vienna: European Central Bank experts worry that 2010 might be the next crisis year for European banks (EZB: Sorge um Bankenkrise 2010. Dauert die Krise zu lange, steht den Banken 2010 die nächste Krise bevor). In: Wirtschaftsblatt Vienna, June 11, 2009, http://www.wirtschaftsblatt.at/home/377926/index.do.

[33] Reuters Germany: European Central Bank worries about new banking crisis in 2010 (EZB befürchtet weitere Bankenkrise 2010). In: Reuters Deutschland, June 11, 2009, http://de.reuters.com/article/topNews/idDEBEE55A00N20090611.

Taken as a whole, the crisis of 2007–2010 was one of the most dramatic crises ever, strictly numerically speaking the biggest financial and economic crisis of all times. It brought the international financial and economic system to the edge of a breakdown. In the end, it could only be managed by the input of billions of dollars, british pounds, euros and other currencies from nation states across the world. Nations had to use taxpayers money to save banks and enterprises by lending them capital, in some cases also by factually donating it to them.

As a result, many "big players" in the financial and economic businesses and in industry (like for example in the US and German car industries) were saved by taxpayers' money, while many small and medium banks and enterprises were not. While many big institutions survived, the main losers of the crisis were the small and medium enterprises of the "real economy," that is, the core productive force "that really creates and works" in our society, and thus forms the backbone of the economies of the West – similarly on both sides of the Atlantic.[34]

A second outcome of the crisis is that the indebtedness of states and nations, already critical before the crisis, has increased to the point that it will take many future generations to repay these debts. In Germany, for example, the total debt of the state and its institutions reached 1707 billion euros (US $2170 billion) as on November 28, 2010, increasing by 7.1% in 2009 alone.[35] This does not take into account the threat of state bankruptcy of Greece and Spain as (at least in part) follow-ups to the crisis, which may put additional burdens upon the national economies of the European Union.[36] In the United States, the national debt has reached US $13,780 billion as on November 28, 2010, with increases of US $2900 billion during the economic crisis in 2008 and 2009 alone.[37,38,39] Many experts

---

[34]Cf. M. Bachner: The Sword of Damocles Hangs over the Small and Medium-Sized Enterprises (Damoklesschwert über den KMUs). In: Der Kurier Vienna, March 19, 2010.

[35]Cf. National debt of Germany (Staatsverschuldung Deutschland), in: http://de.wikipedia.org/wiki/Staatsverschuldung (retrieved August 25, 2010).

[36]Cf. Y. Osman and D. Riedel: The Banks Are the Achilles' heel of Greece (Die Banken sind Griechenlands Achillesferse). In: Handelsblatt Düsseldorf, April 29, 2010, p.1.

[37]AFP: The German National debt reaches new all time high (Staatsschulden erreichen Rekordhoch), March 11, 2010; Staatsverschuldung in Deutschland (German National Debt), in: Bund der Steuerzahler Deutschland (Association of German Tax Payers), http://www.steuerzahler.de/, November 28, 2010; U.S. National debt, in: http://en.wikipedia.org/wiki/United_States_public_debt and The United States National Debt Clock, http://www.usdebtclock.org/ (retrieved August 25, 2010). Additional numbers and statistics can be found in: G. Assenza and A. Martynau: loc cit, pp. 11 ff. On the rising threats for countries and nations as a result of such huge debts, see N. Ferguson: Complexity and Collapse. Empires on the Edge of Chaos. In: Foreign Affairs, March/April 2010.

[38]Some though would question the extent of the impact of the financial crisis on the United States and on the European Union's overall debt development, since their structural origins reach back far before the crisis, and have multiple causes. A more accurate judgment on this topic will be possible only in a couple of years with the help of additional numerical and statistical material.

[39]A case could be made that the previous US and European administration(s) created much of the deficit through a combination of unwise and unneeded tax reductions, expansion of middle class

believe that the growing budget deficits are making the international economic positions of the United States and Europe more and more unsustainable.[40,41]

---

entitlements, and military operations that were very expensive. In any case, the debt will need to be repaid by the future productivity of the population.

[40]Cf., for example, C. F. Bergsten (ed.): The Long-Term International Economic Position of the United States. The Peterson Institute for International Economics, Special Report 20, May 2009. A short summary of the main findings can be found at: C. Bergsten: The Unsustainable International Economic Position of the United States and the Budget Deficit. In: The Peterson Institute für International Economics, http://www.iie.com/publications/newsreleases/newsrelease.cfm?id=150, May 6, 2009 (retrieved April 16, 2010).

[41]Overall, I agree with the analysis of N. Roubini, Stern School of Business of New York University, former US treasury official during the Clinton and Gore administration: "The trouble is that in the bubble phase nearly everyone, the exception being a few critical analysts, (was) swept in a delusional bubble mania of irrational euphoria: households, financial institutions, investors, governments, all of whom profited from the bubble, including Ponzi-schemers [i.e., fraudulent investors], who concoct their houses of cards and financial games. In each bubble there are cranks who argue that this time is different and that this bubble is driven by a fundamental brave new world of ever rising growth and profits. Then, when the boom and bubble turns into a bust and crash, a reality check occurs and financial depression sets in. (But) who is to blame the most for the financial crisis 2007–2010? Who were the culprits of this latest one?

The list of culprits is long. The US Federal Reserve Bank (under the leadership of Alan Greenspan, chairman from August 11, 1987 until January 31, 2006) kept interest rates too low for too long in the earlier part of the 1990s and fed – pun intended – the housing and credit bubble. Bankers and investors on Wall Street and in financial institutions were greedy, arrogant, and reckless in their risk taking and build-up of leverage because they were compensated based on short-term profits. As a result, they generated toxic loans – subprime mortgages and other mortgages and loans – that borrowers could not afford and then packaged these mortgages and loans into toxic securities; that is, into the entire alphabet soup of 'Structured Finance Products' (so-called 'SIVs') like 'MBS's: mortgage-backed securities, or 'CDOs': collateralized debt obligations – and even 'CDOs' of 'CDOs'. These were new, complex, exotic, non-transparent, non-traded, marked-to-model rather than market-to-market and mis-rated by the rating agencies. Indeed, the rating agencies were also culprits as they had massive conflicts of interest: they made most of their profits from mis-rating these new instruments and being paid handsomely by the issuers. Also, the regulators and supervisors were asleep at the wheel as the ideology in Washington for the last decade (i.e., in the years of the presidency of G. W. Bush Jr., R. B.) was one of laissez faire 'Wild West' capitalism with little prudential regulation and supervision of banks and other financial institutions. (...)

In sum, the Great Recession of 2008–2009 was triggered by excessive debt accumulation and leverage on the part of households, financial institutions, and even the corporate sector in many advanced economies. While there is much talk about de-leveraging as the crisis wanes, the reality is that private-sector debt ratios have stabilized at very high levels. By contrast, as a consequence of fiscal stimulus and socialization of part of the private sector's losses, there is now a massive re-leveraging of the debt of the public sector. Deficits in excess of 10% of the gross domestic product (GDP) can be found in many advanced economies, including the United States, and debt-to-Gross-Domestic-Product ratios are expected to rise sharply – in some cases doubling in the next few years." In: http://www.amazon.com/Crisis-Economics-Course-Future-Finance/dp/1594202508/ref=pd_sim_b_1 (retrieved August 15, 2010).

Thus, the financial crisis of 2007–2010 has been ultimately transferred onto the present youth[42] and their children who will have to bear the real costs. They will most probably have lower pensions and will have to work longer.

Additionally, there might be a further devaluation of money, that is, an inflation in the middle and long run, given that many nation states at the peak of the crisis printed billions of dollars and euros to infuse into the economy in order to revive it, for example, by giving huge public work orders (Italy, Spain, United Kingdom), by publicly co-financing the purchase of new cars (Germany), or by conceding tax incentives to first-time house buyers (United States). Given that the newly printed money has only doubtful coverage in real values (as it had before 1971 in the USA, and before 1976 on an international level when currency was pegged to the gold reserves of each country[43]), the value of money might further decrease.[44]

This is because as a general rule, we can say that the value of money decreases above-average inflation levels when the amount of concretely produced goods and services by the "real economy" (i.e. excluding the "real estate bubble" and the "derivative bubble") of a country is not in a balanced relationship with the amount of money in circulation, that is, when you could buy everything produced, let's say, in the United States in 2009, ten times with the money in circulation in the United States in 2009. That is the case today in most countries. Therefore (non-material, i.e., monetary), savings may decline in value in the coming years.[45] As a result

---

[42]Another indication among others for the assumption that the crisis has put particular burden upon the youth is that as a result of the crisis, unemployment, and poverty among young people not only in the United States, but also in Continental Europe, particularly in Eastern Germany and in Eastern nations, have grown beyond the average rate of the overall population. Cf. US Bureau of Labor Statistics: Employment and Unemployment among Youth. Summary. August 27, 2010. In: http://www.bls.gov/news.release/youth.nr0.htm (retrieved August 27, 2010), with hardly half of the youth unemployed. Regarding Europe, youth unemployment at the end of 2009 was more than 21%, see: http://epp.eurostat.ec.europa.eu/cache/ITY_PUBLIC/3-29012010-AP-EN.PDF (retrieved November 25, 2010), i.e. far beyond the average unemployment rate.

[43]There is nevertheless some evidence that the gold standard brings with it other problems, especially at times of liquidity challenges. Cf. L. Arnold: "More Turbulences" ("Weitere Turbulenzen"). In: Die Weltwoche Schweiz, September 5, 2007, http://www.weltwoche.ch/ausgaben/2007-36/artikel-2007-36-weitere-turbulenzen.html.

[44]Some contraindications, though, are found in Handelsblatt Düsseldorf: "It will feel like a permanent crisis" ("Es wird sich wie eine Dauerkrise anfühlen"). In: Handelsblatt Düsseldorf, April 9, 2010. In this article, European experts and CEOs, among others Michael Heise, Chief National Economist of the Allianz Insurance Trust International, assert that the risk of increased inflation is given for the coming years, but it will not reach seriously overproportional levels because of the low capacity utilization and the high unemployment rates in the wake of the crisis. I believe this to be a self-referential, circular, and speculative argument that does not touch the center of things.

[45]Cf. the detailed global analysis (including China) of D. Heilmann, M. Thibaut, A. Grüttner, and M. Eberle: An End of the Crisis is not in Sight (Ein Ende der Krise ist nicht in Sicht). In: Handelsblatt Düsseldorf, March 30, 2010.

of massive amounts of cheap money flooding the market due to worldwide governmental countermeasures to the crisis, the next (housing, derivative, or other[46]) bubble may just be around the corner.[47,48,49]

[46]Many observers think that the next global bubbles may be a food and a water bubble.

[47]It is evident that that if we combine two of the outcomes of the crisis mentioned: the increasing national debts of the United States and Europe on the one hand, and the massive oversupply with money that may lead to its further devaluation on the other hand, how most governments, including Federal Reserve Bank leaders like Jean-Claude Trichet in Europe and Ben Bernanke in the United States, believe the national indebtments can be mastered. To put it in easy terms, they believe in a simple mechanism: That the national debts, which are measured in money, will be manageable through the massive devaluation of money. This is because the more money nations print and put into circulation through their Federal Reserve banks (using it, for example, to carry out public work or to stimulate productivity, or to import real goods like for example oil), the more the value of money decreases, a.o. through inflation. If money is worth less, the national debts will de facto decrease in value, even if their numbers rise. The hope is that the amounts of money with which a national state is indebted will allegedly lose their *real* value more rapidly (due to inflation combined with the increase in productivity) than the strictly numerical increase of the indebtedness. The Executive Board Member of the European Central Bank, L. Bini Smaghi, puts this ideology in just one sentence: There is a widespread belief that national debts can be mastered "through monetary policy. [A country or union of countries like the European Union] can (either) print money to inflate its debt away, (or) depreciate its currency to recover competitiveness … and grow the economy out of debt." L. Bini Smaghi: The Future of the Euro: Why the Greek Crisis Will Not Ruin Europe`s Monetary Union. In: Foreign Affairs, August 10, 2010, http://foreignaffairs.com/articles/66509/lorenzo-bini-smaghi-the-future-of-the-euro.html. Cf. also U. Dönch and A. Körner: Mister Inflation. Ben Bernanke is the president of the US Federal Reserve Bank – and probably the greatest money annihilator in history: He prints billions of new dollars – thus heating prices up and threatening our monetary system (Mister Inflation. Ben Bernanke ist Präsident der US-Notenbank – und womöglich der größte Geldvernichter der Geschichte: Er druckt ungeniert Milliarden von neuen Dollars – das treibt die Preise und gefährdet auch unser Geld). In: Focus. The Weekly News and Analysis Magazine, Nr. 4/2010, pp. 1–13, http://www.focus.de/finanzen/news/konjunktur/tid-17228/wirtschaft-mister-inflation_aid_473550.html. In contrast to what Dönch and Körner assert, I believe that there is no fundamental difference regarding the main mechanism of dealing with national debts between the United States and Europe.

But this overall ratio showed serious weaknesses when the global financial and economic crisis hit. Many of my colleagues and I thus believe in the meantime that this grand strategy is not the path to follow toward a sustainable and balanced economy in a long-term perspective anymore. The reason is that this strategy ultimately follows the slogan: *We don't have to find concrete solutions now. Time is the answer, because it is through time combined with inflation that our debts will decrease. So let's put it on playing with the time factor*. What this implies is that there will be a continuous postponement of the economic and financial reality of today toward the future in contemporary capitalistic societies – by creating a relationship between the real economy and the amount of money that should represent it that is not rooted in the realities of the present, but is permanently anticipating some possible, imaginary realities of the future. Governments in the meantime are printing and distributing money in amounts that would be more appropriate for economies that may have developed in 30 or 50 years in the future, but not now. They are bringing into circulation far too much money compared to the size and the productivity of the real economy.

There are two main implications and effects of this mindset.

3 Origins and Causes of the Crisis: The "Sandglass Principle" of the Mainstream Banking and Finance System Between 1989 and 2007

Overall seen, the crisis of 2007–2010 showed the unsustainability and instability not primarily of the *international economy*, but rather of the widely deregulated global *finance practices* that were established during the "ultra-liberal" period of

---

First, it is clear that this attitude of acting in the "here and now" by speculating on the future as an "imagined reality" playing with money as a time factor to a certain extent mirrors basic mechanisms both of the "real estate" bubble and of the "derivative" bubble, in this case on the level of the long-term strategy of the national economy.

Second, the continuing disproportion between the real products, goods and services produced by the real economy and the amount of money in circulation must sooner or later lead to new bubbles, and thus to new crises.

Some contraindications to this argument though are once again found at: Handelsblatt Düsseldorf: "It will feel like a permanent crisis" ("Es wird sich wie eine Dauerkrise anfühlen"). In: Handelsblatt Düsseldorf, April 9, 2010. In this article, European experts and CEOs assert that Western nation states cannot rely on inflation to reduce their deficits because the then necessary continuous re-financing of short-term debts would be too expensive on the middle and long run, and would cause more damage then the relative "benefits" of inflation could balance. Again, I believe this to be an argument that does not touch the core issue.

[48]Some though speculate that the extraordinary hunger for additional capital revenues by nation states at the brink of bankruptcy like Greece (or by single US states like California) may – now and in the future – indirectly and temporarily (i.e., for at least several years) suck up part of the prospective inflation by detracting liquidity from banks toward nation states, mainly through the emission of an increasing number of – comparatively attractive – government bonds dedicated to cover the growing national debts. I strongly doubt that this hope will hold true in practice, since most of the respective nation states may use at least part of the resulting capital for new investments into incentive programs, hoping to spark a new "growth spiral" that may absorb the debt through the combination of growth and inflation, and thus indirectly repay it, as described above, rather than use it for the "simple" (i.e., direct) repayment of debts and interests. Cf. M. Maisch: Banks run out of the big money. The hunger for capital of over-indebted states becomes a problem for the financial industry (Banken geht das große Geld aus. Der Kapitalhunger der überschuldeten Staaten wird zum Problem für die Finanzbranche). In: Handelsblatt Düsseldorf, April 27, 2010, p. 36.

[49]An option to keep (too) high-inflation rates away from US soil in the past decades was to solicit other countries to keep a "supranational reserve" of US dollars in order to purchase key resources like petroleum, which due to the largely unchallenged political and military power of the United States is traded almost exclusively in US dollars. Therefore, the US dollar has become the de facto "world's reserve currency." This facilitated the US import of real, material goods (like cars, food, resources) for its deliberately printed paper money, since every other country needed a strategic reserve of US dollars and was thus forced to give real goods for paper. Other countries delivered – and continue to deliver until today – real goods to the United States in exchange for paper. Additionally, the United States was able to artificially uphold the value of the dollar despite of the fact that there were – and are – far too many dollars in worldwide circulation if compared with the market value of the US dollar. Considering the amounts of dollars printed in the past (including most recently the issuing of a 600 billion dollar "infusion" into the US economy by the Federal Reserve Bank in November 2010, announced to be made by "alternative" methods) and presently in circulation worldwide, the US dollar's value is too high; in reality, its worth compared

capitalism between 1989 and 2007. In my view, *two* main points have been made clear by the crisis:

---

with other currencies, and with the value of real goods, would be much less. Cf. The Next Reporter: Federal Reserve $600 billion bid defended: Barack Obama says Federal Reserve is independent, has his support. November 9, 2010, http://thenextreporter.com/rj/federal-reserve-600-billion-bid-defended-barack-obama-federal-reserve-independent-support/0810429/.

It is therefore not entirely accurate when President Obama in his G-20 Toronto speech of June 2010 underscored that "after years of taking on too much debt, Americans cannot –and will not – borrow and buy the world's way to lasting prosperity. No nation should assume its path to prosperity is simply paved with exports to the United States." There is some sense and some nonsense in this statement. On the one hand, it is right that the US military supremacy and political power contributed to make European welfare states possible after World War II (and to keep them alive until today), because due to the protection from the US, Europe needs only a comparatively small army and could otherwise not put that much more into governmental programs. Also, it is a fact that the world economy strongly relies on the US economy, its performance and demand. On the other hand, the US wealth is partly also financed through the "dollar hegemony," and thus by the world – which accepts paper for the real goods "exported to the United States" (Obama). That means that the outstanding wealth of the United States is paid for at least partially by the world – that is, by relying on the current status of the US dollar as "de facto" world reserve currency. B. Obama: In: The White House Washington DC, Remarks by President Obama at G-20 Press Conference in Toronto, Canada, June 27, 2010, http://www.whitehouse.gov/the-press-office/remarks-president-obama-g-20-press-conference-toronto-canada.

This situation, created by an interdependent mix between political, military, and economic powers, might change with the emergence of a worldwide reserve system based on multiple currencies, including the euro, the yen, and the British pound sterling. The creation of such a system is currently discussed as one of the main effects of the crisis 2007–2010. Since the crisis showed the dangers of a de facto single world reserve currency, many countries are asking now for a multipolar reserve system as a security against future crises. The result could be a long-term decline for the US dollar, because many countries could gradually sell at least part of their (in the meantime huge) US dollar reserves – as "big player" China, since July 2010 the second-largest economy in the world behind the United States (as well as the biggest foreign holder of US dollars in the world), actually has already begun to do in March 2009. China's strategy is clear: "In March 2009, the governor of China's central Bank, Zhou Xiaochuan, made a splash by arguing that the dollar should be replaced as the world's reserve currency by special drawing rights (SDRS), the accounting unit used by the International Monetary Fund IMF, in transactions with its members and currently composed of a basket of four currencies (the dollar, the euro, the yen, and the pound)." B. Eichengreen: The Dollar Dilemma. In: Foreign Affairs, September/October 2009, pp. 53–68. Cf. R. Paul: The End of Dollar Hegemony. Speech at the U.S. House of Representatives, February 15, 2006, in: The US House of Representatives, http://www.house.gov/paul/congrec/congrec2006/cr021506.htm (retrieved March 07, 2010).

There are several reasons, however, that provide some contraindications to such a development. Among them are the relative decline of the value of the euro due to the threat of bankruptcy of Greece and the huge debt problems of other European countries like Ireland, as well as the adjustment of the value of the British pound due to the notorious structural problems of the British industry. I believe that independently of how these perspectives develop, the main question is not about currencies, but about the amounts of money in circulation on a worldwide level. The main problem are the increasingly disproportionate amounts of money that will need supervision and considerable re-adjustment if above-average inflation is to be avoided in the coming years. I believe this is valid not only for the dollar and the euro, but also for the other currencies mentioned. What is needed is a new relationship between the money in circulation and the productivity of the real economy.

(1) The political deregulation created the bases for the bloating of two artificial, widely unproductive "bubble" side economies "below" the real economy (the "real estate bubble") and "above" the real economy (the "derivative bubble"). They became kind of "hoarding boxes" for the influx of huge amounts of money through the financial industry ultimately deriving from the real economy. These two "bubble economies" eventually became so potent to not only detract capital from the real economy, but subsequently to damage the source of all wealth, the real economy itself by their speculations. The loser was eventually the real economy that through its concrete productivity fed – and feeds – the whole system.

(2) The financial sector not only grew many times bigger in numbers than needed by the real economy, but also ballooned toward over-complexity and created a system of financial instruments that became a labyrinth of "Chinese boxes" nested in Chinese boxes (i.e., derivatives of derivatives, or bets upon bets). The abstraction and "virtualization" of these instruments through the internet and other communication technologies led, together with their highly intransparent interweavement and their overall character of delegating responsibility to others, to financial constructs that were over-intellectualized to the point that basically nobody could understand them fully, and as a whole anymore.[50]

It was emblematic that Nobel Prize Laureate Paul Krugman of Princeton University, who in the past had warned repeatedly against the establishment of the ultra-risky and widely deregulated financial system by going so far to compare it – at the peak of its apparent success at the end of the 1990s – with "the prelude to the Great Depression" of the 1930s,[51] received the Nobel Prize at the very moment when the system crashed (in October 2008).

Krugman in that occasion underscored, as did other leading economists: "This is stunning, it is shocking. We are all scrambling to understand what's happening and come up with answers. I should have seen it coming. I berate myself for not understanding the extent to which we have these financial domino effects [induced, as explained above, a.o. by the "two pillars" of the crisis, i.e. the real estate and the derivative bubbles, R.B.]. I saw there would be a burst bubble and there would be a lot of pain, but I didn't realize how big the pain would be. Lots of people should have seen it coming. In retrospect, how could we have been so blind? We have created a financial system that basically outgrew the defenses we created back in the 1930s to protect against banking crises. We should have understood that because the system

---

[50]It is useless to deny that this development was partly supported by the then prevailing academic thought which during the 1990s and in the first-half of the current decade co-created over-complex financial instruments, and proposed adventurous ways of doing business and getting rich by speculation instead of work. Cf. J. Sapiro: From Financial Crisis to Turning Point. How the U.S. "Subprime Crisis" Turned into a World-Wide One and will Change the Global Economy. In: International Politics and Society, edited by the Friedrich Ebert Foundation Berlin, Nr. 1/2009, pp. 27–44.

[51]Cf., for example, P. Krugman: The Return of Depression Economics. In: Foreign Affairs, January/February 1999.

had outgrown those defenses, there was the possibility of another crisis. But very few people saw it coming."[52,53]

Similarly, the vice chairman of the US Financial Crisis Inquiry Commission (FCIC[54]), Bill Thomas, came to the conclusion that "bank leaders in general did not know what they were doing."[55]

Accordingly, finance expert and Swiss Corporate Management University Professor Fredmund Malik of the University of St. Gallen stated:

> The globalized banking and financial system has become something we don't longer understand: We have deregulated the system to the point that we have created a monster that is out of control. The financial markets are many times bigger than the real economy needs them for their investments and tradings. This volumina are so over-swelled that they necessarily must diminish in the course of this crisis noticeably – at least by a third, probably even by two thirds... The result is that many of us start to think that capitalism has failed – or at least that capitalism is a system that cannot work in principle, because it has the inbuilt trend to become so distorted, over-intellectualized and complex that nobody is able to steer it anymore.[56]

Contrary to Malik, most of my colleagues and I do not believe that capitalism as such has failed. I think to put it that way would mean to gravely misread the crisis. Rather, in the aftermath of the crisis the practices of how the international financial business has dealt – and continues to deal – with money and capital have to be questioned.

So how exactly can we understand what Krugman, Malik, and others meant by their statements of marvel, regret, and disappointment? What precisely is meant by "We have created a monster that is out of control?" Has the finance industry really become a "monster" (as simple as that), or are there other dimensions and potentials in it as well? And where are possible answers, alternatives, or improvements – instead of resignation? Have some of the possible alternatives been issued already before the crisis?

---

[52]In: Krugman Wins Nobel Prize in Economics. In: National Public Radio (NPR), October 12, 2008, http://www.npr.org/templates/story/story.php?storyId=95674011 (retrieved January 20, 2010). In the same interview, Krugman blamed "former Federal Reserve Chairman Alan Greenspan for much of the crisis because Greenspan ignored warnings about the economy."

[53]Cf. Krugman on the Financial Crisis and Spending. In: National Public Radio, October 21, 2008. See also P. Krugman: The Return of Depression Economics and the Crisis of 2008, W. W. Norton 2008; and P. Krugman: What to do. In: The New York Times Review of Books, Vol. 55, No. 20, December 18, 2008.

[54]The United States Financial Crisis Inquiry Commission: http://fcic.gov/.

[55]N. Rüdel: "They did not know what they were doing" ("Sie wussten nicht, was sie tun"). In: Handelsblatt Düsseldorf, April 8, 2010. Cf. N. D. Schwartz and J. Creswell: What Created this Monster? In: The New York Times, March 23, 2008.

[56]F. Malik: Capitalism has failed (Der Kapitalismus ist gescheitert). In: Handelsblatt, July 12, 2009. Cf. in some points similarly R. A. Posner: The Crisis of Capitalist Democracy, Harvard University Press 2010. Cf. contrarily R. Benedikter: Book Series Postmaterialism: The Second Generation, Volume 5: The Capital (Buchreihe Postmaterialismus: Die zweite Generation, Band 5: Das Kapital), Vienna 2005.

Interestingly, the crisis had been foreseen by some attentive observers more or less as it later happened: not only by Krugman,[57] but also by Harvard Economic History Professor Niall Ferguson,[58] by New York University Economy Professor Nouriel Roubini,[59] by investor Warren Buffet,[60] by Republican Member of Congress Ron Paul,[61] and by the independent French civil society think tank "European Laboratory of Political Anticipation" LEAP Paris,[62] to name just a few. Already as early as in the 1980s, the so-called Brandt report, a round table of the world's leading economic and social development experts named after former German Chancellor Willy Brandt (1913–1992), had identified elements of the crisis by projecting systemic distortions of the time into the future.[63]

Even if the theses of all these experts were obviously not always undisputed, most of them predicted unanimously that there were three main factors in the international financial system under the ideological conditions of "neoliberalism"[64] that would ultimately lead to its crisis: *Social irresponsibility, intransparency,* and *unsustainability*. As these three factors, according to all these experts, seem to be the indispensable prerequisite for searching for answers and for drawing some positive perspectives, we have to understand them properly, before making steps toward the potential of positive future outlines. So what would be a clear and simple image to clarify what is meant by these three problematic factors? And how can their specific intertwinement be represented?

In order to try to sketch a general recapitulatory picture of the origins and causes of the crisis as simply and easily as possible, let us take *the image of a sandglass*. In my view, this image can illustrate in a simplified way the main basic aspects of

---

[57]Cf., for example P. Krugman: Will There Be a Dollar Crisis? In: Economic Policy, July 2007, pp. 435–467.

[58]See a.o. N. Ferguson: Banking Crisis: Don't blame the Central Banks. In: The Daily Telegraph, September 30, 2007. Reprint in: The official Niall Ferguson site, http://www.niallferguson.com/site/FERG/Templates/ArticleItem.aspx?pageid=34; and N. Ferguson: Colossus. The Price of America's Empire, Penguin Press, London, 2004.

[59]N. Roubini: 2006 and 2007 Speeches to the International Monetary Fund (IMF), in: http://www.roubini.com/roubini-monitor/253448/2006_and_2007_imf_speeches_by_roubini_predicting_the_recession_and_the_financial_crisisand_the_five_stages_of_grief. Cf. E. Brockes: He told us so: N. Roubini. In: The Guardian London, 24 January 2009, http://www.guardian.co.uk/business/2009/jan/24/nouriel-roubini-credit-crunch (retrieved August 25, 2010).

[60]BBC London: Buffet warns on "investment time bomb". Derivatives are financial weapons of mass destruction. In: BBC London online, March 4, 2003, http://news.bbc.co.uk/2/hi/2817995.stm (retrieved August 16, 2010).

[61]R. Paul: The End of Dollar Hegemony. Speech at the U.S. House of Representatives, loc cit.

[62]Laboratoire Europẽen d'Anticipation Politique LEAP Paris: Global Europe Anticipation Bulletin N°1, January 2006. See also: LEAP Paris, http://www.leap2020.eu/English_r25.html.

[63]Cf. J. B. Quilligan: The Superbubble behind "The Great Moderation": How the Brandt Report Foresaw Today's Global Economic Crisis. In: Integral Review, March 2010, Vol. 6, No. 1, http://integral-review.org/documents/Quilligan,%20The%20Superbubble%20behind%20The%20Great%20Moderation,%20Vol.%206%20No.%201.pdf.

[64]Cf. "Neoliberalism": In: Wikipedia (English), http://en.wikipedia.org/wiki/Neoliberalism (retrieved August 5, 2010).

distortion of the real economy implicit in the creation of "side economies" or "bubble economies" "below" and "above" the "real economy". It may further elucidate how they were – and still are – connected. Last but not least, this basic image may point toward the future of what is needed as a response, in the sense of a constituent "global imaginary" (Manfred Steger). (Fig. 1).

Fig. 1 The sandglass principle of the "neoliberal" financial system

The banking and finance system between 1990 and 2007 that led to the crisis followed – and despite all warnings continues to follow until today – what I would like to call metaphorically a "sandglass principle". The "sandglass principle" can be explained as follows:

(a) The real economy is the area of those creative activities (including industrial, economic, trading activities, but also social and cultural enterprises and endeavors) that concretely "create" values and (maybe more important) incubate the new – even though not always being sufficiently covered by material assets (which particularly in the beginning of economic endeavors are often scarce). In the metaphor of the sandglass, the real economy would be the area between the horizontal dashed lines around the center of the glass. This denotes the area where the real economy is located: in the very center of the economic and creative endeavors, and thus in the center of contemporary society. Here, metaphorically speaking, all "sand" has to pass through on its way through time. But instead of nourishing this decisive dimension, *on the one hand*, many banks preferred to give it to those who don't create much, but would rather trade with already existing goods: foremost to investors and buyers in the real estate market. Most banks were used to lending money *not* as much to the real economy, but to the "speculative economy" in the "real estate bubble". The effect of this practice was that there was in general too much money available for the housing market, thus increasing the prices disproportionally beyond the real value of the objects. We can say that a noticeable, over-proportionate part of the available money – typologically meant to serve the open creativity of the real economy – was "buried" into the soil, that is (again metaphorically speaking), into a dimension "below" the real economy (e.g. the lower part of the sandglass). Thus, this money disappeared from where it was really needed: from the concrete productive process of the enterprises of the real economy, and it became, at least in its basic tendency, "stuck in the soil", thus uncreative. That lack of creativity led to unhealthy swellings. And it ultimately led to the situation where home prices were so high that ordinary middle class home buyers had to take up such disproportionate mortage loans that they ultimately could not repay them – thus triggering the crisis.

(b) However, in the timeframe between 1990 and 2007 banks used to lend money also to another waterhead: to the so-called derivative market (including hedge funds[65]). Structurally speaking, the "derivative" market was an artificial secondary market "above" or "beyond" the real economy (e.g. the upper part of the sandglass), because it did not produce anything by itself, but was in its core about betting on what will happen in the real economy in the future. In the past two decades, hedge funds concentrated in most cases on trading derivatives and other secondary investments contracts on a very short-term basis. These funds were in their essence (and in their majority) huge profit trusts without explicit ties to local, regional, or national communities and without a respective social and environmental commitment. They used – and continue to use – to lend billions of dollars (and euros, as well as other currencies) from banks in order to make profits at any cost anywhere in the world in the fastest way possible, i.e., on a short-term basis, without considering the middle and long-term consequences of their actions on cultures and societies and without thinking in terms of development of the greater good. In fact, the principle of a hedge fund is to use (borrowed) money as a "money magnet": If you have large amounts of capital on hand, you can attract even more money by influencing the markets (including the currency, the real estate and the derivative markets), influencing the prices, by buying and cutting into pieces existing businesses in order to re-sell their pieces with profit, or by artificially devaluating the currency of a country (as it happened with Thailand[66] and partly also with Italy in the 1990s).

Derivative markets and hedge funds together constitute the "waterhead" that we see represented in the upper part of the sandglass metaphor: The derivative bubble. Between 1990 and 2007, large parts of the available money were given by the banks to the "derivative" market and to "hedge funds" in order to circle around the globe in search for short-term profit, without relationship to the real economy – e.g. to concrete creative processes in societal environments.[67] We

---

[65]See "Hedge fund": In: Wikipedia (English), http://en.wikipedia.org/wiki/Hedge_fund (retrieved March 10, 2010).

[66]Cf. R. Benedikter: Warning Signal Thailand (Warnsignal Thailand). In: SWZ – Südtiroler Wirtschaftszeitung. Wochenblatt für Wirtschaft und Politik. Bolzano, 16.04.1999, p. 19. Reprint of an extended version under the title: Warning Signal Thailand. The Asian Economic Crisis Shows the Dangers of the Globalization of the Finance and Capital Markets (Warnsignal Thailand. An der asiatischen Wirtschaftskrise zeigen sich die Gefahren der Globalisierung der Finanz- und Kapitalmärkte). In: Kulturzeitschrift "Die Drei" Frankfurt am Main, 69. Jahrgang, Heft 4/1999, pp. 59–62.

[67]I suspect a large portion of the money in the international hedge funds 1990–2007 came (and continues to come) from institutional investors, many of which are pension funds using the retirement funds of average working people. I would argue that not enough attention has been paid to the impact of choices taken by these large institutional investors, also with regard to their future behavior in the name of the average citizen.

could say that this money was amassed in an artificial bubble that levitated "above" the real economy and that from a certain point in the 1990s on "did not reach the soil of the earth" and the real needs of people and societies anymore. Thus, this money "disappeared" factually from where it was really needed: from the concrete productive process of the real economy, and it became "creative" only in the negative sense that it exploited concretely working communities around the world by the "magnetic" power of capital, and that it created illusive (and in some cases, such as in the case of Thailand, also politically harmful) inter- and transnational games of speculation, which destroyed goods and social cohesion on a global scale.

The point now is that this "sandglass principle" was (and remains until today) *first of all* – by its very nature – *socially irresponsible*. This is because it is not centered in the real economy, and thus not oriented toward the working people, but of primarily speculative character.

In this sense, it was no accident when as early as in March 2003 investor Warren Buffet called the then mainstream "derivative" sector of finance "a rapidly growing ... mega-catastrophic risk for the economy ... These are ... contracts devised by madman ... In fact, such highly complex financial instruments are time bombs and financial weapons of mass destruction that could harm not only their buyers and sellers, but the whole economic system. Large amounts of risk have become concentrated in the hands of relatively few derivatives dealers ... which can trigger serious systemic problems".[68]

In this occasion, Buffet further stated: "Derivatives are financial instruments that allow investors to speculate on the future price of, for example, commodities or shares – without buying the underlying investment. Derivatives generate reported earnings that are often wildly overstated and based on estimates whose inaccuracy may not be exposed for many years. Derivates like (the financial instruments of so-called) futures, options and swaps were developed to allow investors hedge risks in financial markets – in effect buy insurance against market movements – but have quickly become a means of investment in their own right. Outstanding derivatives contracts – excluding those traded on exchanges such as the International Petroleum Exchange – (today) are worth close to $85 trillion, according to the International Swaps and Derivatives Association. (I) warn that derivatives can push ... a 'spiral that can lead to a ... meltdown'."[69]

Later, in May 2007, Mr. Buffett told shareholders that he expected derivatives would inevitably end in huge losses for many financial participants of the system. "I believe we may not know where exactly the danger begins and at what point it becomes a super danger. We don't know when it will end precisely, but ... at some point some very unpleasant things will happen in markets." Noting that the problem

[68]BBC London: Buffet warns on "investment time bomb." Derivatives are financial weapons of mass destruction. In: BBC London online, March 4, 2003, loc cit.

[69]BBC London: loc cit.

of derivatives and leverage was exacerbated by the short-term trading mentality and high turnover in the stock and bond markets, Mr. Buffett added, "There is an electronic herd of people around the world managing an amazing amount of money who make decisions based on minute-by-minute stimuli. I think it's a fool's game."[70,71]

As it turned out, this proved not only to be true for the "derivative" sector. In fact, *both* the waterheads "above" and "below" the real socially productive sector fed themselves (although in different ways) like parasites from the center: from the real economy. This feast was well prepared by the then prevailing cultural and political ideology. "Neoliberal" conditions propagated selfishness as the ultimate "virtue"[72] of humanity that would in the end prove to be good for everybody,[73] as well as ruthless competition as anthropological ideal of "universal" cultural value since anchored in the alleged nature of man.[74] According to this worldview, a system was established where such a selfishness could blossom mainly "above" and "below" the center. The two "waterheads" "above" and "below" obviously did not care about the development of society as a whole; and they were not concerned about the greater good or the common wealth. Since such a system under the "neoliberal" framework was supposed to serve egoism, not the common good, we can call it "socially problematic" or even "socially irresponsible".

Second, the "sandglass principle" was carried out with *intransparency*. That means, as we have pointed out above, that the customer who gave his or her money to a bank was getting no detailed information about what the bank was doing with the money, where the money was invested, and what specific purposes it served. Basically all reports on the crisis confirm that not only the average bank customer, but even the most highly specialized Wall Street finance industry analysts struggled

---

[70]W. Buffet, in: M. Panzner: Buffett on Derivatives: "A Fool's Game." In: http://seekingalpha.com/article/34606-buffett-on-derivatives-a-fool-s-game, May 7, 2007.

[71]The tricky issue here is one of liquidity though. One [of the few] benefits of speculators is that they provide market liquidity, which generally leads to more efficient market pricing.

[72]A. Rand: The Virtue of Selfishness, Signet, New York, NY 1964. As the book states, "Ayn Rand here sets forth the moral principles of *Objectivism*, the philosophy that holds man's life – the life proper to a rational being – as the standard of moral values, and regards altruism as incompatible with man's nature, with the creative requirements of his survival, and with a free society." Cf. "Ayn Rand", In: Wikipedia (English), http://en.wikipedia.org/wiki/Ayn_Rand; and "Objectivism", In: Wikipedia (English), http://en.wikipedia.org/wiki/Objectivism_%28Ayn_Rand%29, (both retrieved August 20, 2010).

[73]A. Rand has been the philosophical and ideological teacher of former US Federal Reserve Bank Chairman Alan Greenspan (born 1926, FedReserve chairman 1987–2006), who notoriously called her "my only teacher." See, for example, S. K. Beckner: Back from the Brink. The Greenspan Years, Wiley New York 1999; and R. Benedikter: The Attention Economy. Perspectives of a New Economic Approach (Die Aufmerksamkeitsökonomie. Perspektiven einer neuen Wirtschaftsform). In: R. Benedikter (ed.): Postmaterialism – The Second Generation (Postmaterialismus – Die zweite Generation), Vol. 2: Man in Economic Culture (Der Mensch), Vienna 2004. Although Ayn Rand distanced herself fiercely from being labeled as "neoliberal," her mindset exemplified in splendid, even brilliant philosophical arguments and astonishing novels the main inspirations for it.

[74]Cf. A. Rand: Atlas Shrugged, New York, NY 1957; and A. Rand: The Fountainhead, New York, NY 1943.

to understand what exactly the banks and their "financial instruments specialists" were doing with the money they administrated by creating derivatives on derivatives on derivatives – and probably even some high-ranking bank managers didn't know that either. Additionally, most economic scientists at universities and think tanks didn't understand the full implications of the "neoliberal" financial practices – not only because the system became so complicated, but also due to the lack of transparency. As the director of the James Martin 21st Century School of Oxford University, Professor Ian A. Golding, previously vice president of the World Bank (2003–2006)[75], presently one of the founding members of the new think tank "Institute for New Economic Thinking" INET New York[76] founded in response to the crisis rightly (and self-critically) pointed out, "there are 20,000 professional academics worldwide in the economic sciences, and not a single one of them foresaw the crisis, even if they are full time employed for it."[77] What does that mean for the state of the economic sciences on the one hand and – probably at least equally important – for the transparency of the financial system for those who try to understand it on the other hand?[78]

Third, the sandglass principle was *unsustainable*. It seems obvious that the "sandglass principle" that dominated the banking and money market between the fall of the Berlin Wall in 1989 and the financial and economic crisis of 2007–2010 was – and still is – not oriented toward sustainability. "Sustainability" means "the capacity to endure. In ecology, the word describes how biological systems remain diverse and productive over time. For humans, it is the potential for long-term maintenance of well-being, which in turn depends on the well-being of the natural world and

---

[75] I. A. Goldin has initiated and directed a wide range of collaborative research programs, including the Programs of the Organization of Economic Co-Operation and Development OECD and of the Rockefeller Foundation on "The Economics of Sustainable Development", as well as of the "Economic Reform, Trade and Development". Cf. "Ian Goldin": In: Wikipedia (English), http://en.wikipedia.org/wiki/Ian_Goldin (retrieved July 23, 2010).

[76] The Institute for New Economic Thinking INET is an independent think tank publicly launched in the framework of a conference held in April 2010 at Kings College, Oxford University, by leading world economists, among them Nobel Laureate Joseph Stiglitz. It was formally founded with an endowment from US investor George Soros in October 2009, and has its main seat in New York City. Its main goal is to rethink the basic paradigms of the international financial and economic sciences given that these sciences have obviously failed to foresee the crisis; as well as to lay the building stones for a new, "integrative" economic paradigm for the post-crisis world. The programs of the INET are of high quality and can be recommended with conviction – even if some initiatives appear rather elitist and are not yet geared toward civil society (i.e. not "participatory" in the broader sense). Nevertheless, the INET is – necessarily, as the post-crisis situation unavoidably requests – concerned with sustainable finance and common wealth development for the future. For a detailed overview see: http://ineteconomics.org.

[77] I. Goldin: In: The Institute for New Economic Thinking INET: The Role of the Economic Profession in the Crisis, http://ineteconomics.org./videos (retrieved August 22, 2010). Cf. similarly R. Skidelsky and C. Westerlin Wigstrom (eds.): The Economic Crisis and the State of Economics, Palgrave McMillan 2010.

[78] Cf. A. Kaletsky: Capitalism 4.0. The Birth of a New Economy in the Aftermath of Crisis, Public Affairs 2010.

the responsible use of natural (and social) resources."[79] The "sandglass principle" of mainstream banking and finance was clearly about speculating on the achievements and risks of others and about taking irresponsible risks rather than about the responsible use of resources, whether natural or social. Strictly economically speaking, the crisis has showed a growing issue of "sustainability of profits" as well, which is becoming increasingly important as the innovation – and thus the change – factor at the interface between technology and economy is speeding up.[80] The "sandglass principle" belongs clearly (and exclusively) to the pre-crisis world insofar as it obviously did not care about any sustainability of profits.

Overseeing the overall picture, the "sandglass principle" of the mainstream banking and finance system between 1990 and 2007 that led into the crisis looks approximately like this (Fig. 2).

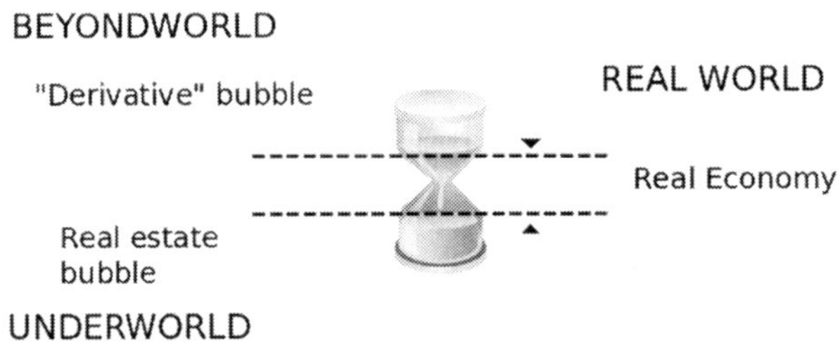

Fig. 2 The typological relationship between the real economy (*center*) and the two "side economies" or "bubble economies" that triggered the crisis: the real estate bubble ("*below*" in the "underworld") and the "derivative bubble" ("*above*" in the "beyondworld")

This recapitulatory image shows the typological picture of how money and capital was distributed in the years preceding the crisis not as much by the mainstream banking and finance *industry*, but mainly by the mainstream banking and finance *system* (which is not the same!).

- Large amounts of money were put into the "underworld" of the *real estate bubble*,
- as well as into the "beyond world" of the *derivative bubble* (including the "hedging" bubble),
- by progressively (although probably in the majority of cases involuntarily) diminishing and thus also devaluating the center-staged "real-world" activities of the *real economy*.[81]

[79]The term "Sustainability." In: http://en.wikipedia.org/wiki/Sustainability (retrieved January 25, 2010).

[80]The issue of sustainability of profits – and its non-consideration by the speculative financial system – is a critical factor in explaining the origins of the crisis. Again, I would argue that the pressure for short-term returns from institutional investors like pension funds was – and remains – one of the key underlying problems not yet addressed sufficiently by post-crisis analysis.

[81]One might argue that while the "sandglass principle" metaphor may be accurate in principle, it would nevertheless be difficult to give any concrete examples of how the real economy in the

As a result of the increasing drain of money from the real economy to the leveraging bubbles "above" and "below" it, the available capital did not only not help the "real economy," but rather put it under speculative pressure, which is what the arrows in Fig. 2 indicate. The bigger the bubbles "above" and "below" got, being in principle unproductive, the more they necessarily fed themselves from the center. At the same time, the money available for the real economy relatively lost importance for the overall system – even if, as said, the real economy feeds all parts of it, because it is the main concretely productive dimension of the system.

As we have seen, at a certain point of the crisis, there was no fresh capital left for the real economy because the two "bubbles" "above" and "below" had sucked up large amounts of it and could not let it circulate anymore back to the system. Since banks were not paid back the money they had pumped into two "bubble" dimensions, a situation of low liquidity first for the real economy and then for the system as a whole developed, which some experts rightly termed "capitalism without capital."[82]

So far, there are very different – and highly contradicting – estimations on what amounts the shift of money from the real economy into the two "bubble economies" comprised and – systemically speaking much more important – how this unhealthy relationship between the real economy, the real estate bubble, and the derivative bubble distorted the balances between the concretely productive sphere in the center, and the "waterheads" aside. In any case, the amounts were enormous, and the balances between the three spheres were distorted noticeably. According to German philosophy and media theory Professor Peter Sloterdijk from the University

---

United States and in Europe was under-capitalized during the pre-crisis years (i.e., between the 1990s and 2007). Money was cheap and relatively accessible for most endeavors back then. In fact, one might argue that on the contrary, the overabundance of liquidity in general was a fundamental cause of the housing and derivative bubbles. While that might be correct to a certain extent, the point remains that large amounts of the available money were put into the "underworld" and the "beyondworld" – and exactly that contributed to the crisis by creating unhealthy bubbles, not only the sheer overabundance of money in the real economy. The subsequent growing liquidity problem of the real economy (experienced probably more in Europe than in the United States) was not the *cause* of the crisis, but it became one main factor of the "domino-effect" *once the crisis had started*, by helping to spread it around and to affect large parts of the productive economy. Fact is, that most traditional banks in Europe and in the United States already in an early stage of the crisis significantly reduced their lending amounts to down-to-earth businesses, industry, and manufacturing because they were afraid of suffering additional losses, after their capital resources were weakened by the losses in the speculative real estate and derivative businesses. Most small- and medium-sized enterprises in the United States and in Europe unanimously report that during the early stages of the crisis they couldn't get the loans and credits they needed, or that they could get them only at a very expensive price they often couldn't afford. A critical amount of liquidity went into government bonds or – now when the worst of the crisis seems to have passed – into high-risk derivative funds again.

[82]D. N. Chorafas: loc cit. Cf. similarly D. N. Chorafas: Financial Boom and Gloom, Palgrave MacMillan, London, 2008. Cf. G. Assenza and A. Martynau: loc cit, pp. 10–25.

of Art and Design Karlsruhe (who in 2005 wrote one of the most well-received German books about the history of globalization[83]),

> "Today's economy suffers from a chronic defect. The virtual financial markets have split from the real economy. Former German Chancellor Helmut Schmidt used a beautiful metaphor describing the ideal relationship between the financial industry and the real economy: the amounts of money of speculative capital should be a kind of dress, which is customized appropriately to the body of the real economy. The dress should be rather casual, and enwrap the body loosely. But in reality, this loose financial couture has developed into a fantastic, spooky encasement [of the real economy], which is fluttering anchorless through the space. The estimations are diffuse: One assumes that the speculative businesses have bloated in the proportion of 1:10 against the real economy; others claim it is 1:50. It is part of the current lack of measurements that we can't even say with full precision in which dimensions we should imagine the disproportion between the real economy and the speculative finance that has been established until 2007. The effect in any case is so far a seemingly universal devaluation of values, which is not only related to economic goods, but basically to all our value scales. Nobody seems to know anymore what is big and what is small, or what is a lot and what is a little."[84]

According to Paul Farrell from MarketWatch, "The derivatives bubble explode(d) five times bigger in five years: Derivatives grew into a massive bubble, from about $100 trillion in 2002 to $516 trillion by 2007 ... Data on the growth of derivatives to $516 trillion in five years comes from the most recent survey by the Bank of International Settlements, the world's clearinghouse for central banks in Basel, Switzerland."[85]

Summing up, the relevant argument I want to make here is that the amount of credit extended to non-productive activities in the "above-world" of the derivative bubble and the "below-world" of the real estate bubble (regardless of its size relative to all credit) was sufficiently large to create a crisis when the markets collapsed. Or to be more precise: What the crisis showed is that regardless of the absolute amounts, the relative amounts put into the systemic distortions of the "sandglass" model are sufficient to create economic havoc when the respective business models are determined to be unsustainable.

A very last point to mention is that this "sandglass principle" has the inbuilt tendency of growing the "waterheads" "above" and "below" always bigger and – if possible – always faster. The dynamics of the "sandglass principle" work(ed)

---

[83] P. Sloterdijk: The Inner World Dimension of Capital (Im Weltinnenraum des Kapitals), Frankfurt am Main, Suhrkamp Verlag, 2005.

[84] P. Sloterdijk, in: E. Karcher: Revolution of the Mind! Peter Sloterijk on the Future. An Interview (Revolution des Geistes! Peter Sloterdijk über die Zukunft. Ein Interview). In: Süddeutsche Zeitung, January 3, 2009, http://www.sueddeutsche.de/kultur/peter-sloterdijk-ueber-zukunft-revolution-des-geistes-1.371816 (retrieved August 20, 2010). Cf. more in detail P. Sloterdijk: In The Inner World Dimension of Capital (Im Weltinnenraum des Kapitals), loc cit.

[85] P. B. Farrell: Derivatives (are) the new "Ticking Bomb." Buffett and Gross Warn: $516 trillion bubble is a disaster waiting to happen. In: MarketWatch, March 10, 2008, http://www.marketwatch.com/story/story/print?guid=B9E54A5D-4796-4D0D-AC9E-D9124B59D436 (retrieved August 29, 2010).

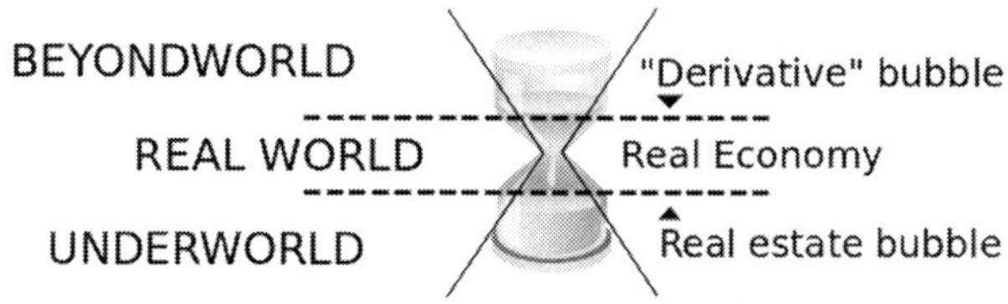

Fig. 3 The dynamics between the three typological spheres of the financial system of 2000–2007

in a way that was (and still is) tightening the center, by expanding the two sides "above" and "below" (at least regarding the relative amounts) in an exponential way: see Fig. 3. Figure 3 does not show the numerical distribution of money in the "old" financial system between 1990 and 2007, but rather the structural tendency of the "neoliberal" system to blow up the two "side economies" by relatively tightening the center. Although the overall system of financial activities established in the "ultra-liberal" period had implemented a mechanism of linear increase, the two "side economies" grew, as the events particularly between 2000 and 2007 showed, to a much bigger extent than the real economy – and ultimately to an extent that went out of control and started to create such an imbalance that this growth "without a real basis" heavily influenced the system as a whole to the brink of collapse.

Taking all the aspects of the – mainly metaphorically and not strictly empirically meant model summarized in the following Fig. 3[86] – it becomes clear that the "sandglass principle" of "globalized" post-cold-war capitalism was neither socially responsible nor transparent or sustainable. It was not focused on the real economy, but – and with increasing fervour – on side aspects of it. As a result of the steady increase of these side aspects at the (relative) expenses of the real economy, the whole construct eventually became a ticking "time bomb" which was just a matter of time to explode, or to implode.[87,88]

---

[86]It is important to explicitly note that the "sandglass model" used in this chapter to explain the basic mechanisms that triggered the crisis is by no means conceived as a representative statistical or quantitative model. It doesn't show the real distribution of money in the current western capitalistic economy. And it does not claim in any way that there is no money left in the real economy in the center, because the two "bubble economies" may have dried all of it up; of course there is still money in the real economy, and even a lot (given that probably overall seen there is even too much money around, as we have seen earlier). The "sandglass model" is *not* about the concrete quantitative proportions between "real economy" and the "bubble economies". Instead, it is useful as a qualitative didactical model of envisioning the entire situation, its inherent dynamics and some systemic features of the pre-crisis finance industry practices at one glance. That is how it can and should be used to understand the crisis, and to build perspectives out of it – not more and not less. Thus, this model should serve as a metaphor for what I believe to be one general mechanism that caused the crisis.

[87]Or as Paul B. Farrell already at the start of March 2008 rightly subsumed: "The derivatives bubble was fueled by ... (some) key economic and political trends (...):

1. (United States' and Europe's) Federal Reserve's cheap money policies created the subprime-housing boom;
2. War budgets burdened the US Treasury and future entitlements programs;
3. Trade deficits with China and others destroyed the value of the US dollar;
4. Oil and commodity rich nations demanding equity payments rather than debt.

In short, despite clear warnings, a massive derivatives bubble (was) driving the domestic and global economies, a bubble that continues growing today parallel with the subprime-credit meltdown triggering a bear-recession . . .. To grasp how significant this bubble increase is, let's put that $516 trillion in the context of some other domestic and international monetary data:

- US annual gross domestic product is about $15 trillion;
- US money supply is also about $15 trillion;
- Current proposed US federal budget is $3 trillion;
- US Government's maximum legal debt is $9 trillion;
- US mutual fund companies manage about $12 trillion;
- World's GDPs for all nations is approximately $50 trillion;
- Unfunded social security and Medicare benefits $50 trillion to $65 trillion;
- Total value of the world's real estate is estimated at about $75 trillion;
- Total value of world's stock and bond markets is more than $100 trillion;
- Bank of International Settlements (BIS) valuation of world's derivatives back in 2002 was about $100 trillion;
- BIS 2007 valuation of the world's derivatives is now a whopping $516 trillion.

(Today's) cascading 'domino effect' was brilliantly described (by) columnist Jesse Eisinger (who) concluded, "There's nothing intrinsically scary about derivatives, except when the bad 2% blow up." Unfortunately, that 'bad 2%' did blow up . . . It only takes a little spark from a 'bad 2%' deal to ignite this $516 trillion weapon of mass destruction. Think of this entire unregulated derivatives market like an unsecured, unpredictable nuclear bomb in a Pakistan stockpile. It's only a matter of time.

The fact is derivatives have become the world's biggest black market, exceeding the . . . traffic in stuff like arms, alcohol, gambling, and (. . .) cigarettes. Why? Because like all black markets, derivatives are a perfect way of getting rich while avoiding taxes and government regulations. And in today's slowdown, plus a volatile global market, Wall Street knows derivatives remain a lucrative business.

Recently Pimco's bond fund king Bill Gross said: "What we are witnessing is essentially the breakdown of our modern-day banking system, a complex of leveraged lending so hard to understand that Federal Reserve Chairman Ben Bernanke required a face-to-face refresher course from hedge fund managers. In short, not only Warren Buffett, but Bond King Bill Gross, our Fed Chairman Ben Bernanke, the Treasury Secretary Henry Paulson and the rest of America's leaders can't figure out the world's $516 trillion derivatives.

Why? Gross says we are creating a new 'shadow banking system.' Derivatives are now not just risk management tools. As Gross and others see it, the real problem is that derivatives are now a new way of creating money outside the normal central bank liquidity rules. How? Because they're private contracts among two companies or institutions.

This chaotic 'shadow banking system' has become the world's biggest black market. Why? Because central banks require reserves like stock brokers require margins, something backing up the transaction. Derivatives don't. They're not real money. They're paper promises closer to 'Monopoly' money than real US dollars. And it takes place outside normal business channels . . . That's the wonderful world of derivatives, and it's creating a massive bubble that could soon implode." P. B. Farrell: Derivatives the new "ticking bomb." Buffett and Gross warn: $516 trillion bubble is a disaster waiting to happen. In: MarketWatch, March 10, 2008,

Summing up, the "sandglass principle" of the "neoliberal" financial system between 1989 and 2007 was a practice that, like the sand in a sandglass, was necessarily, and by its very nature, "running out" of time grain by grain. But while

---

http://www.marketwatch.com/story/story/print?guid=B9E54A5D-4796-4D0D-AC9E-D9124B59D436 (retrieved August 29, 2010).

[88]Again, although the "sandglass model" attempts to explain the basic mechanism of the crisis, it does not explain all aspects of it. To give just *one* – again "alternative" – example of how many phenomena and respective explanations are competitively in play when analyzing the complex and interwoven origins and causes of the crisis, I would like to mention the original approach of Ernst Ulrich von Weizsäcker, former dean of the Donald Bren School of Environmental Science and Management of the University of California at Santa Barbara, considered one of the leading contemporary thinkers on global sustainability. From his point of view, the housing market collapse with which the crisis started (as we have illustrated above) was indeed the activator and catalyst that triggered the crisis in the public perception. But at the same time, the housing market, with its incredible rise and its subsequent sharp decline between the end of the 1980s and 2007, was much more closely connected to US fuel prices than most observers usually noticed. Von Weizsäcker analyses:

"It has been so far heavily underestimated that the crash of the U.S. housing market of 2006–2007 was closely connected with the relationship of fuel prices with the expansion of the real estate market, i.e. with land consumption in the United States. What is meant by that? Assumingly this: Since the times of Ronald Reagan (1911–2004, US president 1981–1989), Americans followed a kind of untold ideology which consisted in keeping fuel prices always as low as possible, and as a matter of principle – i.e., as a kind of 'citizen's right.' Indeed, during the 1980s and 1990s, the oil and fuel prices were and remained low to very low. The effect was that the commuting distances in the USA almost doubled during the past three decades. At the same time, and as a direct result of low fuel prices and the respectively increasing commuting options, a huge expansion in the overall land consumption took place: People built their houses always farther out of the centre, and farther away from their working place, because fuel was so cheap that almost everybody could afford it to commute to almost every distance. Thus, home prices in the periphery went up dramatically. But when in 2006 the oil prices suddenly increased, many Americans had to leave their periphery houses and move to places closer to their place of employment in the centre, because they could not afford commuting anymore. As a result, most houses in the periphery lost in value, in many cases dramatically – not least due to the fact that many of them were built by relying on exaggerated mortgages and lendings. Thus, the owners were left with debts that were higher than the speculative value of the house they had borrowed it for. Summing up, I would say that the crisis has been co-triggered by the decrease in value of peripheric houses that were valuable only as long as fuel was extremely cheap. Many though still want to make us believe that the crisis and its apparently billionary losses were mainly the result of greedy bankers; i.e., the immoral behavior of just a couple of thousands of persons. But this is a far too simplicistic explanation. The crisis was much more due to do how we systemically use resources, and about our basic mindset of how we conceive the use of land, technology, nature and the social sphere." E. U. von Weizsäcker: "Five times wealth from one kilowatt hour" ("Fünfmal so viel Wohlstand aus einer Kilowattstunde"). In: Utopia Magazin, March 10, 2010, http://www.utopia.de/magazin/ernst-ulrich-von-weizsaecker-faktor-fuenf-mal-so-viel-wohlstand-aus-kilowattstunde-energie-ressourcen.

I mention the approach of my friend and mentor Ernst Ulrich von Weizsäcker here only to underscore, for a last time before we move on, the complexity of the crisis; and as a warning to not too easily reduce it to this or to that viewpoint. But I mention it also to point out once again that this booklet does not presume to give the full detailed account of how to explain the crisis. It rather wants to give a basic picture that is meant to give rise to further investigation on the part of the reader. For sure, there are many things still to explore, and to understand regarding the crisis of 2007–2010.

many well-respected analysts asserted years ahead of the crisis that this system necessarily had to undermine its own bases on the middle and long run, the banking and finance businesses continued to practice it – seemingly stuck in a kind of hypnotic group-think and in a mindset that held that "things are good as long as they last, and then everybody for him- or herself."[89]

4 Social Banking and Social Finance: New Approaches to Money and Finance

As a result of this constellation, its underlying systemic features, its many different (be them implicit, or explicit) functional pillars,[90] as well as its – still widely undervalued – behavioral, social and cultural backgrounds[91] (which overall still

---

[89]There is much relevance to the point that bankers were like lemmings marching to the sea. They have done so repeatedly over the last decades. The quote from Chuck Prince from Citibank on "dancing while the music plays" is quite relevant here, see C. Freeland: Investors had little choice but to keep on dancing. In: The Financial Times, October 8, 2009, http://www.ft.com/cms/s/0/7f7260c2-b43d-11de-bec8-00144feab49a.html

[90]A popular – although necessarily eclectic – list of more reasons explaining the origins and causes of the crisis can be found at J. Fox: The Financial Crisis Blame Game. Who and what got us into this financial mess? Here's my far-from-exhaustive list of the guilty. In: Time Magazine, 12 January 2009, p. 17, http://www.time.com/time/specials/packages/article/0,28804,1869041_1869040_1869030,00.html. I am of the opinion that any such list of possible origins and causes does not undermine, but strengthens, the claim that the "sandglass principle" was the core mechanism that triggered the crisis at the very heart of the international financial system between 1990 and 2007.

[91]In fact, to invest money by speculating (not into the real economy) had become increasingly fashionable during the past decades – making speculation not only a financial, but also a cultural trend and an accepted basic civilizational mindset, generally branded as "progressive." Speculation "above" and "below" the real economy was in the process of becoming more important than the real economy – not only regarding the concept of "success," but also in the minds and hearts of large parts of the population. Why? Because, as German philosopher Peter Sloterdijk stated, the general cultural mindset that triumphed in the pre-crisis years between 1990 and 2007 was that of "Harry Potter," the undisputed imaginary hero of the neoliberal years:

"The change apparently took place in what the neoliberals believe as the seemingly universal problem solving power of the markets ... but in reality, it happened in the name of a magical, i.e. neo-mythical world view. The real hero of 'neoliberalism' is Harry Potter. This is because the 'Harry Potter' novels present a fabled world without any reality frontiers. They convinced a whole generation to discover the illusionist and wizard in themselves. Interestingly, the word 'potter' denotes a craftsman who creates hollow containers, or jugs. Containers (or jugs) are media that absorb in order to release. (German philosophy professor) Martin Heidegger has written a deep philosophical reflection about the essence of 'things' using the example of a jug. The jug can fulfill its function only to the extent that it is hollow, e.g. that and can be filled. If it gets replenished, it then lets the fluid go again; by discharging, it donates itself to others. Contemporary finance, in contrast, seems to have blocked the exit of the jug. There is nothing that flows out anymore – and this fact will not be good on the long run. Only losers today believe in work, while all the others try to do magical 'potter' things and let their 'structured financial products,' that is, their hollow containers fly.

have not been modified in their essence and remain factually still in place), many today are seeking "alternative", i.e. more realistic, more balanced, and more sustainable approaches to the topic. This seems to be especially true for the younger generation who will have to deal with money and finance in a better way to avoid similar crises in the future.[92]

Nevertheless, the old system is doing everything to restore itself as quickly as possible, and to make us forget about the crisis of 2007–2010 and its causes. Just one example? The outcry of leading European parliament members in June 2010

So why should we stop 'performing magic' now (after the crisis)? Because 'witching' is an activity that obscures the relationship between cause and effect. The problems begin when the effect is more important than the cause – financially speaking, when profit is no longer in a reasonable relationship with practical, material achievement and performance of the real economy. I would say that it is exactly this imbalance that has stamped the cultural atmosphere of the past three decades. Many indeed wanted to escape reality; in most cases, an average person spent 40 hours per week working and often couldn't receive decent income – whereas at the same time there were others who could achieve great wealth just by spending a couple of hours doing financial 'magic.' Thus, we have invented a dangerous calculation mode for the overall system. And not to forget: The whole system of education will break down, if the logics of cause and effect are suspended. In the current financial culture, nothing will be predictable, because everything goes." P. Sloterdijk, In: E. Karcher, loc cit.

In other words: The "neoliberal" years between 1989 and 2007 produced a culturally broadly accepted – and even celebrated – mindset that held: You don't have to become wealthy by hard work (i.e., through the real economy), but by "witching" (i.e., by speculation in the "upper" or "lower" part of the "sandglass"). "To witch" was to speculate on high risk, short-term profits without care for any consequences. It was to bet on the work of others, and to triumph in an "easy game" by making lots of money in a comparatively short amount of time, and without any "real work." That is what the hype of Harry Potter in the end was all about: Harry Potter incorporates, in the form of a fairy tale, the spirit of the particular time period of "neoliberalism". But this was a destructive and parasitic spirit, in the end, as the crisis of 2007–2010 ultimately proved. Seen through the character of the culture that stood behind it, the crisis was ultimately a necessary outcome, and, to a certain extent a "natural" consequence. If analyzed in-depth, the "Harry Potter" mindset of the neoliberal finance industry and its culture turned the Calvinistic and protestant mindset that founded America on its head. So if we want to change something we have to change the neoliberal "Harry Potter" culture from pure speculation back to concrete reality – from the two "bubble economies" back to the center of reality.

Or put into other words: We must bring the illusions, pathologies, and fantasies involved in the financial "witching epoch" back to a concrete encounter with the "real world," its human needs, and its social options and possibilities once again. We must turn away from an artificial, speculative mindset that characterized the late neoliberal years back to the ordinary American and European spirit that laid the bases for the incomparable wealth of these countries. It means returning to "real production" compatible with the needs of the social community, as it is the task of a functioning and healthy finance. As we are going to see later on, speculative "inventions" may not be compatible with any of the two basic procedures of modern, capitalistic economies: they neither apply work onto nature (1), nor apply spirit (i.e., organization) onto work (2). Instead, they de facto create a kind of a "witching bubble" by applying "spirit onto spirit" and thus become "virtually" (and spiritually) parasitic.

[92]Cf. S. Remer: "Society has not learned from the crisis" ("Gesellschaft hat nicht aus Krise gelernt"). In: Deutschlandradio Kultur, 15.09.2009; and S. Remer: "The Education of Young Bankers Lacks of Knowledge and Morality" ("Es fehlt an Wissen und Moral"). In: Die Zeit Hamburg, November 10, 2008.

for a more intense participation of the civil society and for "alternative" approaches toward a new "Financepeace" destined to counter the increasing activities of old system financial lobbyists, who are trying to obstruct reforms:

"Finance lobbying is obstructing reforms. There has been an unusual cry for help from the European Parliament in Brussels, Belgium: 22 members of the European Parliament's special committee on the financial crisis[93] warn of the intense lobbying by the mainstream financial industry, aiming towards an 'opinion supremacy'. Its intense lobbying must, so they say, be checked by counter-expertises of other groups, who have suggested following the example of the environmental organization 'Greenpeace,' whereby a 'Financepeace' should be set up within the European Parliament. Labor unions, consumer protection and non-governmental organizations have been called into action."[94]

If this is the situation in the European Parliament, then we can assume that things may not be much different in the US Congress. The crisis seems to have triggered a new, unprecedented "lobbying offensive" on both sides of the Atlantic, particularly by those institutions that were at its origins.

But by doing so, the old system is evoking the return of a similar, if not worse, crisis in the future – and thus, it is unwillingly calling for contra-measures. In fact, it is evoking reactions, not only by the European parliamentarians and the civil society but also by world leaders, for example by US President Barack Obama and German Chancellor Angela Merkel.[95]

As early as in January 2010 Barack Obama stated literally: "We have to enact commonsense reforms that will protect American taxpayers and the American economy from future crises. For, while the financial system is far stronger today than it was one year ago, it's still operating under the same rules that led to its near-collapse ... When you see more and more of the financial sector basically churning transactions, engaging in reckless speculation and obscuring underlying risks in a way that makes a few people obscene amounts of money but doesn't add value to the

---

[93]Cf. The European Parliament: Wolf Klinz on European Parliament special committee to tackle the financial crisis. In: http://www.europarl.europa.eu/sides/getDoc.do?pubRef=-//EP//TEXT+IM-PRESS+20091002STO61738+0+DOC+XML+V0//EN, October 7, 2009.

[94]APA/Austrian National Broadcasting Network ORF Teletext: Finance lobby is obstructing reforms. European Parliament calls for "Financepeace" (Finanzlobby behindert Reformen. Europäisches Parlament ruft nach "Finanz-Peace"), June 23, 2010, p. 126. As the following chapters will point out, social banking and social finance are innovative approaches that may be able to contribute to such an endeavor. This is because they can indicate the way toward a sustainabilty oriented "Financepeace" through their basic ideas, but also as "best practice" examples in applied fields of the international banking and finance sector. Thus, social banking and social finance may represent one important pillar for an upcoming civil society initiative by providing it a practically proven applied reference framework.

[95]B. Obama: Obama "Ready To Fight" Banks. In: http://www.youtube.com/watch?v=nRp0UrAmNCs. Cf. J. Calmes: With Populist Stance, Obama Takes on Banks. In: The New York Times, January 22, 2010.

economy – and in fact puts the entire economy at enormous risk – then something's got to change."[96,97] A similar position is held by German Chancellor Angela Merkel.[98]

---

[96]B. Obama in: U.S. News and World Report: Obama Steps Up Campaign Against Wall Street Banks, January 21, 2010, http://www.usnews.com/news/national/articles/2010/01/21/obama-steps-up-campaign-against-wall-street-banks.html. Obama's opinion seems in this case to be relatively representative of his party's overall standpoint. Cf. T. Braithwaite: Democrats adopt hard line on derivatives. Democrats have agreed to a forceful stance on derivatives that could make banks spin off trading desks, but some aids say legislation will stop short of an outright ban. In: Financial Times Europe, April 27, 2010, p. 6.

[97]Going beyond Barack Obama's – overall seen pondered – judgment, some scientists, such as H. N. Pontell from the Department of Criminology, Law and Society at the School of Social Ecology of the University of California at Irvine, went so far to subsume the financial crisis and some of its parts under the label "White-Collar-Crime," a.o. by suggesting that the overall lack of consequences of the crisis 2007–2010 for mainstream bankers and (derivative) traders means to "trivialize lunatic crime." See H. N. Pontell: Fraud and financial crisis. Trivializing the lunatic crime rate. In: H. N. Pontell and S. M. Rosoff (eds.): Social Deviance. Readings in Theory and Research, McGraw Hill, New York 2010, pp. 30–39. Besides that among those who made "obscene amounts of money" through the use of the "sandglass principle" were indeed some criminal individuals who were later brought to trial and convicted to jail sentences, I wouldn't go so far. This is *first* because most of the transactions and business models that led to the crisis were explicitly or unexplicitedly legal at that time. *Second*, like most social bankers do, I believe that the principle of responsibility can be hardly addressed by denoting it negatively in terms of deviance or crime. While new regulations may certainly be necessary, the decisive dimension is a new basic (and systemic) mindset approach to money and finance, which has to be achieved by changing the overall culture of the financial business through education and increased public awareness.

In fact, according to philosophy and media Professor Peter Sloterdijk, business leaders have on average not become greedier than in the past, but rather followed – and in doing so were actively stimulated and rewarded by – the logics of a system that worked in a highly disputable way. The interesting point here is that Sloterdijk blames some reactions to the crisis to have solicitated negative behaviour further: "The world has not become greedier or more avaricious then in previous times. But when the U.S. Federal Reserve Bank in response to the crisis emits money for zero interests, the rational global player has to snap at the chance. Why? Because otherwise he is at a disadvantage to other competitors who will take this easy money.

(Also these disputable reactions) show that the financial crisis has its main cause in technical errors of the world's leading Federal Reserve Banks. Behind these errors stands the conflict between an inflationary and an anti-inflationary course in monetary policies. What we experience today (i.e., as the reactions to the crisis,) is the consequence of the fact, that the pro-inflationists and the debt acrobats have won the game behind the curtains. If the international Federal Reserve Banks attempt to mitigate the crisis by starting the printing presses and printing billions of dollars, we can clearly see how the 'revaluation of values' works. Many governments... are trying to master the turbulences with a hidden strategy of inflation, which in reality is creating an upcoming inflation crisis." P. Sloterdijk, In: E. Karcher, loc cit. Cf. what we have said similarly in footnote 47.

Summing up, if what Sloterdijk asserts is only approximately the truth, it seems to be typical for some temporary, emotionally "heated up" reactions to the crisis by parts of the established social sciences, in particular by (in the broad sense) "leftist" approaches, to exaggerate in the judgment "ad personam" of what happened, and to generalize it in a way that has hardly to do with reality. Thus, by such approaches like the one of H. N. Pontell not much is achieved in the end, because exaggerations usually produce the least impact on reality. Instead, I believe that any reasonable

Following the overall insight that we do need a change, there are two questions that must be answered in order to improve matters:

1. Where do we find an approach to better combine and consistently apply the principles of *social responsibility, transparency*, and *sustainability* to lending and investment practices?
2. What is the role of the individual in reforming the financial system? It seems so hard to make changes in a system as powerful and complex as we have seen in the previous sections. Is there any space for my own contribution? How can I make my voice be heard?

One possible answer to these two questions is *social banking and social finance*. Let us see why; in which sense; to what extent; and how concretely.

In Europe, social banking and social finance have been one of the biggest trends among ordinary bank customers since the 1980s; and some of the important financial players are in the meantime social banks. During the financial crisis of 2007–2010, not only did they not lose any money, but they made the highest gains in their history, increasing their assets with growth rates of about 20–25% per year during 2006–2008 alone. In 2009 – at the peak of the crisis – their average growth rate was about 30%.[99] The combined total balance sheet of European social banks is currently about 12 billion euros (= about US $16 billion),[100] and it continues to grow rapidly. It is expected that the overall growth rate of European social banks will remain

elaboration of the causes of the crisis as well as any proper outline of perspectives consists in making analyses and proposals through balanced and common sense judgments. Some proposals in this sense are found in the following chapters.

[98]Cf. AFP: German Chancellor Angela Merkel wants to cut off financial speculators from business (Angela Merkel will Spekulanten das Handwerk legen), in: AFP News, March 9, 2010.

[99]Info3 News Report Frankfurt am Main, March 1, 2010

[100]C. Scheire and S. De Maertelaere: Banking to make a difference. A preliminary research paper on the business models of the founding member banks of the Global Alliance for Banking on Values. Artevelde University College Gent, in cooperation with the Global Alliance for Banking on Values and supported by the European Social Fund, Artefelde Hogeschool, Gent, June 2009, pp. 19–20; and The International Association of Investors in the Social Economy (INAISE): 12 measures for a socially useful financial system. Four International Social Finance and Community Development Federations put out a call to G-20 Governments. In: http://www.inaise.org/EN/fr_1.html, Paris, Brussels and Washington DC, September 21, 2009. I take only the European banks into account here, and I have inserted the balance sheets as of 2010, where possible (i.e., in the cases of Triodos bank and GLS bank). Cf. Triodos Group News Report: Triodos Group grows by 30%. Stable profit and a record year of lending, in: http://www.triodos.com/com/whats_new/latest_news/press_releases/growth_triodos_group, February 25, 2010; TAZ Berlin: Bank Chief Thomas Jorberg attracts customers (Bankenchef Jorberg zieht Kunden an), in: http://www.gls.de/die-gls-bank/presse/pressespiegel/bankenchef-thomas-jorberg-zieht-kunden-an.html; and NNA News Limited: GLS-Bank: Instead of Financial Crisis Leaps over One-Billion threshold (GLS-Bank: Statt Finanzkrise Milliarden-Hürde genommen). In: NNA News Limited, February 5, 2009.

stable at 15–18% per year throughout the coming years.[101] The reason is simple: during the crisis, many customers gained insight into the above-described practices of "mainstream" banks and shifted their assets to social banks.

Independently from other foresights, Gartner Inc., a UK-based trend analysis and advisory company, predicted as early as in February 2008 that social banks

> "are pushing ... into (traditional) banking and investment services ... [This trend] ... is particularly pronounced in two businesses that are at the very heart of banking, namely lending and payment. Gartner predicts that by 2010, social-banking platforms will have captured 10% of the worldwide market for retail lending and financial planning. So what is social banking and social finance?
>
> Social banking is the combination of social trends, such as green practices, social entrepreneurship, and peer-to-peer lending and financial planning via social networks, with banking products and services. Social banking should not be mistaken for charitable giving. Rather, it combines the social trends in networking communities of interest with financial products, services, capital, and market access for a return on investment and social benefit. Venture capital investment in financial social networks (FSNs) point to the growing prevalence of FSNs and increasing consumer interest in this area.
>
> 'This combination of business, non-profit organizations and social justice is being bolstered by general consumer trends and social causes that appeal to consumers to shop ethically,' said Alistair Newton, research vice president at Gartner. 'In addition, more consumers are generally spending more time in social networks which increasingly form part of consumer purchase processes for new products and services.'
>
> Gartner expects social banking to initially take off in geographies with a developed banking market and widespread adoption of broadband and potentially wireless communication systems. 'Social banking will emerge first where societal cultures have high levels of acceptance for social welfare and potentially where the underserved or unbanked client segments need capital and market access,' said Stessa Cohen, research director at Gartner. 'So we are likely to see this trend first in Western Europe and parts of the United States.' "[102]

The biggest social banks in Europe today are the Germany-based "Gemeinschaft für Leihen und Schenken" (GLS) Bank – its name literally means "Community for Lending and Donating" – (US $2.2 billion), the Netherlands-based Triodos Bank ($6.7 billion), the Italian Banca Etica ($0.8 billion), the Swiss ABS Bank ($0.7 billion), and the Danish Merkur Bank ($0.2 billion).[103] They were founded

---

[101] Cf. Triodos Group News Report: http://www.triodos.com/com/whats_new/latest_news/press_releases/growth_triodos_group, 25 February 2010; and Info3 News Report Frankfurt am Main, March 1, 2010.

[102] Gartner Inc.: Gartner Says Social Banking Platforms Threaten Traditional Banks for Control of Financial Relationships. New Technologies, Ethical Trends and Rise of Social Networking Set to Change Industry Dynamics. Egham, UK, February 6, 2008. In: http://www.gartner.com/it/page.jsp?id=597907 (retrieved February 15, 2010). Interestingly, as a consequence Gartner Inc. "advises (traditional) banks ... (that they) should identify opportunities for partnerships with FSNs ... (and to) urgently invest in customer behavioral and segmentation analysis and re-engineer business intelligence models so that they can better understand the demographic changes taking place in the market." "Demographic change" here means that social banking is strongly connected to the future segments of the financial markets, i.e. that it attracts particularly the young and well educated portions of the population.

[103] C. Scheire and S. De Maertelaere: loc cit, p. 16. The balance sheet of Triodos bank and GLS bank is given as at February 28, 2010; all others are as at February 28, 2009.

in the 1970s (GLS bank), the 1980s (Triodos), and the 1990s (Banca Etica). There are also more specialized, community and environment oriented banks like the German Nürnberger Umweltbank ($2.27 billion).[104] And there are smaller financial lenders that are sometimes organized as non-governmental organizations (NGOs) such as Dutch Oecocredit or the Ecology Building Society (United Kingdom), as well as foundations like the Dutch Iona Stichting Amsterdam, the Swiss Evidenzgesellschaft Arlesheim, or the Swiss Edith Maryon Stiftung, which function as allies for social banks for an overall development that includes profit as well as non-profit elements by sustaining the same social ideals and strategies. While social banks in most cases lend money, the associated foundations donate money (as in the case of the alliances Triodos Bank/Stichting Triodos and GLS Bank/GLS Treuhand). Altogether, there are currently more than 600 ethical investment funds worldwide, with about 480 in Europe, and their number is constantly increasing.[105]

In this situation, there are *three* important questions often asked about social banks:

- What is the institutional framework of social banks and what is their juridical status?
- How is the remuneration of their CEOs, directors, and leaders determined?
- How do social banks survive if they are lending money well below the average market interest rates or even donate money? Where does the money that keeps them going come from? Are they patient "profit maximizers" or are their investors and customers generally willing to accept below-market financial returns (at least over the short term)?

Let us take a look at each of these three questions in sequence.

Regarding the *institutional framework*, all social banks are independent from each other, as well as from thirds. They have different juridical statuses, depending on the country they operate in, as well as on their outreach, their size, and their specific goals. In many cases they are constituted as registered cooperatives, but some also have the status of regular stock corporations, like for example Triodos Bank.

The *remuneration* of CEOs, managers, and executives of social banks is in general much below the (often highly exaggerated) income level of CEOs of mainstream banks. More important, the differences between the different ranks are less accentuated. For example, unlike the big mainstream players, a CEO of a social bank does not earn 500 times the salary of a normal bank employee in the same

---

[104]Glocalist Daily News: Umweltbank Nürnberg performs brilliantly with 30% growth rate (Umweltbank glänzt mit 30%igem Wachstum). In: http://www.glocalist.com/news/kategorie/wirtschaft/titel/umweltbank-glaenzt-mit-30igen-wachstum/, February 2, 2010; cf. Info3 News Report Frankfurt am Main, March 1, 2010.

[105]F. De Clerck: Ethical Banking. In: L. Zsolnai, Z. Boda and L. Fekete (eds.): Ethical Prospects. Economy, Society and Environment, Springer Netherlands 2009, p. 6.

institution, but rather two or three times that amount (which corresponds to his or her heightened responsibility for the destiny of the overall enterprise of the bank).[106]

Regarding the *interest rates* of social banks, we have to differentiate between the interests on *shareholders' capital* and those on *bank deposits by customers.*

There is a broad spectrum of options on the level of *shareholders' capital*: from interest-free cooperative shares (GLS Bank) to regular stocks (Triodos Bank) to so-called dormant equity holdings (GLS Bank), which is a form of shareholdership without the right and/or the duty to (co-) make decisions (and to be held accountable for them). The interest returns for all these shareholderships are generally below those of mainstream banks.

The interest received from bank deposits by customers (daily allowance, time deposits, savings) is in principle the same as in mainstream banks. The difference is that customers in social banks can't choose purely speculative, high-risk hedge funds (with their usually above the market level interest promises), because they don't exist here.

Most of the social banks in Europe work closely together and develop their growth and investment strategies in intense exchange. Simultaneously, they are intensifying their cooperation with social banks worldwide. In March 2009, 12 social banks from around the globe founded the "Global Alliance for Banking on Values"[107] (GABV) with the main seat in London. The official founding statement says,

> This Alliance was created in the belief that trends can be set to change the boundaries of mainstream finance, and contributions can be made to the growth and development of social innovation in the financial sector. The Alliance presents itself as a global alliance of innovative banking institutions, focused on delivering social finance products and basic financial services, while financing community based development initiatives and social entrepreneurs thereby fostering sustainable and environmentally sound enterprises, and fulfilling human development potential including poverty alleviation, while generating ... (equally) for People, Profit and Planet.[108]
>
> (Potential) members of the Global Alliance for Banking on Values are all banks whose central mission is investment in a society that values human development, social cohesion and responsibility for our natural environment.[109]

But the "Global Alliance" is just the most recent strategic joint venture of its kind; it was preceded as early as in 1989 (not by chance the year of the fall of the Berlin Wall and of the start of globalization!) by INAISE, the International Association of Investors in the Social Economy.[110] While INAISE was (and remains) a rather

---

[106] Although important as a matter of principle, I would argue that this aspect is not nearly as critical as the first and third question. There is lots of populist attention surrounding the compensation issue of bankers, but the real issues is what values drive a social bank. I believe that these values will more likely lead to appropriate compensation practices, rather than interventions "from above" (i.e., by governments).

[107] The Global Alliance for Banking on Values: http://www.gabv.org/.

[108] C. Scheire and S: De Maertelaere: loc cit, p. 4.

[109] The Global Alliance for Banking on Values: http://www.gabv.org/ (retrieved January 26, 2010).

[110] INAISE: http://www.inaise.org/EN/frdr_1.html.

colored mix between banks in the strict sense, civil society groups of different origin and interests as well as of local and regional community initiatives "from the bottom-up" in the very broad term, the Global Alliance for Banking on Values is a "hard core" banking alliance that specializes in the "big" international financial sector in a rather restricted sense. Applicants for membership have to offer full banking services and to demonstrate a total balance sheet of more than US $100 million.

Additionally, since July 2009 there is a "hybrid" association between social banks and mainstream financial institutions dedicated to "impact investment": the "Global Impact Investment Network (or GIIN), co-founded by the social banks Triodos Bank and Shorebank Chicago. Partners of this "mixed" approach are, among others, Citigroup, J.P. Morgan, Capricorn, Deutsche Bank, the Bill and Melinda Gates Foundation, and the Rockefeller Foundation. "Impact investment" is a kind of intermediate form between ethically and environmentally aware investment and mainstream banking. It can be considered as a sympathetic sideline to social banking that contains certain elements, but not all features of "pure" social banking and social finance.[111,112] The official self-description of GIIN states, "The Global Impact Investing Network is a not-for-profit organization dedicated to increasing the effectiveness of impact investing. Impact investments aim to solve social or environmental challenges while generating financial profit."[113] It is clear that the profit is in this case mainly meant to strengthen the capital basis, to

[111]The Global Impact Investing Network GIIN: http://www.globalimpactinvestingnetwork.org/cgi-bin/iowa/home/index.html.

[112]The interesting main question here is of course how "pure" a "neo-idealistic" approach like social finance must be to have any long-term effect on the societal whole, particularly on the systemic level. Experience since the 1980s and 1990s has shown that under increasingly complex and multilpolar cultural and economic conditions, only "pure," even if comparatively one-sided, approaches have proven to be specialized and thus focused enough within the system to alter its course at least to a certain extent. Empirical research of the past three decades indicates that in their vast majority, only such rather "one-sided" approaches have exercised any effect on the greater system.

The (philosophical, as well as principal "world view") question for the new generation of socially engaged people is: How "pure" must I calibrate my attempt toward "improving" the world, and toward implementing my ideals, to have any effect on the overall system – given that (most of) these attempts will be "neutralized" by as many contrary approaches? And further: Is it worthwhile to pursue any "hybrid" (or even, to use a more positive term, "integral") approaches at all? As the balance of – and the systemic dialectics between – forces seems to be everything in a democratic society, the question may arise: Does a "balanced" (as opposed to a "one-sided," or "pure") approach not play the game of the opponents of social banking and social finance?

These are "deep", principal strategic questions to discuss – not only between the members of the "new generation" of bankers, but also for everyone that deals with money, i.e. basically for all of us. Further, these questions underscore as such the basic "fundamental ambivalence" (Zygmunt Bauman) of our current civilizational constellation we discussed in footnote 2; and they are fundamental for everyone to reach a clear stance toward the current economic-political scenery.

Like most of my colleagues, I am actively in favor of consciously "balanced" paradigms, but it is still a legitimate debate if these are useful approaches under every circumstance.

[113]The Global Impact Investing Network, loc cit.

balance the impact of inflation upon the shareholder capital, and (in its majority) to be re-invested, instead of being detracted by the capital owners as their profit.

Further, academic research and scientific engagement on social banking and social finance have dramatically increased during the past years. New institutions have been established such as the Skoll Centre for Social Entrepreneurship at the Said Business School of Oxford University in 2003[114] and the Institute for Social Banking in Bochum, Germany, in 2006.[115] This trend is not only due to increased interest by the international academia to innovative issues in the financial sphere, but also a result of the increasing consciousness of most contemporary leaders of social banks that the investment into a sound academic research and teaching is (like educational initiatives as innovative factors are in a more general way) one decisive pillar for developing the mainstream "cultural" attitude toward money and finance in a more inclusive and balanced direction.

Research and teaching is, as we know, potentially at its best when it is globally connected and peer reviewed, and sometimes also if it is tied to global umbrella organizations like the United Nations. Even if these institutions admittedly do not always have the best reputation in the United States and are sometimes seen as the "least harmful compromise," it is probable that they might serve as global integrators and distributors of systemic improvements for the future also in the interest of the U.S.

The Institute for Social Banking in Germany, for example, is an official project of the United Nations' UNESCO Decade "Education for Sustainable Development 2005–2014."[116] It awards a Master of Arts degree (within a couple of years also a Ph.D.) in social banking and social finance in cooperation with the University of Plymouth, United Kingdom. Its study program "MA in Social Banking and Social Finance" has been awarded the Special Prize of the German Continuing Education Innovation Awards 2010 by the German Federal Institute for Vocational Education in Bonn. The institute cooperates with universities worldwide, rapidly expanding its outreach. It publishes extensively on the topics of financial cycles and crises from an ethical viewpoint, including sustainability, ecology (e.g. human ecology), and experimental banking and finance practices,[117] receiving noticeable public attention through media coverage by European "big players" like "Die Zeit," "Die Welt," "Handelsblatt," or "Wirtschaftswoche". The main goal of its research and teaching is to show students and the public the "big picture," that is, to critically point toward the relationship between money, finance, environment, culture, and politics in the current world, and to encourage people to develop complementary, innovative viewpoints. Currently, the Institute for Social Banking is reaching out to the

---

[114] The Skoll Centre for Social Entrepreneurship at Oxford University: http://www.sbs.ox.ac.uk/centres/skoll/Pages/default.aspx.

[115] The Institute for Social Banking Bochum: http://www.social-banking.org/en/news/.

[116] UNESCO Decade "Education for Sustainable Development" 2005–2014: http://www.unesco.org/en/esd/.

[117] The Institute for Social Banking and Social Finance Paper Series: http://www.social-banking.org/en/researchteaching/isb-paper-series/.

United States to form long-term cooperative clusters and partnerships with similar initiatives in the US academia.[118]

All of these different types of institutions:

1. social banks,
2. their global networks like INAISE and GABV,
3. their associated foundations and NGOs, and
4. the related theme-centered research and teaching institutes

are united by the common purpose of seeking to understand, exemplify, and put into practice what is needed today (and what is called for by leading innovative politicians like US President Barack Obama[119] and German Chancellor Angela Merkel[120]): to renew and innovate the financial system through the implementation of *social responsibility, transparency, and sustainability.*[121]

---

[118]Apart from the several existing social banking and social finance initiatives in the United States – which are in part older then their European counterparts (see the following chapters) – there is an increasing number of related academic approaches towards social finance in the United States, even though in most cases with slightly different centers of gravity than in Europe. Among them are the MIT Green Hub at the MIT Boston, Department of Urban Studies and Planning, which includes MIT's Community Innovators Lab (CoLab), http://www.thegreenhub.org/; the Center for Social Innovation CSI of the Graduate School of Business of Stanford University, http://csi.gsb.stanford.edu/; the Center of Ethics in Society of Stanford University, http://ethicsinsociety.stanford.edu/; the Orfalea Center for Global and International Studies of the University of California at Santa Barbara, http://www.global.ucsb.edu/orfaleacenter/index.html; the Bruce Initiative on Rethinking Capitalism at UC Santa Cruz, http://www.rethinkingcapitalism.org/; the Institute for Social Innovation at Fielding Graduate University, http://www.fielding.edu/whyFielding/ci/isi.aspx; the (private) Foundation for the Advancement of Social Theory (FAST), associated with Fielding University, http://www.fielding.edu/whyFielding/ci/fast.aspx; and the Institute for New Economic Thinking INET New York, http://ineteconomics.org/, to mention just a few.

[119]B. Obama: loc cit.

[120]A. Merkel: loc cit.

[121]All those who at this point would like to get additional "hard" statistical numbers – beyond those rendered here – as well as more information about the operative sides of the social banking business in the strict, daily applied sense should consult the websites of the global alliances of social banks mentioned above, the book "Networking Social Banking" published by INAISE of 2010, see www.inaise.org, and the forthcoming book by O. Weber and S. Remer: Social Banks and the Future of Sustainable Finance, Routledge, London 2011. The latter will focus on information about the operative realities and procedures for current and future practitioners in the sector including operative business strategies for the rapidly changing environments of "post-national" finance. Some concrete case studies on a quantitative level can be found in: P. Schwizer, A. Carretta and V. Boscia (eds.): Cooperative Banking in Europe: Case Studies. Palgrave Macmillan Studies in Banking and Financial Institutions, Palgrave McMillan, London 2009. I do not include this detailed information here, because the focus of this short volume is on providing a first introductory image of what social banking and social finance are about; and this endeavor is necessarily tied more to the understanding of a mindset than to the description of concrete everyday operations. Sure enough, these remain important for those who want to go further, or take action themselves by joining the social banking

But what does that precisely mean in detail? And what exactly does social banking and social finance? Is there any more narrow definition for it? And, perhaps most important: Is there a definition that can be used as a "connecting bridge" between the different financial and institutional frameworks of the United States and Europe?

Ok, let us get one step closer to the point now.

5 What Is a Social Bank? Definitions and Practices

The definition of a social bank, and what it is not, is not always easy. This is due to the fact that there are very different approaches that can be subsumed under the term "social banking." This notion currently includes "ethical banking," "cooperative banks and credit unions," the so-called "new social banks", "private and community shared development banks," and "microfinance banks."

All of these initiatives and institutions have a slightly different center of gravity, and they put their focus on different aspects of social change and development. Further, the identity they connect with the term "social" differs often from country to country and from culture to culture. So how can a common definition of what social banking is be delineated?

During the last years, one unifying definition has been attempted as follows: "Social banking is banking that fights poverty," according to Udo Reifner from Hamburg University.[122] But given that most social banks – with the exception of microfinance banks and similar specialized initiatives mainly in the so-called "third

business, and so they should consult the reading list at the end of this volume. An extended collection of highly specialized literature can be found at the "Institute for Social Banking Bochum" reading list, see: http://www.social-banking.org/fileadmin/isb/file/ISBLiteratureResources.pdf.

[122] U. Reifner and J. Ford (eds.): Banking for People: Social Banking, New Poverty Consumer Debts and Unemployment in Europe, Walter de Gruyter Publishers, New York 1992. Cf. U. Reifner and J. Evers, Institute for Financial Services IFF of Hamburg University (eds.): The Social Responsibility of Credit Institutions in the EU: Access, Regulation and New Products, Baden Baden, Nomos 1998. In his writings, Reifner rightly underscores the lead slogan of social finance: "Using money – rather than having it." Sure enough, this may be a good slogan for the financial industry on a systemic level; but it is not similarly appropriate for the individual consumer's use of his personal money. From my point of view, this isn't meant as an incitement to reckless spending and consuming, but rather as an invitation to take bank's money out of the "hoarding boxes" of the upper and lower part of the "sandglass" and to put it to work in "the real world." In fact, one of the causes of the economic crisis 2007–2010 was that the individual consumer on average did not save enough and spent too much, ultimately overstretching his or her credits. See: U. Reifner: Using Money. 20 years Institute for Financial Services, Baden-Baden, Nomos 2007. Cf. U. Reifner: "A Call to Arms." For Regulation of Consumer Lending, in: Whitford, B./Ramsay, I./Niemi-Kiesiläinen, J. (eds.): Consumer Credit, Debt and Bankruptcy: Comparative and International Perspectives. Hart Publications, UK 2009. Reifner's current book on: The Money Society. Lessons from the financial crisis (Die Geldgesellschaft. Aus der Finanzkrise lernen, Wiesbaden 2010) summons up his writings of the last 30 years with focus on the contemporary financial system. Reitner servers currently also as the official speaker of the European Coalition for Responsible Credit (ECRC) (see: http://www.responsible-credit.net/).

world" – are mostly directed toward social innovation, environmental and community development in the much broader sense rather than fighting poverty as such, this seems to be a too narrow definition.

Something similar seems to be true for a second definition: "Social banking is banking directed towards improving the 'financial literacy' of the biggest number of people and populations possible [on the globe, but especially in the 'West'] in order to pave the way for a different, more sustainable public consciousness regarding money and finance."[123]

Again, as plausible as this is, it seems to become reductive if used with the pretense of "core definition." Social banking is indeed decisively centered about changing the consciousness of consumers and the broad public regarding what money is and how it can be best used. Since it wants to provide and increase the societal insight into the connections between money, society, politics, culture, and education in order to reach out for a more just and balanced world, it follows the basic principles of enlightenment: rationalization and emancipation for the largest possible number of people. Thus, the educational aspect (which includes the aspect of serving as an alternative model) is a task of great importance to social banks. Nevertheless, it is just one aspect within a more complex puzzle.

Christophe Scheire and Sofie De Maertelaere, researchers at Artevelde University College Gent in Belgium, propose a broader, more general definition:

> "Let's change the world! Money is there for people! More than interest!" No, these are not slogans by NGOs, neither are they workshop titles from a world social forum, nor are they documentary movie titles. These are slogans by ... who would have guessed it ... banks.[124]

These seem to be descriptions that can be applied to a particularly broad variety of onsets that may reach out from green and ecological to "fair trade" programs as well as to "ethical investment" opportunities within traditional banks, which are in many cases restricted to a certain percentage of their revenue that is re-invested in charity programs, but ultimately functions within the logics of the system as usual. So, it is a good, but maybe even too broad definition in this case.

Frans De Clerck, co-founder of Triodos Bank Belgium and co-founder of the Global Alliance for Banking on Values, has another definition, which is similarly broad, but more elaborated and sophisticated:

> Social, ethical, alternative, sustainable, development and solidarity banking and finance are denominations that are currently used to express particular ways of working with money, based on non-financial deliberations. Standing in the middle of social and economic developments, bankers are well positioned to have an overview and a feeling for what matters ...
>
> The common bond and specificity of what is often described as "ethical, sustainable, social, alternative, development or solidarity" banking and finance ... is that they are characterized by *value driven* impulses and practices at the core of their business, while

[123]U. Reifner: Financial Literacy in Europe, Nomos Publishers, Hamburg 2006.

[124]C. Scheire and S. De Maertelaere: loc cit, p. 3.

> values are (usually) poorly developed in the field of mainstream commercial banking and finance . . .
>
> The private sector and financial institutions in particular are increasingly expected to play an important role in helping to create a truly sustainable world. Conscious consumers, ethical investors, enlightened businesses, non-governmental organizations (NGOs), cultural creators, and leading international institutions are working to make a *triple bottom line (People, Planet and Profit)* a reality. These people and institutions want solutions for poverty, injustice, war, widespread diseases, educational inequalities, destruction of nature and the planet. (. . .) Money, intelligently and wisely invested as an instrument for improving (the) quality of life, can have a major impact on human development. Because of this impact, a neutral attitude to investment and lending is irresponsible . . .[125]

What De Clerck is inducing here is a *first* common core feature of social banking and social finance that makes a difference, because it seems to be a unique characteristic of social banks and social finance institutions. It consists in the fact that they are working with a "triple bottom line." What is that?

The term "triple bottom line" means that unlike traditional banks that judge lending and investment opportunities with a "single bottom line," i.e., with the criterion of profit alone, social banks are defined by applying *three different standards to judge investment and lending opportunities that take into account three different criterions*, all of them equally considered:

- *Profit* (respectively, economic rationality; there can't be losses that threaten the development of the bank as a whole),
- *Environment* (natural habitat, protection, and sustainable handling of resources),
- *People* (the primacy of the community and the balanced advancement of society, seen as a whole).

If applied with consistency and coherence and in a systemic dimension, this "triple bottom line" can be a valid measurement of what defines a social bank.

But there are at least two more features that define a social bank.

The *second* feature is that social banking and social finance are characterized by *maximized transparency*. That means social banks let the customer know in every detail, where his or her money goes, where it is invested or lent to by the bank, and what it concretely produces. Social banks publish at least once a year (many of them twice a year) detailed reports what has been financed, what the losses and returns of the respective operations are, and who concretely is the main beneficiary.

That leads to a situation where the customer not only enjoys the returns on his bank account, but also has full insight into what his money has "done" in the world. He or she is then free to see if this is what he or she wants, if he or she wants to keep that engagement, or if it is time to give the bank advice about better opportunities that "make more sense" (in the literal meaning of the term, i.e. with regard to the realization of values).

---

[125] F. De Clerck: loc cit, pp. 1–2.

De Clerck explains,

> Transparency of ethical banking operations – showing what is financed – is a prerequisite for open dialogue between the bank, clients and civil society.
>
> Conscious bankers can transform feelings of powerlessness (of individuals and groups) into an understanding that something can be done. To practitioners of ethical banking, raising consciousness and responsibility are essential in their missions and ambitions. They make the choice to only finance projects and organizations that contribute to a more sustainable society, and they define absolute criteria about who they will not lend money to, for example, non-sustainable products and/or services and those involving unsustainable working or production processes. Their specific products and services reflect these values and intentions.
>
> In the best circumstances, ethical screening and investor pressure is contributing to a process of intensified observation, questioning, reflection, measurement, ethically amended business principles and consequently adapted decision-making.[126]

There is a third and last core criterion that social banks try to pursue: *human development*. Social banks put much emphasis on emancipating and evolving communities and capacities rather than profit. They operate from the assumption that human development toward a more just, sustainable, and "green" lifestyle is more important, and in the end more beneficial for all, than making profit at all costs for a given number of shareholders.

De Clerck has the point:

> While money is a catch-word of our age, to ethical banking institutions and their shareholders, savers, investors and borrowers, money and ethical banking practices are instruments for human development. These characteristics differ with those of mainstream finance, mainly driven by market forces, shareholder value and financial return...
>
> [Social Banks] focus on the capacity building force of bringing savers and borrowers, consumers and entrepreneurs together for investment – for example in organic agriculture, school education or care for handicapped people. [They] see banking as a continuous and conscious process of directing the money flow to where it is needed in [a] societal and human development perspective...
>
> [They aim toward] using money as an instrument for social change, and that can bring a breath of fresh air to the banking sector.[127]

6 What Is Money and What Is Capital According to Social Banking? The Concept of "Liberation Finance"

Summing up, *social banks consider themselves as "catalysts for social change" without the primacy of profit.*[128] Or to put it in other words, "Social banking we define as where suppliers of financial services take a positive interest in the social outcomes and effects of their activities."[129] In short, social banks conceive themselves as – not only *philosophical*, but, probably much more important, as

---

[126] De Clerck: loc cit, pp. 5–6.

[127] De Clerck: loc cit, pp. 5, 8, 10.

[128] De Clerck: loc cit, p. 9.

[129] C. Guene and E. Mayo (eds.): Banking and Social Cohesion. Alternative Responses to a Global Market, Jon Carpenter Publishing, Charlbury, 2001, p. 1.

institutional – incorporation of the basic post-neoliberal insight "that the pursuit of economic efficiency and social progress (are) complementary."[130] They are about implementing elements of equality into (so far practiced) capitalism – as many have theoretically asked for, but not succeeded in practically.[131]

From my point of view, apart from the ideals stated in the programs of social banks themselves and their respective declarations of intents, these are the best – and most balanced – definitions of what a "social bank" is.

Similarly, De Clerck draws the conclusion,

> although private community and development banks, microfinance banks, ethical, environmental and social banks and ethical funds differ in terms of focus, accents, clients, products and business culture, they have in common to practice banking and investment with *a social development mission*. The differences tend to be rather complementary qualities that can be fertile in combination with each other. They are all delivering an innovative and human value contribution to the value-neutral financial system . . .
>
> (Social) banking as it has been described . . . stands in a historical line of (the) continuous search for the application of ethical principles in banking; and is in line with (the) broader trends in the 20th and 21st centuries such as the emergence of civil society and the new social class of cultural creatives, growing consumer awareness, social justice and environmental movements, and the growing recognition of social entrepreneurship . . .
>
> Ethics are now more than ever a subject of personal choice, behavior and responsibility. At the same time, more and more people are individually looking for values to incorporate in daily life. As contemporaries on their way, (social banks and finance institutions) are part of an ongoing process of search and practice linking up and networking with other people, creating new forms of social cohesion.[132] Instruments such as ethical banking processes, products and services and money as a subservient tool can be helpful.[133]

---

[130] G. Banks: Markets – How free? In: G. Banks: An Economy-Wide View: Speeches on Structural Reform. The Australian Government Productivity Commission, Commonwealth of Australia, Melbourne 2010, p. 265. To be found a.o. at: The Social Science Research Network, http://papers.ssrn.com/sol3/papers.cfm?abstract_id=1614664, August 15, 2010.

[131] Cf. M. Friedman: Capitalism and Freedom, University of Chicago Press, Chicago, 1962 (2002).

[132] There is little doubt in social research today that networking – that is, establishing social cohesion based on mutual trust and on personal contact – creates social contexts that are becoming increasingly useful prerequisites of economic and financial success not only individually, but also collectively. This is the case specifically in progressive environments of economy and society. One of the best examples is the success story of Silicon Valley, as currently researched by Stanford's economic sociologist Mark Granovetter. Mark is conducting research on the sociology of industrial organizations: "One study is called the 'Silicon Valley Network Analysis Project' (SiVNAP). Though everyone agrees that the most crucial aspect of Silicon Valley's dramatic success is its networks, there has been virtually no systematic study of their history, structure, and functioning. Mark's study explores these networks and their evolution over time, and also investigates the institutional complex that supports local industrial activity, including financial, educational, legal, and political sectors." In: Stanford University, Department of Sociology, http://www.stanford.edu/dept/soc/people/mgranovetter/index.html (retrieved April 27, 2010). Regarding the increasing importance of trust in societal relationships (including economy), see the seminal contributions of Stanford sociologist K. S. Cook: Trust in the Economy. In: J. Beckert and M. Zafirovsky (eds.): International Encyclopedia of Economic Sociology, London 2005, pp. 690–696; and K. S. Cook, R. Hardin and M. Levi: Cooperation Without Trust? New York, NY 2005.

[133] De Clerck: loc cit, pp. 12–13.

Might be nice and satisfying on the philosophical level, maybe, but what does that mean in practice? What is the consequence for concrete, applied business and finance endeavors?

To a certain extent, the best criterion that summarizes all the definitions that we have seen so far can be expressed in one slogan: *Freedom through a more just distribution of financial funds and potentials.* What does that mean?

Money and capital (and their inbuilt mechanisms of facilitating and incentivizing creativity) bear immense potentials of empowering the individual and groups; and *is this sense capitalism is – until proof of the contrary – the best available system of unlashing productivity human beings have so far developed.* At the same time, the main problem with capital is that it bears the "inbuilt" tendency toward creating dependence – for all sides involved:

- for those who "have";
- as well as for those who "haven't",

that is,

- for the rich and the middle class, as well as
- for the poor

alike.

This is because the *poor* in general must work for those who hold the money (or to be more precise, for those who control the amassments of capital in different forms, including the means of production). They are unfree by serving the interests of others.

The *rich*, who have to let others work for them, become dependent as well: they depend on the need of capital to grow and to multiply itself, i.e., on maximizing profit and returns. Thus, the rich become unfree by depending on the mechanisms of their own (monetary or material) property.

As for the *middle class*, its members are always "suspended" in the middle ground between these two poles. They thus are dependent in a twofold way. On the one hand, they depend on capital in the sense that they yes have a wide range of choices (much wider than those of the poor of course), but these choices are limited by the mechanisms of how money operates in a given society in a given place in a given time (for example, by the above described laws of the mortgage market in 2006 or by material goods as an expression of social status). On the other hand, they are dependent on the pressure of money also in the sense that they must always be aware to not become the next "poor" class. That means that their driving force is, typologically speaking, to "not go down," that is, to keep their status, which is connected to continuous income. Once this income fails to arrive, things can get pretty bad in just a moment.

The poor, the rich, and the middle class are thus to a certain extent "exploited" by the laws of money and capital, as well as connected in exploitation. In other words, they are all to a certain extent, though at different levels, left unfree by the mechanisms and effects of money and its accumulation as capital.

As the economic crisis of 2007–2010 has shown with unmatched clarity, the concentration of large parts of the worldwide capital in the upper and the lower parts of the "sandglass" model (instead of at their meeting point, where it would belong "naturally" because it is there that the real process of economy in time and space takes place) has aggravated this situation of dependence. The developing of the real estate and the derivative bubbles combined put a lot of pressure on all three classes. And when the bubbles eventually blew up, the pressure on the poor, the middle class, as well as the rich was further increased. As it seemed to many observers and consumers, the crisis demonstrated that money and capital develop their own "laws" and mechanisms – independently of the people who handle them. What does that mean?

It means that in many cases capital unfolds its own laws and (unconsciously) controls people, not vice versa. And one factor that decisively co-created this situation was the "single bottom line" standards and "profit only" habits of the banking and finance business that played with the mechanisms of dependence, and were in many cases their expression. But the mechanisms of fostering dependence that ruled the international banking and finance system in the past decades tended to create always less winners and always more losers because they evoked a situation where capital became concentrated in always fewer hands, and the middle class went down.

As post-crisis statistics concordantly show, social inequality dramatically increased between the 1990s and 2007, both in the United States and in Europe. One indicator among many for a deepening rift in Western societies is the percentage growth in real after-tax income in the United States, 1997–2009, with 16% increase for the bottom 20% of the population, 95% increase for the top 20%, and 81% for the top 1%. Household debt in the United States rose from US$ 680 billion in 1974 to US$ 14 trillion in 2008.[134] "In the United States, wealth is highly concentrated in a relatively few hands. As of 2007, the top 1% of households (the upper class) owned 34.6% of all privately held wealth, and the next 19% (the managerial, professional, and small business stratum) had 50.5%, which means that just 20% of the people owned a remarkable 85%, leaving only 15% of the wealth for the bottom 80% (wage and salary workers). In terms of financial wealth (total net worth minus the value of one's home), the top 1% of households had an even greater share: 42.7%."[135] A similar, though slightly mitigated development is visible in Europe.

As a response to this "innate" bonding force of money and capital, social banking's quest is about liberation in a twofold way:

- *Liberation from restriction*: Social finance is about liberating people from some of the restrictions, which the lack of money causes (and sometimes even the possession of money as an end in itself).

[134] F. Zakaria: Restoring the American Dream. In: Time, November 1, 2010, pp. 14–19.

[135] G. W. Domhoff, University of California at Santa Cruz: Who Rules America? Wealth, Income and Power. November 2010, http://sociology.ucsc.edu/whorulesamerica/power/wealth.html.

– *Liberation to unfold potential*: It is about liberating the largest number of people possible to explore their own potentials of creativity, by making them more independent from the immediate pressures of the bonding laws of money and capital.

Both liberation strategies depart from the assumption that the more people are free, the more they will be productive – and that the more people are free, the more society as a whole will benefit from their unbound creativity.[136]

Both these two "liberation strategies" are enacted by social banks according to the slogan *Using money, not having it.*

This slogan suggests that the banking and financial business is not about hoarding money, in what sense and way ever. Money as such was – and is – never meant to be "kept" or "stored," but to be circulated. And it is meant to facilitate creative movements by its circulation: production, work, culture, social encounter (the latter often referred to as the "multiplier effect" inbuilt in money).[137]

Or as a friend (who is a self-made multimillionaire based in Connecticut) once expressed, "If you want to get wealthy, one of the first principles to follow is to not keep your money for yourself; you have to spend it, that is, give it to others in order to get it back. You have to create a giving and receiving cycle that is constantly moving, and never stops. You have to create a circulating flow."

For those who are reminded here about the blood circulation in the human body that strangely seems to follow a very similar, if not the same, principle: You are absolutely on the right track to understand what money is!

Money, from the viewpoint of social banking and social finance, is the "blood" of the "social organism." It works best if it circulates; but it becomes a problem if it is concentrated in too great amounts in a single part of the body. It is not good

---

[136]This assumption is to a certain extent also the ideological basis of the European "welfare states." Unlike in the United States, most countries in Europe offer their citizens free health care, free social services like kindergardens and schools, as well as extended, publicly financed security nets against unemployment and social disadvantaged. For example, every citizen in the European Union has the right to get public health care, wherever she or he is; there are in principle no differences in the quality of treatment related to money. This is a "social finance" aspect inbuilt in the overall public spending of most European states. Sure enough, the other side of this coin is that many European states are currently at a point where they face great difficulties in maintaining this system, because health care and other social features are becoming too expensive due to advanced technologies, and given that people's average age in the Western countries is rapidly increasing thus growing the financial needs for public welfare.

[137]This aspect is at the center of the view of most social bankers that social banking is a return to banking's original roots, where the circulation of money to build a community (and its individuals) is what has historically made local and regional banks successful (and also the communities in which they exist). Or as David K. Korslund, lead independent director of Chicago-based social bank, Shorebank, and senior advisor of the Global Alliance of Banking on Values GABV London puts it: "I believe that we make too much of the fact that social banking is new. I would argue that it is merely returning to the roots of banking which is how to use money in a community to develop its potential. By doing so the community has a stronger economy which is good for a bank." D. K. Korslund: Letter to the author, April 8, 2010.

for the health of the body if "blood pressure" is too high; neither is it good if it is too low.

Similarly, it is not good for the "health" of society if "money pressure" is too high or too low. And more importantly, blood in the body is not meant to become "more blood," it is not an end in itself. It serves the body, and it fulfills its duty best if it is evenly distributed and nurtures all the organs necessary for its proper functioning. Like blood in the human body, money as the "social blood" of modern societies is nothing for itself; it is not meant to become "more money." As blood in the human body is but a medium to transport oxygen to the cells, money is but a "medium" to transport and facilitate the work of the "cells" of the "social organism" – i.e., the work of those who produce concrete economic, technological, social, and cultural life in the real economy.

Therefore, money is much more a *social relationship between productive people*, rather than a "material good" in itself, or an abstract tool of speculation upon the work of others.

If we depart from such an understanding of money, the view on how to handle it advances. We will not "hoard" money "into the soil" anymore (i.e., into the real estate bubble) nor will we put it "into the clouds" again (i.e. into the derivative bubble).[138] Rather, money will be given (lended as well as donated) to those who produce the concrete new in "real life." Such an understanding takes us away from the illusions of exaggerated value connected with the real estate market; and it equally distances us from the lifeless speculations of the international derivative market, as we knew it in the past decades. It brings us back to "real life", i.e. to the real economy. *Social banking and social finance are about* "bringing money back to real life" in the real economy.

But if money is the "blood" of modern societies, and thus a medium of service, not a tool of power plays through mechanisms of dependence, what is capital then?

The question of capital is a little trickier, but ultimately not much more complicated than the question of money. Let us use a simple example to exaplain.

Think of a person who works his or her whole life with diligence and commitment, like most of us do. This person will save some money over time, because she or he will earn more than she or he can consume: she or he will produce what is called a "surplus value."[139] This may vary in time, and there might be times when this person needs more money than she or he actually earns; but over the course of a lifetime, most individuals, and most groups in civilizations that are based on the division of labor and on the advancement of technology, produce a surplus. One reason for this is that the division of labor, that is, the specialization of individuals in a certain field in order to share and exchange the results then, allows us to be more

[138]Nevertheless, it remains an interesting challenge for social banks to use money appropriately to finance real estate on the one hand, and to anticipate concrete futures on the other hand *without* creating bubbles. Some potential answers to this challenge can be found in the following chapter.

[139]I use this term here in a non-Marxist, humanistic (and thus more simplifying, not class and exploitation specific) sense.

productive and to achieve more goods in a much shorter timeframe than if we were self-supporters.[140,141]

Now imagine that this person comes to the end of his or her life. If things have gone as they in average do in Western societies, she or he will have created surplus values that consist in owning a house, a computer and a car, other material goods, and a bank account, for example, to take any number, of US $100,000 in savings. When the person dies, these surplus values remain – and another person, say the son

[140]The division of labor and the development of technology are the two main structural causes of capital formation; they are at least as important as the effort of individual work as such. As one of the theoretical forerunners and pioneers of modern social banking and social finance, Austrian philosopher Rudolf Steiner (1861–1925) asserted, there are two basic modes through which values are created: (1) The application of work onto nature; (2) the application of intelligence onto labor, as in the form of the organization of work by the division of labor and through technology. The result of (1) is material goods; the result of (2) is material capital (i.e., the means of production, such as machines) and money capital. Cf. R. Steiner: Seminar on National Economy (Nationalökonomischer Kurs) (1922), Basel 1979, in: Dreigliederungsportal Deutschland, http://www.dreigliederung.de/download/340.pdf (retrieved January 10, 2010); and R. Steiner: Capital and Credit (1919), in: Rudolf Steiner Archive online, http://wn.rsarchive.org/SocialIssues/CapCrd_index.html (retrieved January 10, 2010).

The outstanding usefulness of the division of labor and the use of technology that a.o. leads to a "surplus" in the form of savings (capital) is one main reason why the dream of "going back" to self-supporting ways of life, often interpreted as "return to nature" and thus to a better life, must be ultimately an illusion; it would make us much poorer, reduce our life options and get us less creative. Social banking and social finance are about consciously using all the modern forms of labor and productivity, including the division of work, technology, and high-level specialization, and they are about producing capital, and using it. Social banking and social finance are not about going back to the "natural world" that, for example, the hippies or the "flower power generation" of the 1960s and 1970s dreamed of. The reason is that such a return, besides hindering technological progress and leaving the facilitating powers of money and capital unused, would basically limit us to daily survival. Once self-sufficient ways of life produce more than they can consume, we would be already in a "capitalistic" society again, because the surplus starts to produce its own laws and structural features – even if most social dreamers were (and remain) reluctant to admit that. Overall, I believe that self-sufficient ways of living can be a good addition to the benefits of the capitalistic society; but they can certainly not replace it.

[141]Of course, both the core creation modes of (material) values: (1) the application of work onto nature and (2) the application of intelligence onto labor have to be enacted with common sense and responsibility, as not least the current grave environmental crisis shows. There are limits of applying work onto nature; as well as dangers inherent in the overuse of intelligent working capacities due to the increasing power of technological tools. For an exemplary interactive introduction into these issues, see: A. Leonard: The Story of Stuff. An interactive learning project, in: http://www.storyofstuff.com/ and http://storyofstuff.com/index.php (retrieved April 12, 2010). While I regard Leonard's – and other environmental activists'– critique on the *overexploitation* of nature through the overapplication of intelligence onto labour and the *overuse* of technology as legitimate and necessary, I do not agree with its generalizing, anti-economy tone. While the *wrong use* of applying work and technology onto nature must be criticized in order to improve things, the principles of value creation explained above, as well as their validity for creating wealth for the greater social progress, in my view are not touched by it.

or the daughter, does not have to start his or her productive life from the bottom-up, as they already have a head start by using these assets. And that means, they have the advantage of achieving their goals much easier, and that they are more free.[142]

Additionally, and this is the decisive point, that US $100,000 saved by the person is not gone; it "lives on", circulating in the form of loans by the bank in which it is placed to its customers, allowing them to create new products and services, and thus generating interests for the holder of the account, thus increasing the amount continuously.

Looking at what is typologically happening here, there is one surprising observation. The US $100,000 on the bank account appears as the surplus result of the "real work" of the person[143] put into an abstract (numerical) form. And in this abstract form, the work of that person continues to live on even after the person has died. That means: What we call capital has been the real work of a person (or many persons) that has been put into the abstract and arbitrary form of a social convention called money.

This is also true if the person in our example does not die, but if she or he lives on. Once you have a certain amount of "surplus value" transformed in the abstract form of money as capital, you suddenly have not only one, but in principle two "working forces" at work: The biological person that continues to work and the accumulated money or capital that becomes a second working force of independent stature and ontology. What does that mean?

It means that capital, not only in the form of money (money capital) or of goods (material capital, means of production), but also in the form of education (knowledge capital) and so forth, is in its essence something what the Greeks called "logos" (law, or principle of origin) and what the English language calls "spirit" – an immaterial, but absolutely concrete origin, cause, and logical organization of reality. Exactly in this sense, capital is the "logos" (or "spirit") of the modern social sphere. And summing up what we have seen, capital is in its basic tendency a quite positive "logos" or "spirit," at least in principle, and as such. Why? Because it is a "spirit" that ultimately is destined to work for us; that is destined to set us free; that is the (abstracted) heritage of our lives that lives on after us and that facilitates the work of others by giving them the means to create.

---

[142] Cf. A. Sen's seminal tract on the role of freedom in human development: A. Sen: Freedom as Development, Oxford University Press, Oxford 1999.

[143] Again, this is only true if the expression "real work" is understood either as "physical work" (i.e. as applying physical work onto nature) or as "thought work" (applying intelligence onto work). Pure speculation on the work of others can't be considered as "real work" (derivative bubble), nor can the speculation on material goods be classified as such (real estate bubble).

As a consequence, "Capital is spirit" was exactly one of the core slogans at the origin of the foundation of most European social banks in the 1970s and 1980s.[144] Considering what we have seen, we may now understand why.

We must be aware of misunderstandings here, however. Capital is not "spirit" in the sense of being something religious or something that has in itself a "higher" meaning. That would be a mystification, and mystifications are never appropriate. Capital is "spirit" exclusively and only in the sense that, exactly because it is abstract, it is a working force that does in principle not work mainly for itself, but enables others to work. It is a kind of active force that is the abstraction of the real work of a person, the "saved essence" of a life. Thus, capital is not a "value" in itself, but rather a "reminder of life," or, to put it in better terms, it is a "living potential" that enables productivity and creativity of other "real persons" – and, most important of all (and as the prerequisite of everything else) it is a force that is capable to increase freedom.

Exactly in this sense (and in no other), capital can be considered as "logos" with regard to the needs and mechanisms of modern societies. In this sense, capital is in principle the most positive and enduring embodiment of social relations in modern societies.[145]

But why is all this so important for the proper understanding of what a social bank (and a social finance enterprise in the broader sense) is at its core, and in its basic motivation?

One of the leading questions that has driven social banking and social finance forward right from the start is to understand the very nature of what money, and especially what capital, is. These questions seem to have been forgotten or are at least never made explicit on Wall Street, because there they are considered superfluous or because the answer seems self-evident: Money is what it is, it is value.

---

[144]One of the most influential thinkers that incepted such an unusual approach to money and finance, and thus gave birth to the first "green" movements in Europe in the 1970s and 1980s (including the German political "Green party") was the famous German artist Joseph Beuys (1921–1986). In fact, the slogan "Capital = Spirit" is mainly his invention (as it was, for the rest, also the slogan "Art = Capital"). It was originally the *leitmotif* of his professorial chair as ordinary professor of Art and Society at the University of the Arts Düsseldorf (1961–1975), and it later became the slogan of the "Free International University," which he co-founded in 1973 in order to promote new approaches to social and societal questions, including economy and finance. Cf. J. Beuys: What is Money? A Discussion. Clairview Books, Forest Row 2010.

[145]In contrast, influential US theorist Immanuel M. Wallerstein's (Yale University, born 1930) definition of capitalism is something to the effect of "capital is always and necessarily the pursuit of capital per se." This definition implies that capitalism, as Wallerstein understands it, is fundamentally and by its very characteristics unhealthy for the greater societal good. In contrast to Wallerstein, I think that such a view, while correctly pointing to the *wrong use* of capital, does not take into account several positive aspects that are decisive in the overall structural judgment. Cf. I. M. Wallerstein: World-Systems Analysis: An Introduction, Duke University Press, Durham 2004 (1987); I. M. Wallerstein: Historical Capitalism, with Capitalist Civilization, Verso, London 1995; and I. M. Wallerstein: The End of the World as We Know It: Social Science for the Twenty-First Century, University of Minnesota Press, Minneapolis, MN 1999. See also http://www.yale.edu/sociology/faculty/pages/wallerstein/.

But instead of this naive realism that does not take into account that every value is already an individual and social interpretation, money is not what it seems: According to what we have seen, it is much less and much more than we believe it to be.[146]

Interestingly, there is a clear analogy between what social banks see as the *in principle* and *potentially* liberating power of money and capital and what innovative social approaches to technology regard as the *in principle* and *potentially* liberating power of technology for our age.

For example, since January 2009 the "Program on Liberation Technology"[147] at the Freeman Spogli Institute for International Studies at Stanford University "seeks to understand how information technology can be used to defend human rights, improve governance, empower the poor, promote economic development, and pursue a variety of other social goods . . . The last few years have seen explosive growth in the use of information technology to . . . fight corruption, deter electoral fraud, expose government wrongdoing . . ., protect the environment, educate consumers, (and) improve public health . . . Lying at the intersection of social science, computer science, and engineering, the Program on Liberation Technology seeks to understand how (and to what extent) various information technologies and their applications – including mobile phones, text messaging (SMS), the Internet, blogging, GPS, and other forms of digital technology – are enabling citizens to advance freedom, development, social justice, and the rule of law."[148]

As an analogy, social banking and social finance pursue similar goals in an adjacent field. They pursue a program that could be summarized as "*Liberation Finance*" or "Liberation Capitalism." Similar to the "Program on Liberation Technology," social banks seek to understand how money and capital can be used to "defend human rights, improve governance, empower the poor, promote economic development, and (to) pursue a variety of other social goods." In doing so, they try to create alternatives to the system of "dependence finance" as it was mainstream since the 19th century, by using capital in a value-oriented way.

[146]Cf. The actuality of German poet J. W. Goethe's (1749–1832) poem "Faust," where it is stated (in part II) that money is the "deepest riddle" – in the positive and negative sense alike – that characterizes the social sphere and the cohabitation of human beings in the age of modernity; and that thus money and capital have to be understood in their ontological essence if modern man as such is to be understood. Cf. J. Ackermann und H. C. Binswanger: "Money is missing. Good then, let's create it!" Goethe's poem "Faust" and the Modern Use of Money ("Es fehlt das Geld. Nun gut, so schaff es denn!" Goethe's Faust und der moderne Umgang mit Geld). In: Frankfurter Allgemeine Zeitung (FAZ), 20.06.2009, http://www.faz.net/s/Rub58241E4DF1B149538ABC24D0E82A6266/Doc~E10569058E50A4F888BFCCAD3B5A4648C~ATpl~Ecommon~Scontent.html; H. C. Binswanger: Money and Magic, Chicago University Press, Chicagos 1994; and H. C. Binswanger: The Magic of Money (Die Magie des Geldes), in: St. Galler Tagblatt, June 3, 2005, http://www.iep.uni-karlsruhe.de/download/Die_Magie_des_Geldes.pdf

[147]The Stanford Program on Liberation Technology at the Freeman Spogli Institute for International Studies: http://fsi.stanford.edu/research/program_on_liberation_technology/

[148]In: http://fsi.stanford.edu/research/program_on_liberation_technology/ (retrieved January 15, 2010).

Social banking as a whole, lying at the intersection of economy, social science and ethics, seeks to understand how (and to what extent) various financial instruments and their applications – including lending and donating, investment strategies, and the respective assessment criteria – have the potential to enable citizens to advance freedom, development, social justice, and the rule of law. Social banking is indeed about protecting the environment (and) educating consumers by incepting a different, to a certain extent, more evolved and more realistic understanding of money and finance – and by aiming toward collective progress through the empowerment of the individual.

So the analogies between "liberation technology" and "liberation finance" are obvious. But while there are many joint initiatives between social finance and environmental and community endeavors, strategic cooperation between "liberation technology" and "liberation finance" have still not been developed sufficiently. Given that both initiatives share similar ideals and goals, it maybe would be worth a try.

7 What Is the Philosophy of a Social Bank?

We have seen that social banking and social finance are about liberating creative potentials (1) by making decisions with regard to the "triple bottom line" of people, planet, and profit, which are seen as of equal importance; (2) by putting values first instead of interest rates and profit; and (3) by cultivating a different concept of what money and capital in principle are.

To realize the resulting pretension, sober business expertise in dealing with the system is as important as values and ideals. Dealing with reality is more important than dreaming. "Liberation finance" is as much an economic as an ethical endeavor. It must not only work philosophically, but hold true in the practice of working effectively with the money available under the given conditions of the globalization of financial markets, i.e., without losses and by achieving overall growth. Only if both aspects, economic *and* ethical success, are concomitant factors, the greater social good inherent in social banking can be achieved.

The result is (necessarily) a combination of realistic and idealistic viewpoints in the underlying mindset: an approach that could be denoted as "realistic idealism".[149] Accordingly, social banking's aspiration toward its own constituent philosophy is what we could call a "financial humanism."

Financial humanism is not an ideology, nor is it a worldview of well-defined stature. Social banking does not want to impose an ideology. Rather, the philosophy of social banking is in a very general way freedom and its facilitation – including the freedom to choose specific values, opinions, and beliefs, as long as there *are* values,

[149]Dutch philosopher Jaap Sijmons (* 1959), in an attempt to combine idealism and realism into *one* attitude, describes this approach as "Phaenomenological Idealism," which would be a good denomination for the basic world view of social banking and social finance. See J. Sijmons: Phaenomenology and Idealism. ZENO Research Institute of Philosophy of the University Utrecht, Series "Questiones infinitae," Volume 50, Utrecht 2004.

opinions and beliefs at all. Social banking at its core wants to enact, to stimulate, and to enliven a social dialogue about the values for our time. It wants this dialogue to be at the center of the socio-economic system; and it wants to keep this dialogue permanently alive. But social banking does not suggest which specific values are "the right ones" – except those that are basic humanistic requests and more general denotations such as sustainability, social responsibility, or the "human measure." Social banking wants to engage an in-depth dialogue about ethical individualism and the "common good." Social banks take their decisions, as far as possible, in the light of the results of this ongoing (and in principle open) dialogue. For example, most social banks not only practice transparency regarding their investments, they also regularly question their customers about their values, their possible shift of values, and where the capital should be invested accordingly.

Seen as a whole, the philosophy of social banks can be embraced in one sentence: *Practice-oriented value orientation without presetting in detail of what is valuable.*

Theoretically speaking, this philosophy is (in essence) a kind of "secular essentialism." It is an idea-driven worldview with a non-ideological stance based upon and oriented toward ethical individualism. In this philosophy, the orientation toward material aspects of development constitutes the *relativistic* (or secular) aspect; the orientation toward facilitation of individual and social creativity constitutes the *idealistic* (or essentialistic) aspect.

This secular essentialism is based on one central assumption: for social banking and social finance, *it is the human being as such, and only the human being in its real life process that is the only absolute value.* This value has to be enabled to unfold itself in the most consistent manner possible. In assisting this unfolding, money and finance find their ultimate meaning, sense, and aesthetics.

Applied to the sandglass model previously sketched that gave birth to the financial and economic crisis of 2007–2010, the basic consequence of this philosophy is to take money out of the two sandglass bubbles: from below (the real estate market) and from above (the derivative market) and to put it "to work" in the real economy at the center.

Accordingly, social banks seek the return of the financial system to what they call the "core business of banking": the sourcing of the real economy, which is seen as the most important task of the financial industry.[150] The real economy is, as we have seen, the intersection area between the upper and lower parts of the sandglass. And it is exactly in this area where the creative individual unfolds herself or himself. Thus, social banks urge the financial industry to transfer money not eclectically, but systemically both "from below" and "from above" to that "medium area."[151] This shift

[150] I. Schönauer: "Return to the core business of banking." CEO states that the sourcing of the real economy is the most important task of the financial industry ("Rückbesinnung auf das Banken-Kerngeschäft." Institutschef bezeichnet die Finanzierung der Realwirtschaft als wichtigste Aufgabe der Finanzbranche). In: Börsen Zeitung Düsseldorf, Nr. 29, 12.02.2009.

[151] My hypothesis is that core banking in the "medium area" of the real economy is (a) asset accumulation in safe warehouses, (b) building solid productive assets using borrowed funds, and (c) facilitating cash payments.

is seen as the necessary consequence of the philosophy of "realistic idealism"; and it is regarded as one of the "post-crisis" challenges necessary to foster an improved kind of financial circulation and logic.

Last but not least, there are *two last points* that we have to consider if we want to understand the philosophy of social banking and social finance to the full extent.

First is the importance of culture. Not least because of the crisis, parts of the mainstream banking system have discovered the importance of sustainability, ecological and ethical aspects for the future of globalized societies. But what is still lacking is the full inclusion of culture into most mainstream concepts of sustainability. Most of these concepts are too narrowly conceived. In most cases, culture and education are not sufficiently included.

But given that culture is by definition the dimension of behavior in the social sphere that can be "inherited" and thus passed on from generation to generation, or in better terms, "culture is the hereditament of the social,"[152] culture becomes a decisive factor for building lasting sustainability solutions. Changing an attitude depends on how we think about attitudes; it depends on "changing the mind." Mind-innovating with regard to "bad habits" on the one hand, and heredity transmission of "good attitudes" on the other hand, are two core functions of culture. Both are features of every inclusive concept of sustainability in the long run. This is because to change the *zeitgeist*, and to develop the existing paradigms towards centers of gravity that focus on inclusion and sustainability, means not only to change the economic investment streams, but also to invest into education and science. To change the mind is social banking and social finance (at least) as much as it is the methods and criteria of investing. Therefore, what social banking and social finance do is to include the concept of culture into the concept of sustainability of finance, and they try to invest into ideas "which time has come" (Victor Hugo) as much as in profitable businesses.[153]

Second is the question of ethics in the strict sense. According to the viewpoint of social banks, money is in its essence not a value in itself, but the expression of a social relationship of mutual trust and help. This is valid especially in our age where paper and electronic (immaterial) money have become the standard forms of transactions, as well as the standard expressions of values. But in reality, the value of paper money is not based on any real value (like it is in the case of gold[154]),

---

[152] J. Heinrichs: The Logical Principles of the Social Sphere. Origins of Society (Logik des Sozialen. Woraus Gesellschaft entsteht), Varna 2005. Cf. M. Opielka: Community in Society, Sociology after Hegel and Parsons (Gemeinschaft in Gesellschaft. Soziologie nach Hegel und Parsons), Wiesbaden 2006.

[153] Cf. the excellent short overview over the interweavement between economic, technological, and cultural factors in innovative processes in F. Knauß: How Innovation Functions (Wie Innovationen entstehen). In: Handelsblatt Düsseldorf, 15 March 2010.

[154] Admittedly, though, the value of gold is in the end nothing "natural" or "given," but is ascribed by the community of human beings to it. The only difference is that gold has a greater material consistence, and most important, that it is a limited resource on this planet – while paper and electronic money are basically not limited resources and can therefore be multiplied ad libitum.

because paper by itself is (almost) without any real value. For example, nobody would accept ten sheets of colored paper in exchange for a car. The same is even truer for electronic money, which is just an information code in a machine and has no material reality at all.

Nevertheless, the factual value of money in our society is based on the trust in a social contract – which is expressed in the principle that there is *artificially ascribed* value to colored paper or to an electronic information (what we call money), which we are willing to accept in exchange for "real" goods. That means that money is in its essence a relationship *created by* the sheer will of a community of human beings – and that accordingly it has to be *used for* the community, not according to alleged "autopoietic laws"[155] of capital per se or of abstract financial mechanisms (like those we have seen at work in the real estate and derivative bubbles that led to the crisis). Social banking is, to put it that way, the place where the very relationship that is expressed in the arbitrary form of modern money[156] finds its "heart": a bank is in principle nothing else than the place where money "comes together" and is redistributed according to the ethics of "the best for all," i.e., the community in the greater dimension.

If this is the case, then one remaining question arises: Exactly what kind of ethics, *consequentialist* ethics or *principle* ethics, do social banks in principle follow in their pursuit of the "greater good" through the use of the social convention of money?

There are two main options of "how to be ethical" in our modern world – i.e., how to apply ethical considerations to reality:

1. *Consequentialist moral reasoning*. This attitude departs from the assumption that the *consequences* of an act decide if it is morally appropriate. From this viewpoint, morality consists in the outcome of actions, not in the specific quality of

---

That means that gold has a more concrete and more realistic relationship with the economic and social reality than paper money or electronic money.

[155]Cf. F. Varela: Monte Grande. What is life? Icarus Films 2004. In: http://www.montegrande.ch/eng/home.php.

[156]The change of currency from national European currencies (the German d-mark, the French franc, the Italian lira, the Dutch gulden, the Spanish peseta and the Greek drachma, etc.) to the European euro on January 1, 1999 (book money) and on January 1, 2002 (cash) as the joint currency of the European Union has helped many Europeans to understand that money is nothing more, and nothing less, than a social convention, or a social contract between given parts. In the United States, the founding moment of its currency, the US dollar (derived from the German word "taler," a medieval currency used mainly in Central Europe) in 1792, seems too long ago for an average citizen to remember that at the basis of the unmatched wealth of this nation – the richest nation on earth at the present, and presumably also in the foreseeable future – there has been, and still is, a social contract about values, and thus about money, that is unparalleled in the history of humankind. Cf. B. M. Friedman: The (American) Economic System. In: P. H. Schuck and J. Q. Wilson (eds.): Understanding America. The Anatomy of an Exceptional Nation, Perseus Books, New York 2008, pp. 87–120.

the action itself. That is an attitude that can justify ethically problematic endeavors – like investing in "unethical" stock markets in order to *first* make profit by exploitation or through the destruction of nature in order to *then* invest it into "ethical" projects. The main proponents of this attitude were (and are) the followers of so-called Utilitarianism, i.e., people inclined to the philosophy of English philosopher Jeremy Bentham (1748–1832). Most current bankers on Wall Street seem to be indeed eager disciples of his teachings until today – at least in order to appease their conscience.

2. *Categorical moral reasoning*. This posture "locates morality in certain *absolute* moral requirements, certain *categorical* duties and rights, regardless of their consequences."[157] This approach departs from the assumption that an action has to be judged by the intrinsic moral quality of itself, not by its outcome. The act itself, not its outcome, decides upon its moral value. One of the main founders of this attitude was the German philosopher Immanuel Kant (1724–1804),[158] interestingly a contemporary of Bentham. It was hardly an accident that both Bentham and Kant were living in the age of early modern capitalism. "Categorical moral reasoning" can probably be attributed to most of the "ethically strict" worldviews at least in Europe, among them the majority of contemporary European civil society's approaches to money and finance.

The interesting aspect is, which of these two ethical options do social banks base their decisions to lend their money on – and where to invest it according to their understanding of the "greater social good," as well as to their concept of the very nature of money and capital? And on which of these two options do they base their long-term strategic decisions? Is it *consequentialist* or *principle* ethics that social banks and social finance institutions follow?

The answer is not easy (as always in the case of reality). But it is nevertheless more or less obvious, if we consider what we have seen so far. If social banks' philosophy consists in a "realistic idealism," then they must cultivate an ethical strategy of integrating both consequentialist and principle ethics.

In fact, social banks have (almost) always chosen the "hard way," that is, the way of "productive ambivalence" between consquentialist and principle ethics. They must always ponder both: consequentialist ethics and principle ethics, in every single case, case by case. Sometimes it is better to choose a consequentialist approach; in other cases it might be necessary to insist on the principles. Only the intense examination of every concrete case can decide in the end which option is the best to achieve the goals of the greater good. Why? Because according to their very characteristics, social banks have to ponder reality and ideal very carefully – as it

---

[157] M. Sandel: What's the right thing to do? In: Harvard University Justice Course, Episode 1, http://www.justiceharvard.org/index.php?option=com_content&view=article&id=11&Itemid=8 (retrieved February 25, 2010).

[158] Cf. M. Sandel: What's the right thing to do? In: Harvard University Justice Course, http://www.justiceharvard.org/ and http://www.justiceharvard.org/index.php?option=com_content&view=article&id=11&Itemid=8 (Episode 2 ff.) (retrieved February 25, 2010).

seems inbuilt in the very nature of investment and money itself in abeyance between present and future.[159]

Nevertheless, overlooking the ethics of social banking, we have to make a distinction between *strategy* and *tactics*. While the everyday short-term *tactics* of how to steer the interests and achieve the goals of social banking best may follow a rather consequentialist approach, the overall long-term *strategy* of where social banking wants to go, and to which better society it points at, is guided predominantly by principle ethics. The art then is to combine both approaches by taking into consideration the surrounding events on a day-to-day basis and the bigger picture of economic and social development.

It is to a certain point understandable that there are people who assert that because of this "dual" approach to ethics, social banks are philosophically speaking "more banks" in the strict sense that most of the mainstream banks. Why? Because they seem to represent the "productive, innate dualism" and face the difficult choices of the money and finance sector *as such* in a more consistent way than many mainstream banks.

Social banks thus cultivate a reality-oriented mixture of consequentialist and principle ethics; therefore, they have disappointed both one-sided realists and one-sided idealists alike. Many "hard core" financial experts believe that idealism in the banking and finance sector is suicide; and many "hard core" idealists of civil society believe that dealing with money and finance not only to do the good but also to generate profits corrupts the character. Both these views are wrong if we look at the naked facts. The last decade has shown that idealism in finance did not lead to suicide, but on the contrary was – strictly economically speaking – the most successful approach that generated the highest growth rates. At the same time, the focus and attitude of most social banks did not change; on the contrary, they never invested more money into ethical purposes than when they made the greatest profits.[160]

---

[159]In contrast, religious institutions, in the United States and Europe alike, traditionally favor principle ethics over consequentialist ethics. For example, the catholic pope Benedict XVI. (Joseph Ratzinger) has included a long passage on the characteristics of modern economy and capital in his so far most important Encyclica "Deus Caritas est" ("God is Charity," December 25, 2005), dedicated to social progress: Chapter 26 ff., see: http://www.vatican.va/holy_father/benedict_xvi/encyclicals/documents/hf_ben-xvi_enc_20051225_deus-caritas-est_en.html. There he states that economy and finance are among the most important fields of action for "socially engaged people" of the present and the future, if there are principle ethics (i.e., Christian ethics in his case) applied. The chapter has assumedly been written in part by experts in modern economic history. While there are many good ideas produced for the whole of society and the sphere of social organizations, the inclination of traditional religions toward principle ethics that is once more exemplified in this Encyclical (as well as in similar writings and teachings by other religions) is one reason – among many – why social banking and social finance, like other socially progressive initiatives rooted in (and working with) the civil society paradigms and mechanisms of today's world, have to consider themselves independent from every religious affiliation. That does not exclude the appreciation of and cooperation with religious charity trusts.

[160]Cf. the detailed comparative statistics in C. Scheire and S. De Maertelaere: loc cit, p. 10 ff. and p. 16 ff.

Thus we could draw the conclusion that a philosophy of finance that tries to integrate realism and idealism, consequentialist ethics and principle ethics, proves to be more appropriate and successful within the specific constellation of modernity than pure realism or pure idealism.

But is such a view justified? And, if the answer is yes, to which extent? What, if at all, can this mean concretely for the future of our Western "economy-driven" societies?

In order to answer these questions, let us take a – very brief – look into what has ideated in this regard in the past, and where the historical origins of social banking and social finance are located.

8 Where Do Social Banks Come From? A Very Short History

We have seen so far that social banking is about solidifying timely ideas like social responsibility, transparency, sustainability, ethical individualism, and value orientation without fixing specific values. And we have seen that it is about pondering "consequentialist ethics" with "principle ethics," by bringing both these approaches together in the perspective of an "idealistic realism" for our time.

But where do all these ideas come from? And who were the first pioneers to make them fertile for the modern finance business?

Harvard historian Niall Ferguson rightly states, "The study of modern history is simply inseparable from the study of economic history. I get a little frustrated by how history is conventionally taught in high schools and indeed in many universities, because the economics and particularly the finance tend to get left out. And yet you can't really imagine the renaissance without the Medici, and the Medici were bankers; and you can't really imagine, if we come to the 20th century, the rise of fascism without the great depression . . . So my sense is if we want to understand the historical process from the renaissance down to the present, we need to understand finance as well as the usual kings, queens and dictators."[161]

If this is plausible, we have to take a brief look at where the ideas of social banking and social finance come from, and who were the great pioneers that inspired the foundation of this new field of economic action.

In Europe, two of the main great pioneers between the 19th and the 20th century (and their respective problems and perspectives) were Rudolf Steiner (1861–1925), an Austrian philosopher and social reformer,[162] and Silvio Gesell (1862–1930), a German merchant, anarchist, and theoretical economist.[163]

---

[161] N. Ferguson: On the Financial Crisis. In: The Agenda with Steve Paikin, http://www.youtube.com/watch?v=By8n0Rkmzik. Cf. already in 2004 N. Ferguson: Colossus. The Price of America's Empire, Penguin Press, London 2004; and most recently N. Ferguson: The Ascent of Money: A Financial History of the World, Penguin Press, London 2008.

[162] See: http://en.wikipedia.org/wiki/Rudolf_steiner.

[163] See: http://en.wikipedia.org/wiki/Silvio_Gesell.

Both Steiner and Gesell thought about money and finance in different ways than most of their contemporaries. Both founded their own political movements of social reform and innovation after World War I in the 1920s. Steiner founded the so-called threefolding movement, which was dedicated to create a differentiated, multidimensional society that would respect the mutual independence of politics, economics, and culture from each other[164]; Gesell founded the so-called Free Economy movement, which tried to establish autonomous local and regional forms of money and an economic system based on individual abilities.[165] Steiner put his emphasis on creating a "down-to-earth" banking and finance system that would systematically combine lending with donating and thus would differentiate between "lending money" and "gift money" in order to put "lending money" into the small and medium economical enterprises and "gift money" into the cultural and educational sector. Gesell dreamed of the equalization of the rich and the poor by diversifying interest rates and rent charges according to wealth and the respective needs.

Interestingly, independently from each other, Steiner and Gesell developed an anthropomorphic concept of money and capital that was similar in many regards. The basic thought of both was that money should become a mere tool rather than a "hoardable" good in itself, because hoarding money would detract productivity from the "real economy" and to create not only individual, but systemic imbalances. In order to achieve a more productive use of capital, Steiner and Gesell similarly proposed to conceive money as something that should follow the life cycle of a human being: Money should be "born" (i.e., printed), should become old (be devalued by law within a certain timeframe), and eventually "die" (become worthless) to pave the way for newly printed money, that would follow the same cycle, and so on. The result would be that everybody would spend his or her money as fast as possible in order to avoid devaluation and in such a way money would no longer be hoarded, but would circulate with the maximum speed within the "real economy," thus increasing productivity and employment for all.

To understand that rather unusual thinking about money, let us take an example of how Steiner and Gesell conceived the "anthropomorphic aging of money".

Let us assume you work for a day and you get $100 in payment after you finish. By law, in Steiners and Gesells view of "aging money" that money would be devalued by 10% of the original sum per month (that's how it "ages"). That means that during the same month in which you got your money, the $100 is worth 100%, but the month after, the $100 is worth only $90, and if you spend the money that second month, you will get the equivalent of $90. On the third month, it is worth only $80, on the fourth $70, etc., until after 10 months, the money "dies": Its value has expired and it is not worth anything anymore. What would you do in this case? Of course, the most reasonable thing in this case would be to spend your money as soon as possible, in order to use it at its maximum value. You wouldn't keep the

---

[164] For more information, see: http://en.wikipedia.org/wiki/Social_threefolding.

[165] For more information, see: http://en.wikipedia.org/wiki/Freiwirtschaft.

money, but you would spend it immediately, for example, by letting another person work for you on something that you are not qualified to fix by yourself, the roof of your house maybe. The overall, systemic economic result envisaged bei Steiner and Gesell would be a strengthening of the real economy, and an an increase in the exchange of services and goods for the benefit of all. And more important, the result would be that nobody would be "hoarding" money anymore in order to speculate with it on the work of others.

It is important to note here though that neither Steiner nor Gesell thought of this model as being appropriate for the whole economy, that is, on the national and international level. They conceived the "aging money" merely to be a secondary level of local and regional money destined to create additional, locally and regionally limited circulation streams of productivity. That means that both Steiner and Gesell thought of an (at least) twofold money system in a given country, consisting of an official currency valid for the whole nation that had to correspond to rather traditional notions, and a second currency varying from region to region, city to city, and even town to town that had to follow the principles of "aging money" in order to create additional economic and financial opportunities. Such a twofold money system is necessary if the ideas of Steiner and Gesell are to be put into practice, because if there would be *only* the "aging money," it would be impossible to have any savings to perform bigger investments: let's say to buy a house or a car; with the "aging money" alone, you would have to buy them "step by step" (which is quite impossible in the case of a sophisticated machine like a car, or a computer) or by incurring long term debts, which could become quite complex and problematic (if not impossible) for the individual within an universal "aging money" system.

But there are also important differences in Steiner's and Gesell's philosophies. One main difference is how they viewed capital. Steiner was convinced that capital was in principle something good, because it facilitates heightened productivity and, as abstracted outcome of practical labor that lives on in time beyond the working capacity of its "creators," is in principle something like an abstraction of humaneness, and thus something positively "spiritual" (as we explained above). According to Steiner, the challenge is how to handle capital best, that is, for the sake of the community as a whole. In contrast, Gesell had the tendency to look at capital as something that had to be overcome as a systematic feature of modernity, since he believed that it were the mechanisms of capital that allowed the exploitation of communities and the dependence of politics, culture, and society from what he called the few great capitalistic conglomerates. While Steiner pointed at using capital in a better way to serve all three dimensions of modern society, i.e. economy, politics, and culture alike, Gesell in many ways pointed toward a society where capital would lose its own "life" in order to become a mere money tool distributed among all members of society according to their talents and to their needs.

A second difference between Steiner and Gesell is the focus of how they thought to improve the cohesion of economy, finance, and community. While Gesell pointed toward re-distributing wealth in a socialist way through national and local governments to "set people free" from the power of capital (the idea of a *"Free Economy"* for everybody), Steiner focused on what he called a capitalistic "Dialogue Economy" or "Associative Economy": Producers, traders, and consumers should systematically come together with the funding financial institutions to agree upon what goods are needed in what timeframe to which extent for whom. "Round tables" between all these actors would have to be organized in local, regional, and national settings alike; together, all parts involved would constitute a kind of "permanent parliament" of the diverse levels of economic and financial productivity meant to interact. The result would be a much more "human," down-to-earth, real economy, consumer- and need-oriented production instead of what Steiner called the artificial creation of needs for the masses by the producers, regardless of the societal facts and contexts. What Steiner hoped for was not a socialist approach, but in many ways the contrary: A "Dialogue Economy" that in Steiner's view means "economy from below"; that is, a radically democratic, consensus-based economy instead of the interest- and profit-driven "predatory economy" of the "everybody against everybody" financial industry controlled by small entrepreneurial elites.[166]

Interestingly, like most innovative movements in early 20th century Europe, both Steiner and Gesell came from the same tradition of German idealism that was also the origin of their fierce antagonists Karl Marx (1818–1883) and Ludwig Feuerbach (1804–1872), who dominated not only the leftist, but paradoxically also the bourgeois understanding of money, capital, banking, and finance throughout the 19th and 20th centuries. But unlike Marx and Feuerbach who invented the concepts of "communism" and "socialism" that in the hands of their successors created a totalitarian "state capitalism" as opposed to liberal private capitalism, Steiner and Gesell were not socialists, but financial humanists (even if Gesell had some affinities with Russian Marxism during the Bolshevik revolution toward the end of World War I). While Gesell's experiments were limited in their concrete outreach and never achieved a sufficient audience to unfold mentionable practical effects, Steiner's "Threefolding movement" became a serious and widespread political alternative to Marxism on the one hand and National Socialism (fascism) on the other hand during the early 1920s in Central Europe, to the point that the Nazis attempted several times to murder Steiner, forcing him eventually to flee to Switzerland where he spent the rest of his life in exile and was most probably eventually murdered by the Nazis in 1925.

---

[166]One important cluster of respective *contemporary* "bottom-up" initiatives (among an increasing number of similar approaches philosophically and systematically opposed to the "bottom-down" directives of the traditional elites) is "Transition towns." See: www.transitiontowns.org. "Transition towns" are towns and cities where parts of the civil society deliberately (i.e., without the command of the government, or other public institutions) choose to address all those aspects of life that the community needs in order to sustain itself and thrive: for example, how to significantly increase sustainability by drastically reducing carbon emissions to mitigate the effects of climate change. "Transition towns" are about "forming (civil society) groups to look at all the key areas of life (food, energy, transport, health, heart & soul, economics & livelihoods, etc.), thus creating complementary pools to governmental and institutionalized power by civil society activity, and by including money and finance at the very core that empowers them." In: www.transitiontowns.org.

The works of Steiner and Gesell were banned between the 1930s and 1940s by the Nazis and the Communists alike, and the Nazis burned their books. Their ideas were rediscovered only after World War II starting in 1946, when both their movements were re-examined mainly by academics seeking new, innovative approaches. In the 1950s and 1960s, European social reformers such as Wilhelm-Ernst Barkhoff (1916–1994) and Wilhelm Schmundt (1898–1992) in Germany or Bernard Lievegoed (1905–1992) in the Netherlands took up their ideas and developed them further. With the student protests and the emancipatory movements of the 1960s that began at the University of California, Berkeley, and reached out to Europe at the end of the decade, the first social banks were founded with direct reference to the ideas of Rudolf Steiner.

Today, most social banks in Europe, and all of their big players, have their roots in Steiner's ideas of an "associative" economy: from GLS Bank in Germany to Triodos Bank in the Netherlands, from Ekobanken Sweden to Merkur Bank in Denmark. But in the meantime there are also social banks that do not attribute their foundations to Steiner (like the Banca Etica in Italy or the Alternativbank Switzerland ABS, as well as most ethical programs within mainstream banks). However, a large portion of today's social banking business is still inspired by Steiner's thoughts on how to reconcile humanism and social justice (the famous slogan of the French Revolution revived by him: "Freedom, Equality, Brotherhood"[167]) with the "hard" realities of money and finance; on how to create dialogical forms of economy by bringing banks, producers, and consumers together to discuss how best to serve the real needs of a given population in a given space in a given timeframe; and thus ultimately on how to reconnect the money and finance business to the "real economy" again.

Summing up, both Steiner and Gesell coined alternative approaches to money, capital, and finance that lasted longer than the "short" 20th century[168] – including Marx's and Feuerbach's ideas – and which eventually became the seed for the new humanistic approaches of social banking and social finance for the 21st century.[169] Nevertheless, it is important to note that their ideas were (and remain) disputed right from the start and in principle, and that these ideas were never implemented directly by any social banking institution, but served merely as inspiration for developing contemporary new ways of handling money and finance.[170] This is due to the fact

[167]In the gender-attentive society of today, we would rather prefer the slogan "Freedom, Equality, Siblinghood."

[168]E. Hobsbawm: Age of Extremes: The Short Twentieth Century 1914–1991, Little Brown & Company, London 1994.

[169]Other sources include rural and civil society cooperatives, trade unions, charity organizations of the churches, ecological (green) movements, and the microfinance movements, all of them active in Europe mainly since the 1950s and 1960s, the microfinance movement since the 1980s.

[170]Cf. G. G. Preparata: Perishable Money in a Threefold Commonwealth: Rudolf Steiner and the Social Economics of an Anarchist Utopia. In: Review of Radical Political Economics, Vol. 38, No. 4 (2006), pp. 619–648, Sage Publications, London 2006; and S. E. Usher: Rudolf Steiner and Economics. The Threefold Social Organism: An Introduction.

that most ideas of Steiner and Gesell, particularly their ideas on how to reorganize the financial system as a whole, were obviously dependent on the historical circumstances of their times and can't be taken as direct blueprints for the completely different world of today. Still, their works remain worth reading and have a lot to say about the relationship of humaneness and finance.[171,172]

It is no accident that many leading economists of the 20th century have pointed out the continued educational value of these ideas – particularly John Maynard Keynes, who judged that "Gesell's chief work is written in cool and scientific terms, although it is run through by a more passionate and charged devotion to social justice than many think fit for a scholar. I believe that the future will learn more from Gesell's than from Marx's spirit."[173] Similarly, the doctoral father of current Deutsche Bank's CEO Josef Ackermann, Hans Christoph Binswanger, pointed out that "Steiner was maybe the first who thought that economy and finance could be a dialogue based endeavor, i.e. a democratic endeavor."[174]

9 The State of Social Banking and Social Finance Today: A Brief Comparison Between the United States and Europe

Now, to turn back to our days, let us ask the question: What is the state of these traditions today? And how can we describe the relationship between these mainly European forerunners and the contemporary finance and banking sector of the still economically most influential nation on earth, the United States?[175]

In: http://www.rudolfsteinerweb.com/Rudolf_Steiner_and_Economics.php (retrieved January 15, 2010).

[171]Cf. R. Steiner: Towards Social Renewal (1921), Rudolf Steiner Press 1977; R. Steiner: World Economics (1922), Rudolf Steiner Press 1972. Most texts by Rudolf Steiner about social economy and social finance can be found online at: http://www.rsarchive.org/SocialIssues/.

[172]Cf. S. Gesell: The Natural Economic Order (1906), translated by P. Paye, in: http://www.ces.org.za/docs/Gesell/en/neo/index.htm.

[173]J. Maynard Keynes: General Theory of Employment, Interest and Money, Harcour, Brace and Company, London 1935 p. 355. See also online: University of Adelaide, http://ebooks.adelaide.edu.au/k/keynes/john_maynard/k44g/.

[174]H. C. Binswanger (St. Gallen University): Money and the Alchemistic Form of Being. A Dialogue (Geld und die alchemistische Seinsweise. Ein Dialog). In: Institute for Social Threefolding Stuttgart, June 1994, http://www.dreigliederung.de/essays/1994-06-015.html.

[175]I deliberately focus here on the "Western" constellation only: *first*, because the large majority of existing social banks and their global networks (as well as most of their global leaders) are found here; *second*, because the worldwide financial system is still guided, and dominated, by the West; and *third*, because of the comparative scope of this volume. Nevertheless, there are many useful theories on social banking from other cultures, societies and traditions. A useful reading list that includes elements of non-Western experiences can be found at the Institute for Social Banking Germany's recommended reading list: http://www.socialbanking.org/fileadmin/isb/file/ISBLiteratureResources.pdf (retrieved November 15, 2010).

As we have seen previously, there are about 600 social banks and social finance initiatives today around the world, the majority of them in Europe. Nevertheless, it would be wrong to describe social banking and social finance exclusively with the notion of being "European"; and it would be equally inappropriate to label them solely as "answers to the financial and economic crisis of 2007–2010."

To start with the second point, social banks existed long before this crisis, in Europe and the United States alike; and as plausible as it is to look at some of their approaches as answers to this recent crisis, they are not the result of it. As much as they might have taken advantage of the crisis, their fate does not depend on its outcome.

With regard to the first point, there have been social banks in the United States even before the main big players in Europe were founded. For example, the Chicago-based Shorebank was founded in 1973, earlier than the GLS Bank and the Triodos bank. Others like Wainwright Bank and Trust Cy were founded in the 1980s; and the New Resource Bank in 2006. Currently, two US-based banks are members of the Global Alliance for Banking on Values: Shorebank in Chicago and The New Resource Bank that is active in California. Others might join in the coming years. According to INAISE, there are currently about 20–30 social banking and social finance initiatives in the United States, and the number is growing in the wake of the crisis.[176] Since the mainstream system is rapidly restoring itself though, it can't be predicted how many of these initiatives may be sustainable ones and how many may disappear within a relatively short period of time.[177]

As in Europe, the scope, focus, juridical status, and size of social banks in the United States and Canada vary noticeably. Besides the relatively few "regular" banks there is a relatively broad number of social finance initiatives that have been constituted by trade unions or as community shareholderships like the National Community Reinvestment Coalition (NCRC),[178] the Caisse d'Economie Solidaire Desjardings (founded in 1971) in Canada,[179] or the Vancouver City Savings Credit Union (Vancity) Bank (founded as early as in 1946). Others are constituted as "non-profit social finance foundations" like the Rudolf Steiner Social Finance Foundation RSF San Francisco.

Regarding their size, most of the US social banks are relatively smaller than their European counterparts; nevertheless, they are growing to a similar extent (with a

[176]Cf. R. Kropp: Sustainable Investment Strategies Earn Respect in the Aftermath of the Financial Crisis. Having sounded warnings for years about the possible causes of the economic crisis, sustainable and responsible investment may be embraced by more mainstream investors. In: Sustainability Investment News, October 17, 2008, http://socialfunds.com/news/article.cgi/article2567.html.

[177]For a continued oversight, see the largest U.S. website devoted to socially responsible investing "Social Funds": http://www.socialfunds.com/.

[178]NCRC: http://206.130.110.176/index.php?option=com_content&task=blogcategory&id=50&Itemid=104 and http://206.130.110.176/wordpress/. NCRC's projects are funded in part by the Ford Foundation New York, http://www.fordfoundation.org/.

[179]F. De Clerck: loc cit.

few exceptions like Shorebank, which faced some setbacks in the aftermath of the crisis). Among the bigger players in the United States are Shorebank Chicago (US $2.6 billion balance sheet total as on December 31, 2008) and the New Resource Bank California (US $0.17 billion).[180] The Rudolf Steiner Foundation for Social Finance San Francisco had consolidated assets of about US $120 million at the end of 2007 and was growing at a rate of more than 30% per year between 2006 and 2008.[181] In Canada, Vancity, which does not consider itself to be a social bank in the strict sense, but rather a "green citizens bank" (sometimes also describing itself as a "community-oriented civil society bank"), that is, an intermediate institution between the mainstream and the alternative financial businesses (in many regards closer to mainstream though), is the biggest community credit union in the nation, with 14.5 billion Canadian dollars (US $14.2 billion) of total assets at the end of 2009.[182]

If we compare the social banking and social finance institutions (in the broad sense[183]) in the United States and Canada with those in Europe, there are many similarities in the history, philosophy, strategies, and the overall goals. Nevertheless, there are also some differences. Among the latter are the following:

1. *The founding impulse*. While many US social banks and social finance institutions departed from a rather locally specialized focus – for example, on green agriculture, biodiversity, environment, social housing, or specific community concerns – most of their European counterparts started with a rather general impulse that was, in many cases, less locally and community oriented, but directed toward broader societal ideals and ends. While many US institutions today focus in a very realistic manner on concrete and down-to-earth goals in their direct neighbourhood without challenging the system as such, historically seen most European institutions had stark idealistic impulses of changing the ways of how capitalism works in general (even if in a realistic and segmental

180 C. Scheire and S. De Maertelaere: loc cit, p. 16.

181 Xigi.net, http://www.xigi.net/index.php?en=426 (retrieved February 1, 2010).

182 Vancity: https://www.vancity.com/AboutUs/.

183 I do not include here the mainstream community development financial institutions (CDFIs) in the United States, even if they present features that qualify some of them as *potential* social banks. The reason is first that average CDFIs are the result of a U.S. Government designation to make sure local communities are sourced (i.e., a designation "from above", while social banks are in principle developments "from below"). Second, the vast majority of CDFIs do not share many of the proceedings (triple bottom line), the values and ideals, and the concepts of money and finance of social banks. For more information about CDFIs, see: The CDFI Fund of the United States Department of the Treasury, http://cdfifund.gov/who_we_are/about_us.asp; and The National Community Investment Fund NCIF, http://www.ncif.org/index.php/CDBIindustry/CDFIs/. See also R. Kropp: Treasury Department Will Invest $1 Billion in Community Development Financial Institutions. With unemployment rates still at record highs and big banks unwilling to lend to small businesses, CDFIs welcome the infusion of capital when demand for their services is greater than ever. In: Sustainability Investment News, February 10, 2010, http://socialfunds.com/news/article.cgi/article2885.html.

way).[184] Both approaches have their pros and cons. The ideal in the age of globalization would probably be to melt both approaches.[185]

---

[184]I would suggest that this difference is an interesting overall cultural comparison between Europe and the United States.

[185]As always with comparative cultural issues, it is a delicate task to seek explanations for the differences between the United States and Europe with regard to the societal embedment of capitalism. The reason is that every such explanation is by its very nature unavoidably full of potential exaggerations and misunderstandings, which is always dangerous because it generalizes and functions necessarily as a reduction that presents some advantages and many problems. Thus, every such attempt has to be handled with extreme caution and carefulness. Second, every such attempt has to consider that most aspects involved present their pros and cons *to an equal extent.*

That said, *one* aspect for the different approaches toward "improving the capitalistic system" in Europe compared with the United States might consist in the fact that capitalism as a form of modern economy and the United States as a nation formed an indivisible unity right from the start, so that most US citizens face certain difficulties in "culturally" rethinking how capitalism should work. To many, this would mean to "change the United States as such" (especially to the conservatives of course). In contrast, in Europe there has been a long history of experiments with non-capitalistic and alternative forms of economy since the very first forms of capitalism during the crusades and the renaissance (i.e., between the 12th and the 15th century) emerged. Although basically all of the experiments with alternative approaches have failed, Europeans seem to find it generally easier to imagine the possibility of alternative approaches to "classical" modern capitalism than Americans.

On the other hand, a *second* aspect might be that the different approaches in the "cultural psychology" toward capitalism could be the result of the fact that modern capitalism was "invented" in Europe (let us think of the Fugger family in Germany in the late Middle Ages, or the Medici in Florence during the Renaissance, to mention just a few); so that Europeans in general might have it easier to be critical, given that they have had such a long story with witnessing its many faults in the early and "axial" periods; while Americans might be necessarily less distanced, that is, "closer" to capitalism as a functioning "natural" cultural practice given that they became a nation when capitalism was at an already developed stage.

A *third* cause of the typological differences between social banks in Europe and the United States may consist in the different political framework of the history of capitalism in the United States and in Europe, i.e. in the fact that in the United States, unlike Europe, democracy predated the rise of industrial capitalism. Cf. the accurate observation of L. Zingales in: Capitalism After the Crisis, In: National Affairs, Number I, Fall 2009, pp. 22–35: "In America, unlike much of the rest of the West, democracy predated industrialization. By the time of the Second Industrial Revolution in the latter part of the 19th century, the United States had already enjoyed several decades of universal (male) suffrage, and several decades of widespread education. This created a public with high expectations, unlikely to tolerate evident unfairness in economic policy ... Unlike in Europe – where the most vibrant opposition to the excesses of business came from socialist anti-market movements – in the United States this opposition was squarely pro-market. When Louis Brandeis [1856–1941, US Supreme Court Justice from 1916 to 1939] attacked the money trust, he was not fundamentally trying to interfere with markets – but was only trying to make them work better. As a result, Americans have long understood that the interests of the market and the interests of business may not always be aligned." It is clear that this difference between the histories of capitalism in the United States and Europe continues to be influential on the system until today, and that it also influences the differences in the basic attitudes of social banking and social finance on both sides of the Atlantic.

A *fourth* reason is the different relationship with debts and indebtedness as such: "Another distinguishing feature of American capitalism is that it developed relatively untouched by foreign influence ... As a result, American capitalism developed more or less organically, and still

2. *The concept of "social."* Overall, European social banks cultivate a broader concept of what is meant by the term "social" than their US counterparts. While in the United States "social" is often confined to charity and work with the disadvantaged and is concerned in many cases with social and financial justice (for example, to provide people chances to get a house in a given neighborhood by helping them find cheaper credits), the concept of "social" in Europe embraces a rather broad interdisciplinary field of action that includes sustainability also in the sense of ecology, technology, environment, and culture, and that involves all social classes. In Europe, these different dimensions are in fact seen in many cases as interdependent, if not inseparable from each other. Respectively, the strategies in general seem to be more diversified in Europe and more focused in the United States – again, with all pros and cons involved on both sides.

---

shows the marks of those origins. The American bankruptcy code, for instance, exhibits significant pro-debtor biases, because the United States [as a colony] was born and developed as a nation of debtors." L. Zingales, l.c. Cf. G. C. Herring: From Colony to Superpower, Oxford University Press, Oxford 2008. On the one hand, this has the advantage of making indebtedness something "normal" in the United States (which is not the case in Europe); on the other hand, it has the disadvantage of unconsciously favoring debts over donations, de facto excluding the latter from "regular" business and constricting them into philanthropy.

Finally, a *fifth* reason might be a more narrow cultural one: The close connection between the "American dream" and capitalism, which made of the dollar sign a symbol of promise of a "good life," and thus a proto-religious symbol. Something similar does not exist in Europe, because Europe has no "American dream." Instead, most European societal dreams already since the late medieval social reformers (for example, Michael Gaismair, 1490–1532) were (at least in their basic tendency) more or less oriented toward "social" dreams of society ("social" in the sense of "community oriented" and "collective-relied"). R. Haskins rightly stated that as a consequence of the economic and financial crisis "there is a real threat to the American Dream." In: R. Haskins: Getting Ahead in America. In: National Affairs, Number I, Fall 2009, pp. 36–37. The question is not whether this is positive or negative because I regard the American dream as a positive ideal inherent in a progressive and open society, and its potential decline as worrisome. The question is rather, can the American Dream of individuality, self-reliance and vertical mobility and the common good be structurally better combined than it has been the case so far? I regard this question as important for the United States and Europe alike. While the United States may have to supplement the American dream with a stronger community orientation, Europe may have to introduce something like a "European dream" on a systemic level, and to use it to balance its often one-sided dreams of a communitarism in crisis already since the 1970s.

Again, all these five points present their pros and cons on both sides involved. America has the inestimable advantage of being culturally so "close" to – and involved with – capitalism that it is kind of a "natural" habit that facilitates the use of money; and the outcome is that America has become – by far – the richest nation on earth within only two centuries. The relative advantage of Europe is that it may be more inclined to experiment with institutional and governmental options, although this is a two-edged sword insofar as innovations in the financial markets can only take place on a global level; that is, in exchange between Europe, the United States, and other nations, if they want to be sustainable. That is one reason (among others) why I believe that the future of the beneficial use of capital and money, and the improvement of how the capitalistic system works, consists in the combination of both the cultural habits and relative typological strengths of the United States and Europe. Cf. similarly F. Zakaria: Restoring the American Dream, l.c.

3. *The principle of donation.* In Europe, the principle of donation is seen as an integrative part of the institutional core business of social banks, involving economic, social, and cultural recipients. In the United States, donating is often seen as the exclusive business of philanthropists who have "made it" in their jobs and then "give back"[186] to their communities and thus to the nation that made them

---

[186]Cf. B. Gates' exemplary lecture: Giving Back: Finding the Best Way to Make a Difference. 2010 Payne Distinguished Lecture, Freeman Spogli Institute for International Studies, Stanford University, 19 April 2010, in: Stanford University, http://news.stanford.edu/news/2010/april/bill-gates-setup-040910.html.

With an endowment of $34 billion (as at April 2010), the Bill and Melinda Gates Foundation holds assets that are almost double the amount of the combined total balance sheets of all social banks worldwide. In managing such huge amounts of money, Gates – as one of the most successful and influential businessmen of all time – is perhaps the best example of the *diachronic* principle that is followed by many philanthropists: *First* you make money by "playing tough" and "playing rough" with the mainstream rules of the "everybody against everybody" economic and financial mainstream, not excluding occasional ambivalent or even questionable behaviors and practices (see, for example, the various trials brought by the US and European governments against Microsoft for monopolistic and anti-competitive practices). *Then* you go into the "helping and community principle," that is, into administrating the achieved profit and donating it according to your preferences.

Sure enough, modern capitalistic societies will always need these great individual entrepreneurs, since their work has to be considered as exemplary in many ways as it is inspiring to many. Furthermore, like most of his kind and at this exceptional level, Gates certainly puts the principle "using money rather than having it" convincingly into practice, at least with part of his fortune (Gates' overall fortune is estimated to be about $53 billion net worth as of April 2010). But while it is more then commendable (as well as honorable) that great individuals put their money into philanthropy, and while these "great achievers" deserve unreserved admiration for their contributions to progress and wealth for the broader public, there are a few questions that should be openly discussed.

First, is it possible to follow a *synchronic* principle of "doing business" and "doing the good" *at the same time*, instead of doing *first* the one, and *then* the other? It it possible to combine profit and philanthropy for the benefit of all within "regular" business; that is, without going into philanthropy in the narrow sense? Social banks and social finance institutions are about lending and donating money to sustainability-oriented enterprises; but they are also about making profits, and they function like normal banks, while following a "triple bottom line" for people, profit, and planet. They are trying to do business and to do the good at the same time without separating the one from the other.

A *second* possible question to discuss with regard to the relationship between philanthropy and social finance is a more general one: Is it better for the overall development of modern societies if the social good is taken care of by "great individuals" according to their personal world views (even if in some cases in close cooperation with the governments), or is it better if the benefit of all through the handling of money becomes a systemic factor, i.e. an institutionalized function within society that is in principle independent of single, charismatic pioneers? Social banking is about implementing the use of money to the benefit of all as a systemic factor in today's financial business, and it is exercised according to decisions not taken by great individual donors (and their advisers), but by communities of shareholders, customers, and consumers in a democratic – or "associative" – way. Could it be that it is exactly this cooperative and dialogic *procedure* that makes the biggest difference over time, not the input of money as such?

Interestingly, in his answers to the questions posed by the audience in response to his Stanford lecture of April 2010, Bill Gates gave a definition of sustainability centered on the demand of the community: "Sustainable probably means that you wanna do something that even once

rich – like, for example Bill and Melinda Gates, Warren Buffet, Oprah Winfrey and their foundations, as well as "the rich, the beautiful and the famous" in general. While the core business of social banking and social finance in the United States is in many cases regarded as lending money at conditions that foster social and community development, in Europe, social banks are organized in a way that values lending and donating as in principle equally important activities.

4. *The focus of ethical investment.* Ethical investment in stock markets and bonds has its historical origins in the trade unions and local community shareholder trusts of the post-1945 United States[187] and was later taken over by some mainstream European banks as a niche business. In contrast, the idea to found whole banks as institutions dedicated 100% to social finance was an idea that gained a broader momentum mainly in Europe at the end of the 1960s (of course, with some exceptions like the first US social banks that were founded earlier than their European partners, mentioned above).

Are these differences elements of potential separation or of potential conjunction between US and European social finance initiatives?

It cannot be overlooked that there are cultural differences.[188] But it is also easy to see that if put into dialogue, these differences instead of being a disadvantage for

---

you're not there giving that either the practices, or the government funding allows that benefit to continue. So it is gonna be something ... that is so dramatic in its impact ... that it will continue ... It's easy to be unrealistic about it ... a lot of virtual philanthropy comes in that isn't able to sustain that ... So it's a smart question to thinking about that from the very beginning ... and only those solutions that are very effective and have incredible demand from the people involved will be the ones that get adopted." In: B. Gates: Stanford Open Office Hours, 20 April 2010, http://www.facebook.com/home.php?#!/video/video.php?v=672651583673&ref=mf. Cf. A. Gorlick: Bill Gates pushes students to focus on the "important problems." In: Stanford Report, April 19, 2010, http://news.stanford.edu/news/2010/april/bill-gates-lecture-041910.html. See also R. Benedikter: The Case of Microsoft. Economy between the Principles of Individuality and Community (Der Fall Microsoft. Wirtschaftsleben zwischen Individualität und Sozialität), in: Kulturzeitschrift "Die Drei," 70. Jahrgang, Nr. 9/2000, Stuttgart 2000, pp. 7–23.

[187] Some social bankers in the United States see an additional aspect of their ethical roots in the 1920s and 1930s, when churches, particularly the Methodists and Quakers, established trade-union-like community funds that excluded the production of alcohol and the funding of prostitution.

[188] Cf. as just one – though symptomatic – example the famous initiative of the US "super-philanthropists" Bill Gates and Warren Buffet who in July 2010 tried to motivate (private) billionaires first in the United States, and then around the world, particularly in Europe, to dedicate 50% of their wealth by donating it to charity through public foundations and funds. See: The Giving Pledge, http://givingpledge.org/. Although all those who agreed to donate did so in a non-binding manner, the initiative was read by many as the opening up of a "new age of commitment" of the rich as an effect of increased consciousness produced by the crisis. Regardless if this is the case, and independently of the open question if private, voluntary philanthropy by a selected group of billionaires may be the right way for society to evolve its social bases and to improve participation, the interesting point is that there were widely different reactions in the United States (where 40 billionaires joined) and Europe (where only a few agreed). The different reactions pointed toward the existing cultural divide between the two shores of the Atlantic when it

the global networking of social finance can prove to be fruitful engines of progress and mutual enrichment. The exchange about diverse backgrounds, cultural habits, political and societal mechanisms is already becoming a factor of strength, diversification, and mutual support both of governments and banks, as the economic and financial crisis of 2007–2010 has impressively shown. Thus, I would agree with experts Sven Remer and Frans De Clerck that these differences have the potential to become useful catalysts benefiting the greater impulse of social banking and social finance on an international level.[189]

10 Seven Answers to the Financial Crisis

If we sum up what we have seen about the philosophy, the history, and the current state of social banking and social finance on both sides of the Atlantic, the questions remain: What is the outlook with regard to the immediate needs of change and innovation that surfaced as an effect of the economic and financial crisis of 2007–2010?

---

comes to social issues: Whereas in the United States, "social finance" is still comparatively widely identified with private donations, the same task is identified in Europe almost automatically with a core function of the state (respectively, the government). In the United States, the government has traditionally kept a low profile and low interference with the citizens; the culture of private initiative for the greater good still prevails (depending obviously also on the single states and their different "sub-cultures;" California, particularly northern California, is not Texas, in the sense that even within the state of California, and between the states of California and Texas, the common good is looked at differently). In contrast, in Europe, private care for "social progress" is not appreciated to a similar extent, and thus does not enjoy the same prestige. This is because Europeans believe that it should not be left to the voluntary decision of the richest segment of the population to contribute according to their possibilities to public concerns; instead, social issues should be regulated systemically and by law. The issue here is that different financial and societal systems have incepted different "cultures of finance," particularly when seen in their relationship to public affairs. It is clear that this unavoidably creates different presuppositions and contexts for social banking and social finance. On the other hand, it may be exactly this potential complementary between different systemic embedments of social banking and social finance that could result as one great advantage fostering flexibility and adaptability. In any case, the "50% donation" initiative of Gates and Buffet made it once more clear what we have discussed above: Philanthropy is (1) not the same, (2) it is not of equal systemic valence, and (3) it is no substitute for (and no alternative to) social banking and social finance – even if there might by (hopefully) some alliances in the future.

In short, the question here is about the greater vision on tomorrow's society. Do we want to have a financial system based on ruthless speculation on the one hand, and a donating pole of philanthropists and private foundations on the other hand – without connection between them, and with the latter often building the profits that create the charity endowments in the "opposed" sector? Is it not desirable to have something "in between" these two poles? This would indeed be social banking and social finance. They are a part of the working financial system, and they are at the same time functioning as its corrections with regard to social issues. Thus, social banking is neither part of the one, nor of the other pole: it is part of both, and thus a functioning and feasible "third way" to serve as a "systemic bridge." Cf. Handelsblatt Düsseldorf: The Nice Billionare Next Door (Der nette Milliardär von nebenan), in: Handelsblatt Düsseldorf, August 29, 2010.

[189]Cf. S. Remer: "Society has not learned from the Crisis" ("Gesellschaft hat nicht aus Krise gelernt"). In: Deutschlandradio Kultur, 15.09.2009; and F. De Clerck: loc cit, p. 12.

What constructive proposals do social banks have as answers to the crisis? And what do they concretely claim to be able to accomplish in the long term?

Typologically speaking, there are *seven* main solutions to the economic crisis discussed in the international public debate: (1) return to the state of things before the system crashed, (2) restore the system with some ethical improvements, (3) implement better regulation, (4) permit further deregulation, (5) create alternative models within the system, (6) create alternative models against the system, (7) change the system from the bottom up.

While social banks would obviously not recommend returning to business as usual (option (1), requested by large parts Wall Street), there is also broad agreement among them that to restore the mainstream banking and finance business only with some minor improvements such as the introduction of basic ethical minimum standards foremost for bank leaders and for aspects of their investment practices, will not suffice (option 2). Although an encouraging move, ethical standards imposed on a culture of unethical behavior from the outside are in most cases ineffective, and their concrete implementation is difficult to measure.

On the other hand, to point toward changing the system of the capitalistic economy all at once (option (7), suggested by the "new left" movements that have been re-encouraged by the financial crisis in many countries, including the United States), seems to be unrealistic, as well as dangerous and contraproductive.

So the remaining rational options for debate seem to be options (3)–(6). And it is exactly in the range of these four options that social banks have made their theoretical and practical contributions during the past 2 years.

Altogether, there were *three* concrete in-depth proposals by the global social banking networks during the years 2008–2009, all on initiative and under the leadership of their leading European players. The Global Alliance for Banking on Values GABV proposed three theses for a better future in February 2009[190]; and the International Association of Investors in the Social Economy INAISE proposed 12 measures to improve the resilience of the financial system in September 2009.[191] Earlier, in December 2008, an assembly of European alternative banks under the leadership of the GLS Bank Bochum proposed an eight-point program in response to the crisis.[192]

[190]The Global Alliance for Banking on Values (GABV): The Upside of the Downturn: How Sustainable Banking Can Deliver a Better Future. Three Theses. In: http://www.gabv.org/News/Triodos.htm, February 5, 2009.

[191]The International Association of Investors in the Social Economy (INAISE): 12 measures for a socially useful financial system. Four International Social Finance and Community Development Federations put out a call to G-20 Governments. In: http://www.inaise.org/EN/fr_1.html, Paris, Brussels and Washington DC, September 21, 2009. These 12 theses have also been signed by the European Federation of Ethical and Alternative Banks (FEBEA), by the US National Community Reinvestment Coalition (NCRC), and by the Global Coalition for Responsible Credit (GCRC).

[192]T. Jorberg (Chairman of GLS Bank): European Alternative Banks Call for an 8 Point Plan (Alternativbanken Europas fordern 8-Punkte-Plan). In: http://www.gls.de/die-gls-bank/presse/pressearchiv/detail/datum/2008/12/08/alternativbanken-europas-fordern-8-punkte-plan.html, December 8, 2008.

In order to catch what the future may bring, let's take a look at these three proposals, see where they converge, and what their common essence might be. In conclusion, we will have to ask how applicable they are with regard to the existing international financial system.

First, the three theses of the GABV, developed under the leadership of Peter Blom, CEO and chairman of the Executive Board of Triodos Bank, state the following:

> Sustainable banking has been developing for decades, but it has accelerated rapidly as the financial crisis has taken hold. Why? What makes these apparently unconventional financial institutions more crisis-resistant than their mainstream contemporaries? And can they offer a viable alternative, plotting a path for the future that other banks can follow?
>
> Sustainable banking is becoming a significant force in the world's financial markets. The ten best known sustainable banks in the developed world have assets of around $30 billion, not including the much wider-reaching, more mainstream institutions like the cooperative banks. These commercially solid, growing banks focus on financing environmental projects, social entrepreneurship and community businesses. Even though they operate in emerging markets, microfinance banks have realized extraordinary growth rates in both volume and profit. The total assets of all microfinance providers are estimated at $50 billion; they serve 150 million people in the developing world.
>
> As the sustainable banking industry has flourished, so have some of the key institutions driving it ... Perhaps surprising, these organizations have been propelled forward by the credit crunch and the turbulence that followed it.
>
> That (they have) been able to side-step the worst impact of the crisis, and prosper despite it, is not a matter of luck. Social finance institutions finance sustainable business, delivering clear social, environmental or cultural benefits. As such, social banking and social finance is directly connected to the real economy, only financing business and projects that provide services and products that people need. In essence, we offer basic banking. A decent profit, a strong capital base (15% Bank for International Settlements ratio[193]) and a stable funding base from savers' deposits are integral parts of our business approach. And the GABV thinks this straightforward model is the way banking should be.
>
> Investing depositors' money in packaged and repackaged sub-prime mortgages (as mainstream banks did prior to the crisis) is precisely the opposite. The issue is not so much the sub-prime mortgage itself. It's the demise of the relationship between bank and home-owner that characterizes it that has led to such catastrophic consequences for the markets and millions of people connected to them. Banks bundled these mortgages together and sold them to "the market," but the buyer had no idea what to do if the borrowers failed to pay interest or missed their repayments. The relationship between borrower and lender was lost, and we're now living through the consequences.[194]
>
> How did we get into this mess?
>
> For many years basic banking – raising deposits and granting loans – has meant high operational costs for banks, and limited profits. Shareholders came to expect ever-increasing returns, and substantial management bonuses created incentives for the banks that delivered them. Together they created a voracious appetite for ever more profitable products

---

[193]Cf. Bank for International Settlements: http://en.wikipedia.org/wiki/Bank_for_International_Settlements. Insertion by Benedikter.

[194]To be more precise, we have to record that this habit was not only practiced by mainstream full banks, as the whole process involved many intermediaries (mortgage brokers, underwriting banks, servicing banks, packaging investment banks), all of which took fees to make a profit, and none of whom maintained a long-term relationship with the client. Addition by Benedikter.

and services. This shifted the mainstream bank's emphasis away from basis banking and the real economy, into potentially lucrative but more complex and less transparent products. Securitization of assets became common, creating markets for Collateralized Debt Obligations (CDOs) which created massive profits – as long as a volatile market continued to go up.

This approach led to unprecedented profits[195] – and also to the enormous losses banks face today. Banks like Triodos, which were not prepared to invest in these riskier, complex leveraged financial products, have fared much better. Indeed, at the height of the crisis, Triodos Bank grew its deposit base by 15% in just two months. Many of the new customers are increasingly savvy about what a bank should, and shouldn't do. People who used to be skeptical about smaller banks now understand that staying close to the real economy is safer than being big and involved in global markets for leveraged financial products.

Another factor helped determine which banks won and lost in the financial crisis: whether or not they are listed on a stock exchange. (Most social banks) deliberately (choose) not to be listed, not least because the conventional shareholder relationship is anonymous. Instead, (they) want to be close to (their) shareholders and explain (them their) long-term strategy.

While the shares of social banks aren't liquid on a (stock) exchange, they are issued and can be sold on a match bargain market, which matches buyers with sellers, and vice-versa, at regular intervals. And the principle used to calculate their price is based on the value of the underlying businesses we finance, not on the vagaries of market sentiment.[196] The quality of our loan portfolio determines (social) bank's value, not the market. This approach is straightforward, grounded in real companies and the people who run them, and prevents speculation.[197]

---

[195] It is decisive to understand however that these profits were only short-term and *apparent* profits. If the accounting had captured all costs including cost of capital and risk, these profits would not have existed. I suspect that if you look at the profits in the "fat" years until 2006 and compare them with the losses of 2007–2010, there would be no net profits at all, even if the incredible levels of unsettled compensation were repaid to the banks. Addition by Benedikter.

[196] Sure enough, there are many issues about markets that cannot be fully addressed here. On the one hand, the markets allow individuals to move their funds to social banks (i.e., voting with their wallets). On the other hand, some markets are intransparent and provide insufficient information. Given the premise of social banks that capitalism is not a bad thing, but on the contrary the best form of working with money and finance available, there is a large question as to the role of markets in a capitalistic system. Addition by Benedikter.

[197] Again, as much I share P. Blom's and the GABV's basic viewpoint here, I would not at the same time devalue the importance of markets too much. In my view, while I agree with the need to change things, from a scientific viewpoint the reality of markets and their role for the proper functioning of the capitalistic system is more complex than Blom's statement, and therefore it has to be seen in a more sober and pondered way. I would in general agree with G. Banks (The Australian Government) here who in my view correctly states: "Not all societies have been persuaded by the logic of [capital driven] markets. However experiments around the world with alternative systems have only served to demonstrate their value. And indeed we have seen a progressive shift towards, or back to, markets across the globe in recent decades; a move which has generally paid off for the countries concerned. Since 1980, world Gross Domestic Product (GDP) has risen by two and a half times, or an unprecedented 40 per cent per capita, with millions of people rising out of extreme poverty ... (The) gaps or deficiencies in market provision all involve things that civilized societies care about. They have to do with fairness and quality of life. It could be said that they have to do with the *productivity of societies,* not just the *productivity of economies.* But we shouldn't condemn markets for failing to produce them. Markets make an important contribution, but they

In contrast, listed banks have to fight the perception of being weak as stock prices drop. And, because they've dropped (during the crisis) depositors have become anxious, transferring their money quickly via the internet. This left some banks facing systemic problems and needing government intervention to rescue them.

These problems have a profound impact on the public, making increased regulation inevitable. Because, if nothing else, the financial crisis made it abundantly clear that the financial markets are not able to regulate themselves.[198]

What does the future hold? How can we learn from what has happened, and change the way we handle our money, so our banks can become ... solid pillars of our financial system and not the biggest threat to its longer-term health? And is there a role for sustainable banks? (...)

The (crisis has) shown that banks are not just ordinary businesses with money as their core product. Money, especially savings, is fundamental to the way we live our lives – just like clean drinking water, electricity, healthcare and education. In this sense, banks provide a public service, looking after our money when we're not using it, and allowing us to send it to each other. But if we do not want to nationalize these core functions, we need bank regulation that is clear and linked to a reliable savings guarantee program, one that protects savers' money, should a bank go under.

The only way to make sure this happens is to separate basic banking from the extraneous financial functions now offered by so many modern mainstream banks.

(That means): To regulate savings, loans and payment facilities ... is simple, transparent and makes a depositor's guarantee scheme affordable. Other functions, like insurance and investment banking need to be kept separate. This should be the first challenge for governments and regulators alike.[199]

This request is to a certain extent similar to the US Glass–Steagall Act of 1933, a law proposal that tried to enact similar standards in the pre-WWII era. Its goals were to separate basic business activities of banks from their speculative activities, for example, by introducing different modes of taxation and differentiated juridical rules and restrictions.[200] The Glass–Steagall Act was proposed by the Democratic

---

cannot satisfy every societal goal or need. They cannot do it all. That is why we have governments and why, realistically, electorates require them to perform a larger role than the minimalist functions advocated by libertarian philosophers." G. Banks: loc cit, pp. 267–270.

[198] In this regard, I again only partly agree with Blom, because I regard such a "total" judgment in danger of becoming imbalanced in its tendency. Again, things are slightly more complex. I rather agree with G. Banks' smart statement: "Problems *in* markets should not be conflated with problems *of* markets. It is easy to lose sight of the simple function of markets. They are a means of connecting willing buyers and sellers, to their mutual benefit. That is all they do. Of course, if they do it well, they achieve a lot. But, like the old saying about oils, 'markets ain't markets': some operate a lot better than others. History tells us that those societies with better functioning markets have been the most successful economically, and often the most successful socially as well." G. Banks: loc cit, p. 267. I wouldn't necessarily contrapose Banks' position to Blom's however. Both have their points, and both these positions have to be seen as "unity in diversity," if we want to catch the multifaceted – and often contradictory – nature of contemporary (financial) markets.

[199] GABV: The Upside of the Downturn, loc cit Accentuations by Benedikter.

[200] My assertion is that Glass–Steagall separations worked as they kept more risky proprietary trading off the books of "commercial" banks and in the hands of "investment" banks where any losses would be at the cost of the owners. Therefore, I believe that the combination of public trading of investment banking shares with the elimination of Glass–Steagall relative to certain proprietary trading in the "neoliberal" era co-created the underlying circumstances leading to the crisis.

Senator Carter Glass and by Congressman Henry B. Steagall, a Democrat as well. It is regarded as one main model for new regulations proposed for the post-crisis financial business by US President Barack Obama and German Chancellor Angela Merkel.[201]

Blom continues with a second point:

> What should we expect of our banks?
>
> *A solid banking sector is needed to finance solutions to the real problems we face*, especially climate change and poverty. Worldwide, a significant and growing minority of people want to invest their money in a more sustainable future, and (they) need the banks to help them do (so). (Banks) should respond, *not least because they can*. Instead of generating artificial profits from complex financial instruments and unacceptable risks, banks are in a unique position to facilitate lasting change.
>
> The paradigm taking over now, whether we like it or not, is that financial capital is no longer the limiting factor for growth and prosperity. We need a new, better balance between the three key elements of production: natural resources, labor and capital. Despite the financial crisis, we're not short of money[202,203]; we just have to make better use of it. Banks play a critical role in this process. Sustainable banks, including microfinance banks in emerging economies, have proved that their core business works. They service their

[201]Cf. R. Heakal: What was the Glass–Steagall Act? In: http://www.investopedia.com/articles/03/071603.asp (retrieved March 10, 2010); and Handelsblatt Düsseldorf: Glass–Steagall Act of 1933 (Glass–Steagall Act von 1933). In: http://www.handelsblatt.com/politik/international/obamas-vorbild-glass-steagall-act-von-1933;2516803, January 21, 2010.

[202]In fact, as I have already mentioned above, we might have too much money if compared with the size of the real economy. After all, the amount of money in circulation globally is enough to buy and sell the entire biosphere several times over. All that money sloshing around is bound to create disturbances. Addition by Benedikter.

[203]Some analysts thus paradoxically even assert that the real estate and the derivative bubbles may be to a certain extent a relative benefit for the stability of the value of money, since they bind a lot of it in artificial "hoarding boxes"; if the huge amounts of money "hoarded" in the real estate and the derivative markets would be taken out and put into the real economy (as social banks propose), inflation could explode to unprecedented levels, so these analysts say. I believe this is an assertion that could be challenged from various viewpoints, and with a variety of arguments. Nevertheless, if the proposals by social banks to leverage the bubbles by pulling out the money from the derivative and the real estate markets in order to stimulate "real" economic productivity were followed on a systemic level by the national and international economic and financial systems, it would be indeed necessary to drastically reduce the overall amount of money in circulation. An interesting contribution to this debate about how much money is appropriate for what economy at which time is the theory of "100% money," also called the theory of "Plain money" developed by I. Fisher (Yale University, 1867–1947) and J. Huber (Halle University, Germany). See: http://de.wikipedia.org/wiki/Irving_Fisher and http://de.wikipedia.org/wiki/Joseph_Huber_%28Soziologe%29. Some actual texts of Huber on the topic of monetary reform can be found at: http://www.soziologie.uni-halle.de/huber/publikationen.html#a11, as well as at http://www.soziologie.uni-halle.de/huber/publikationen.html. I especially recommend J. Huber: Seigniorage Reform and Plain Money. Paper prepared for the Forum for Stable Currencies, House of Lords, London, June 20, 2001, in: http://www.soziologie.uni-halle.de/huber/docs/london2001.pdf; and J. Huber and J. Robertson: Creating New Money. A monetary reform for the information age. The New Economics Foundation NEF London, London 2000, in: http://www.neweconomics.org/sites/neweconomics.org/files/Creating_New_Money.pdf (retrieved April 15, 2010).

> customers, helping them to become successful social entrepreneurs and contributing to sustainable development. They are profitable social innovators in the financial sector. Three important lessons can be learned from their success:
>
> 1. *Sustainable banks focus on the relationship with their customers.* They institutionalize the relationship between the depositor and the borrower, not just with money but by highlighting the interdependence between the two. The result (are) committed depositors who understand what their bank is using their money for, and borrowers who feel supported by (this knowledge). Equally important, the increasingly controversial reward systems that offer inflated financial bonuses (to bank leaders) need to be informed by the "value" of relationships, not just transactions.
> 2. *Sustainable banks know their shareholders, and most (shareholders) are listed (by name).* The relationship of social banks with their shareholders goes well beyond a financial return. Instead, shareholders and sustainable banks share a common mission. This makes (social banks) robust in the face of external shocks (and shocks don't come much bigger than the most recent financial crisis). Questions of ownership are critical. Banks . . . can choose to follow clear, strong codes for socially responsible shareholding, so shareholders know exactly what they're letting themselves in for if, and when, they invest.
> 3. *Sustainable banks are about core banking.* They focus on the sectors they know well, financing business in the real economy. And they provide inclusive financial services in emerging markets for poor, but commercially astute people. Their success highlights the need for a regulatory framework that makes sure (that) banks only work in savings, loans and transactions creating capital as a buffer for depositors: (i.e. in) the core business they came from, and (which they) know best. If that approach is implemented consistently, banks will . . . make the margins they need to deliver healthy, effective and key banking services.[204]
>
> The frontrunners in this field are established, solid, profitable and fast-growing (social) banks. Brought together, they (can) be a powerful force for change. . . The . . . goal (of the networks of social banks) will be to show . . . just what is possible if banking moves from a place of opportunistic self-interest, to serving the public and meeting the great challenges of our time.[205]

Besides the partly too euphoric tone of this manifesto, we recognize some "sober" core elements of social banking and social finance here that we already know:

- return to the core business of banking, that is, to financing the "real economy";
- refuse to participate in artificial secondary financial markets like the real estate bubble and the derivative bubble, including the market in collateralized debt obligations (CDOs);
- ensure there is transparency and personal relationship between bank and customer;

---

[204] Admittedly, though, from a strictly empirical point of view it is still not fully clear if the current economics of banking allow a sufficient margin to be generated by basic banking in the long run. There are also issues of scale given the increased use of technology in banking. I therefore think that substantial research into the economics of basic banking is needed to determine what level of capital can be supported by social banks under which conditions for how long. Addition by Benedikter.

[205] GABV: The Upside of the Downturn, loc cit, Accentuations by Benedikter.

- make investments in innovative markets, even though some of them may be initially unprofitable (among them renewable energy, green technology, the environment, the cultural and educational sector, as well as global agriculture and fair trade);
- make social responsibility the most important imperative, in principle regarded as more important than pure profit;
- push the greater good as the primary goal;
- urge investment into human development in a broad, interdisciplinary perspective that includes cultural change (or behavioral development) as one decisive measure of the success of sustainability.

But there are also some new elements in this statement oriented toward a proper reaction to the crisis not only by social banks, but at least potentially by the entire finance sector:

- Governments should establish new national and international banking and finance regulations that differentiate between the core business of financial institutions (commercial activity) and their speculative activities (betting on derivatives, real estate speculation, etc.), including different taxation;
- Banks should refrain as much as possible from being listed in the anonymous stock exchanges and incentivize instead toward a more direct relationship with the shareholders on a community-based level of direct contact, involvement, and co-responsibility.[206]

Given the reception of these ideas by leading statesmen in the United States and Europe, they seem to be worth an in-depth debate of how to implement them best in given local, national, and international constellations in a short-, middle-, and long-term perspective.

But before we come to further conclusions, let's proceed quickly to the *second* important manifesto coined in response to the financial crisis by social banks, the 12 measures proposed by INAISE:

> On the occasion of the G-20 summit in Pittsburgh on 24 and 25 September 2009, the International Association of Investors in the Social Economy (INAISE) and the European Federation of Ethical and Alternative Banks (FEBEA), joined by the National Community Reinvestment Coalition (NCRC) and the Global Coalition for Responsible Credit (GCRC), demand that the G-20 governments consult with the institutions of social finance and community reinvestment to reform the (overall) financial system. They propose 12 measures to ensure that the countries members of G-20 commit (themselves)... to the creation of a new financial system: (more) effective, socially useful and inclusive ...
>
> The (following) 12 proposals are based on the tested methods and practices of financial institutions, members of the (social banking) federations, and (they are) founded in research

[206] Personally, while fully agreeing with this point, I would make one exception here: I would assert that there is a need for some very large banks to provide global reach. These banks are unlikely to find enough capital to support their role in this manner. Therefore, while the principle is right, it might need some differentiation. Addition by Benedikter.

... Some have already been implemented by G-20 nations. If carried out by all G-20 countries, our proposals would put in place an international duty to exercise responsibility:

- Financial services providers and all related firms would be required to follow clear principles of responsibility, and to have transparent mechanisms in place to enable citizen oversight, in order to ensure that these principles guide behavior in practice.
- Remuneration policies within the financial sector would be reshaped in the light of this goal.
- This affirmative obligation would include (also) the obligation for financial firms properly to consider financial inclusion and the social and environmental impacts of their actions – as well as their inactions – on all neighborhoods and households, including those on rural, low income and minority communities and territories, when designing and offering financial products and services. (...)
- Our proposals would create stronger regulators to enforce uniform regulations in each G-20 country, consistent with safety and soundness.

The 12 proposals for ... reform of the world financial system of INAISE are as follows:

Proposal 1: Regulators in each G-20 country should ... require that banks and bank holding companies demonstrate that their commercial banking activities are legally and financially fully separated from (their) speculative financial activities; and that they are fully supported by adequate, dedicated capital reserves. G-20 fiscal authorities should tax revenues from speculative financial activities at rates higher than those levied on commercial bank activities.

Proposal 2: Excess executive remuneration has promoted irresponsible behavior along the entire chain of financial services production and delivery, leading to risk-taking, misrepresentation and fraud that continue to damage local and national economies. Furthermore, over-remuneration in the financial services sector distorts employment markets, weakening long-term growth by luring many of the brightest young people away from research and production. G-20 governments should cap aggregate financial services compensation at levels comparable to that practiced in a basket of other industries.

Proposal 3: The lack of standardization, documentation and comparability among financial products weakens regulatory enforcement while it increases bank regulatory cost. It hinders truthful pricing of risk and enables fraud. Regulators must insist that all retail and market traded financial products (might) be standardized and documented by their producers, (in order) to ensure full traceability of the chain of (origin, and of) production. Agencies which rate and label financial products and institutions and their subcontractors should be licensed, and their fees covered by taxes on financial services.

Proposal 4: Purely speculative financial transactions produce no sustainable value for communities, regions and countries, yet generate massive risks for them.[207] G-20 countries should implement an international tax on (purely) speculative financial transactions.[208]

---

[207]There is evidence though that some level of speculation provides useful market liquidity. The question is how much of it is healthy for the overall system. Addition by Benedikter.

[208]In fact, a first step in that direction has been induced by the G-20 group (i.e., by the 20 most industrialized countries of the world) in March–April 2010 by sketching and discussing the draft for a homogenous global financial services tax. "The G20 ... called for more work on the International Monetary Funds' (IMF's) proposal for a levy on the balance sheets and profits of financial services companies, which is designed to fund future bank rescues. [But] the proposals have already faced protests from the [mainstream] banks, as well as from countries such as Canada and Australia, whose banks did not suffer greatly from the financial crisis. There have also been complaints from the private equity and hedge fund industries that fear they too will be

Proceeds should be used to finance oversight of systemic risk, and to support economic development in less developed countries.

Proposal 5: All bank and other retail financial service executives, experts, agents, products and services should comply with a rule of *I do no harm to my clients* ... As is currently required under the European Union's Marketing and Financial Institutions Decree of 2004 (the Markets in Financial Instruments Directive, or MiFID[209]), distributors of retail financial services products should be required to identify all retail and small business clients according to their level of financial literacy, and be held to enforce fiduciary responsibilities, specific to each level.

Proposal 6: Retail financial products are not covered by rules of traceability and quality that are standard for most products (food, pharmaceutical products, etc.). G-20 regulators should be required to ensure that all financial institutions adhere to an affirmative obligation to guarantee the traceability of fiduciary engagement, and (that they) document the risk of all financial products they handle as producers, (re)sellers or buyers. Regulators should enforce penalties for violation of these standards. (...)

Proposal 7: Financial exclusion and discrimination in the access to credit weakens the economies of G-20 countries, and leads to disinvestment. As is currently the case with the U.S. Community Reinvestment Act (credit & investment)[210] and the French Code of Financial Institutions (bank accounts),[211] G-20 regulators should be required to hold all financial institutions to an affirmative obligation to serve the financial services needs of all communities and territories, consistent with safety and soundness.

Proposal 8: Statistical oversight of all financial institutions is necessary to ensure that each equally respects its service obligations directly as well as through subsidiaries and holdings. To this end, G-20 regulators should require financial institutions to publish annual data on their production, as is already the case in the United States under the Home Mortgage (Disclosure) Act.[212] This data should cover all territories served in any fashion by a financial institution, and enable the disclosure of discrimination in the quality, price and availability of products and services.

Proposal 9: G-20 governments should require public representatives to sit on the board of financial institutions in which there is a public investment, guarantee, deposit or a loan.

Proposal 10: All G-20 Regulators should be required to take into account the statements, complaints and requests of individuals, community groups, local elected officials and consumer organizations. Regulators should reply with fully documented responses in a timely fashion.

Proposal 11: Access to affordable, appropriate financial services including credit are a fundamental condition of economic citizenship in modern society. It is a (citizens') right which imposes a duty to service on all financial institutions. In addition, G-20 regulators

---

caught by the tax." P. J. Davis: Top 80 insurers hit out at being included in IMF global tax plan. In: Financial Times Europe, April 27, 2010, p. 13, http://www.ft.com/cms/s/0/1957afc4-5193-11df-bed9-00144feab49a.html (retrieved April 27, 2010).

[209]For further information, see: MiFID, http://en.wikipedia.org/wiki/Markets_in_Financial_Instruments_Directive (retrieved April 1, 2010).

[210]Community Reinvestment Act: see http://en.wikipedia.org/wiki/Community_Reinvestment_Act (retrieved March 16, 2010).

[211]Monetary and Financial Code. Statute of the Banque de France. In: http://www.banque-france.fr/gb/instit/telechar/histoire/mfc.pdf (retrieved March 30, 2010).

[212]The US Home Mortgage Disclosure Act: http://www.ffiec.gov/hmda/ (retrieved March 29, 2010).

should develop that right by encouraging the development of credit unions, bank and non-bank social finance and community development organizations, micro-credit organizations and cooperatives. This should include favorable tax treatment.

Proposal 12: Capital markets have weakened competition by creating international banking conglomerates. Their size alone presents a systemic risk to the international economy. This trend hinders the creation of a diverse, resilient financial system. It should be countered by regulation, by taxation and by affirmative policy. G-20 regulators should test any proposed new regulation of finance by whether it increases the variety of financial service providers while ensuring safety and soundness. (The) current *one size fits all* capital standards and accounting rules… are inappropriate and should be adapted to meet the safety and soundness needs of diverse institutions … Banks that generate high systemic risks should apply higher solvency ratios in order to meet the higher risk incurred by governments responsible for their supervision.[213]

It is clear that these 12 proposals by INAISE, similarly as the 3 proposals by GABV previously mentioned, are in line with what we have seen as the general worldview, philosophy, and business strategies of social banks in Europe and in the United States alike. Even if the INAISE recommendations seem more inclined to implement rather European than US standards on the international system, they are in line particularly with the request to "return to the real economy" by pulling capital from both the derivative funds and the real estate bubbles and by making it available to the productive activities of the "real economy." But there are additional, regulative features in this catalog of measures proposed by INAISE, which in many cases remind us of the proposals of US President Barack Obama and German Chancellor Angela Merkel or are identical to them, even they were coined independently from them. While proposal 9 was implemented temporarily during the crisis by President Obama (the biggest banks that were supported by billions of US taxpayer money were put under direct supervision of the government), there have also been some efforts regarding proposal 2: the limitation of the remuneration of bankers, though with rather poor effects and no clear outcome. Most other proposals are still in the discussion phase and have not led to bigger formal, explicit changes so far.

Nevertheless, most of the proposals made by INAISE are in direct accordance to what Barack Obama and Angela Merkel proposed between August 2009 and January 2010:

- differentiation between commercial and speculative activity of banks, including different taxation;
- limitation of compensations for bank leaders and executives;
- regulative measures to obtain a greater transparency of financial products for the average customer, including the obligation to publish details about the investments and transactions of the bank;
- introduction of binding ethical standards;

[213] INAISE: 12 measures for a socially useful financial system, loc cit.

- obligation to banks to serve their local communities instead of putting their money into global speculation,[214] including a new "citizens right to be funded" and the respective right of local communities to complain;
- incentives for the creation of social and community banks and for social financing in the overall sense, including favorable taxation;
- limitation of the size of banks in order to avoid the return of the dilemma of "banks being too big to let them fail."[215]

Most of these ideas, though not directly related to the proposals of social banks, GABV and INAISE, have been among the main concerns of US President Barack Obama during his first two years in office and of German Chancellor Angela Merkel during the crisis. The result is that in the future it should be possible for governments on both sides of the Atlantic to prevent banks from becoming too big, if necessary by breaking banks up if their size becomes a threat to the national or international economy and/or the financial system.[216]

This option is supported even by global mainstream banks. For example, Vikram Pandit, CEO of Citigroup (which calls itself "America's global bank"), in a remarkable lecture about the "Global Financial Crisis" at Columbia University, New York, on April 28, 2010, confirmed most of what has been said in this volume about the twofold origins and causes of the crisis. With regard to the future of the financial system he stated that

1. banks should return to the core business of banking;
2. a new capitalistic culture is needed, and that the existing capitalistic system has to be considerably improved;
3. banks "should be banks" and thus should serve the communities they are surrounded by, not merely speculate; and
4. the reputation built upon the trust of customers is the most important asset of a bank.

In addition, Pandit stated literally:

> Regulation needs to change, as well as our commitment to what we call responsible finance ... (We need) first to return to the basics of banking. To be a bank means to take deposits, make loans, provide payment systems and custodial services, finance trade, facilitate capital flows through trading, all with confidence and trust, by focusing on banking basics ... In addition, we (have to) change our business model from one of capital deployment to

[214]Of course, the tricky question here is: When is investment on a global level the right thing to do? There is a risk that if the regulations against global speculation are implemented too tightly, there could be a lack of funds for needed investments for improving communities in developing countries. That is one reason (among several) why I am in general against overregulation of the banking and finance business.

[215]Cf. AFP: German Chancellor Angela Merkel wants to cut off financial speculators from business (Angela Merkel will Spekulanten das Handwerk legen), in: AFP News, March 09, 2010.

[216]U.S. News and World Report: Obama Steps Up Campaign Against Wall Street Banks, January 21, 2010, http://www.usnews.com/news/national/articles/2010/01/21/obama-steps-up-campaign-against-wall-street-banks.html.

client centricity. We (have to) focus clearly on client interests ... because often transactions trump(ed) relationships, often with an emphasis on trading for the bank's own accounts ... A best bank serves the interests of its shareholders and employees, by concentrating on what is best for its customers, and on building relationships with them. That is one of the clear, clear lessons of this financial crisis ...

Another priority is cultural change, built on the values of responsible finance, and it is absolutely essential. No one wants to see a repeat of 2008 or 2009, but here is the problem: In five, ten, twenty or thirty years, people in the midst of a volatile economic bubble, are unlikely to see beyond the illusions it creates. Their memories of what happened in 2008–2009 will be dim, maybe even nonexistent, and they could repeat history, they could succumb to all due familiar pressures that we just saw over the last many years ...

So what do we do? How can we make sure the lessons that we learned are embedded in our collective memory, so that we can at least mitigate future crises? How do we make sure the system internalizes the learnings?

I know only two answers: One is regulation, to try to hardwire the learning from this era into the financial system; and the other is culture. Each financial institution can create a culture of responsibility ... We do need a new global order for regulators, bankers, administrators, that will either substitute or supplement existing frameworks ... A strong culture of responsibility (has to have the purpose) to serve the interests of clients and to be a force for positive change in the world ...

By returning to the basics of banking, we are helping to set the fundamental tone of the culture we want...: Banks should be banks, focused on serving clients; banks should not speculate with their capital; markets need to be transparent; derivatives should be cleared centrally and settled centrally (...); (and) we should end once and for all the phenomena of 'too big to fail' ... (We should remember that) our reputation (is) quite literally our most valuable asset.[217]

Similarly, Deutsche Bank CEO Josef Ackermann in April 2010 started to speak openly of "oligopolistic" structures in the international banking sector due to the exaggerated size of the biggest banking conglomerates,[218] including his own bank, which controls 22% of the worldwide foreign exchange trade alone. Other examples include Switzerland where the combined total balance sheet of only two banks – UBS bank and Credit Suisse – are more than four times as big as the gross domestic product of the country; and the Netherlands, where the three biggest banks together hold a market share of 95%. Something similar, though on a more restricted geographical level, is true if we consider that the bank of one single city alone, Switzerland's Geneva, administers 10% of all private wealth worldwide.[219] In the United States, a similar role probably belongs to the banks of New York City.

As a result, European institutions are working on respective regulations that may allow governments in the future to intervene if a bank – or a banking conglomerate – gets too big or if it exerts too much control over the capital and money market.[220]

[217]Columbia University News Release: On Campus News from Columbia University: Citigroup CEO Vikram Pandit Underscores Need for Banking Reform and "Responsible Finance" at Columbia's World Leaders Forum. April 29, 2010, including full video of the lecture in: http://news.columbia.edu/oncampus/2015.

[218]T. Riecke, M. Maisch und R. Benders: The Power of Banks Challenged (Die Macht der Banken im Visier). In: Handelsblatt Düsseldorf, April 8, 2010.

[219]Austrian National Broadcasting Network ORF 2 Teletext, August 25, 2010, pp. 137.

[220]T. Riecke, M. Maisch und R. Benders: loc cit.

Similar regulations may be an option for the United States, where the ten biggest banks control more than 50% of all customer assets – more than half of the savings of the entire nation.[221] If some of them fail, the United States as a nation may be threatened.

At the same time, some of my colleagues and I worry about the tendency of governments to interfere too much into the free decision making of banks. We don't think that overregulation by governments is the optimal long-term solution. Banks have to be free to make their choices even in the future, and this is especially true if they make the wrong choices. Why? Because every other solution hinders individuality to unfold at its own full level of responsibility and freedom – both on the side of banks, as on the side of customers. I agree in this regard again with Australian government representative (chairman of the Australian Productivity Commission), G. Banks, that the future of the financial and banking system after the crisis of 2007–2010 is mainly about "achieving regulatory balance"[222] – that is, not exaggerating with regulatory governmental interventions, on the one hand, and avoiding doing nothing at all, on the other hand.

I would emphasize this crucial aspect of regulatory balance. There should be a much more engaged debate on how to provide for maximum responsibility of financial systems to allow investors to make informed choices – and how to balance regulation and deregulation on the short, middle, and long run. I am convinced that in the end, every balanced solution may eventually lead to more capital flowing to social banks.

Interestingly, there is a potentially even more important thought hidden in these efforts of balancing regulation, of limiting the size of banks, and of breaking through toward new cultural standards of behavior. It is the thought: *What is the right size of a financial institution at all?* Or, to put it in other words, *What is, overall, the human measure in banking and finance?*

This is, and this has been right from the start, one of the core questions that led to the foundation of social banking and social finance, as opposed to mainstream banking and finance. Social banking and social finance were, and are, about regaining the human measure in the size and activity of financing, as well as about a new "human relationship" of lenders, traders, and customers with money in general. That regards not only the amounts in which money is traded and handled, but also its very basic concept. While "small is beautiful"[223] is not necessarily the main law to follow in globalized banking and finance, the balance between size, outreach, and human relationship should become a much more important measure for the success of a bank than it has been in the past.[224]

---

[221] T. Riecke, M. Maisch und R. Benders: loc cit.

[222] G. Banks: loc cit, p. 271.

[223] E. F. Schumacher: Small is Beautiful: Economics as if People Mattered, Blond and Briggs Publishers, London 1973 ff.

[224] Cf. H. Glauber (ed.): Slower, Less, Better, More Beautiful. 15 Years of Dobbiaco Sustainability Colloquia: Cornerstones for the Future (Langsamer, weniger, besser, schöner. 15 Jahre Toblacher

Something similar seems to be valid if we look at the current international discussion about regulation of the international financial markets. In general, the – fundamentally integrative – mindset of social banking and social finance is about balancing things, and this should be true here also. Most social bankers would judge: Neither overregulation nor underregulation of "the right size" will be healthy, because extremes always tend to do more harm than good. Instead, both regulation and deregulation have to be integrated within a sound view of the whole picture, its long-term development, and with the basic prerequisite of freedom. While some additional regulation seems to be necessary, overregulation of the size of banks could lead to even more restrictions for the customer, particularly for the small and medium businesses that are in desperate need of credit. How to balance overregulation versus underregulation depends on the specific fields of intervention, on the overall constellation, and on the respective application modus. I would argue that looking for the simplest forms of regulation should be a goal.

It is obvious that the measures proposed by GABV and INAISE can only achieve tangible effects if imposed on an international level – possibly not only among the G-20, but on a global level. But it is also clear that even if they are implemented in some parts of the global financial system by unilateral or bilateral agreements (for example, between the United States and the European Union), they will leave their sign and will change the system as a whole in the middle and long term.

As much as these proposals are doomed to fall into oblivion once the crisis has been over for a couple of years, they may prove to be *principally* useful for the global financial system also in the long term, and independently of further crises. This is because they in my view present innovations that can be positive for the financial and banking system as a whole, independent of the needs of further regulations or deregulations.

But let us come now to the *third and last* catalog of proposals, the eight-point program as proposed by an assembly of European alternative banks. Issued as early as in December 2008, it states,

> Across Europe, there is a growing awareness of the importance of a sustainable handling of money. The crisis indeed has underlined this importance. Many citizens therefore ask themselves, what their money is doing while in the bank.
>
> Based on the experience of the alternative banks business model(s), the following points (may) be important to consider, (if) a new framework for the financial sector has to be shaped:
>
> 1. Financial service providers (should) in future clearly focus on the needs of the "real economy" and thus concentrate on those services. The yardstick must be a clear reduction of financial instruments (which point towards) speculation, and which thus do not serve the real economy.
> 2. Alongside the fight against inflation for consumer goods, international monetary stability should also take account of inflation risks with regard to assets. (Example: the property bubbles in Denmark and in the United States). This inflation on assets has a

Gespräche: Bausteine für die Zukunft), Munich 2006. See also: The Dobbiaco Sustainability Colloquia Academy, http://www.toblacher-gespraeche.it/index_e.php.

clear tendency to blow up lending, and to make the economy addicted to infusion of money from loans.

3. It should be incumbent on the community of states to undertake real efforts to close so-called "offshore financial centres" or "tax havens." It is not acceptable that it is still possible to a wide extent to avoid tax paying and to exploit differences in regulation.[225]
4. The size criteria laid down in European national supervisory regulations with regard to the system relevance of institutions should be transferred to (the regulation of) global finance. It (should) not be possible for financial institutions to be created whose size ... is sufficient to cause a crisis of the system to collapse.[226] (Some appropriate lessons should be learnt from the example of Iceland and its banks[227]).
5. The rules by which the rating agencies work should aim to remove conflicts of interest. Just like the rated institutions, the rating agencies themselves should be subject to financial supervision.[228]
6. The transparency rules in financial services transactions must satisfy precisely (the) regulatory framework conditions. The focus must be on the long-term interests of consumers and citizens, more than of shareholders. Regulation should not in itself cause excessive administrative burdens for ... market participants, which has been the case for many rules implemented in recent years (...), without creating a real benefit from a citizen point of view.
7. The design of products must be simple with regard both to the way they work and (to) their contract terms. Transparency is the key ... (to) avoiding future crises.
8. Alongside these proposals, mostly with the regulatory framework in mind, there is a need for a wide-ranging information and education campaign on financial topics. The way in which money is invested, bears interest, is used and shapes our society must be brought to public awareness to a much greater extent than it is so far the case".[229]

"While we observe different developments in the European countries, we are convinced that the European Alternative Banks can serve as examples of how the financial sector can further evolve for the benefit of the greater community ...

Alternative banking may serve as 'best practice example' for diverse aspects and proceedings of a progressive banking system ...

---

[225]Sure enough, without a universal tax system (not likely to be agreed in the near future), there are many open issues to address here. Addition by Benedikter.

[226]Similarly, L. Zingales states, "we stand at a crossroads for American capitalism. One path would channel popular rage into political support for some genuinely pro-market reforms, even if they do not serve the interests of large financial firms. By appealing to the best of the populist tradition, we can introduce limits to the power of the financial industry – or any business – for that matter ... This would mean abandoning the notion that any firm is too big to fail, and putting rules in place that keep large financial firms from manipulating government connections to the detriment of markets. It would mean adopting a pro-market, rather than pro-business, approach to the economy." In: L. Zingales: loc cit, p. 35.

[227]Cf. T. McVeigh: The party's over for Iceland, the island that tried to buy the world. Almost overnight, its population became the wealthiest on Earth. The credit crunch is making the cash disappear. In: The Observer London, October 5, 2008, http://www.guardian.co.uk/world/2008/oct/05/iceland.creditcrunch; and The Financial Times: Iceland, http://www.ft.com/iceland (retrieved March 15, 2010).

[228]Perhaps the more relevant question here is: What should be the role of rating agencies in an improved capitalistic system at all? Addition by Benedikter.

[229]T. Jorberg: European Alternative Banks call for an 8 point plan, December 8, 2008. English version in: http://www.inaise.org/doc%20download/Press%20release/Merkur%20press%20release%20Dec%202008%20EN.PDF.

> We agree that one priority for the global networks of social banking and social finance after the crisis is to provide political leaders around the globe with concrete examples of 'best policies'; and we are willing to enact this in cooperation with the World Future Council.[230,231]

Taken together, there are several points in these three programs and proposals by the GABV, INAISE, and the Assembly of European Alternative Banks that can be of importance for the future of the international banking and finance system.

While it is important to take notice of them, their immediate and mid-term impact on the existing system should not be overestimated. Rather, most of these proposals can serve as an inspiration on the long term; and many of them have still to be concretely adapted to the circumstances. Additionally, most of these proposals are destined to improve things in specific sectors of the international banking and finance activity, rather than changing the system as a whole, and as such.

Overlooking the three proposal catalogs, it is important to stress two main aspects in particular:

1. If we look at the seven solutions to the financial crisis that are currently being discussed by the international community: return to the state of things before the system crashed, restore the system with some ethical improvements, implement regulation, permit further deregulation, create alternatives within the system, create alternatives against the system, change the system – then it becomes clear that social banking and social finance claim for a sound balance between new regulative measures (like limiting the remuneration of bankers and the size of institutions), transparency, and the introduction of binding ethical standards. But it also turns out that social banking networks are in principle against overregulation. While social banking as a "realistically idealistic" philosophy suggests the return of the financial business "to the real economy" as being critical, and while it is against the renewal of the speculation in the "beyondworld" of the derivative (including the hedge funds) bubble as well as in the "underworld" of the real estate bubble, it does not suggest to turn everything upside down all at once. Rather, social banking and social finance are about developing alternatives of "best practice" examples in order to show how the money and capital streams can be used more effectively, by being more directly connected with the community's surrounding banks.
2. The common center of gravity of all the proposals by social finance institutions clearly underscores that social banking and social finance are *not* about "revolutionizing" the system and the principles of capitalism, free trade, and

[230] The World Future Council (founded by Swedish writer and activist Jakob von Uexküll, born 1944): http://www.worldfuturecouncil.org/english.html?lang=1.

[231] T. Jorberg: European Alternative Banks call for an 8 point plan, December 8, 2008. In: http://www.gls.de/die-gls-bank/presse/pressearchiv/detail/datum/2008/12/08/alternativbanken-europas-fordern-8-punkte-plan.html. This eight-point plan has been signed by Banca Etica (Italy), Cultura Bank (Norway), Ecological Building (United Kingdom), Ekobanken (Sweden), Freie Gemeinschaftsbank (Switzerland), GLS Bank (Germany), Merkur Bank (Denmark), and Triodos Bank (The Netherlands) – i.e., by European Social Banks only. Translation from the German version: Roland Benedikter.

> open markets as such. To the contrary, they are about making a better, socially and environmentally more sustainable use of them – exactly like the Stanford Program on Liberation Technology (previously mentioned) efforts to make better use of technology by implementing its productive features in a more socially liberating way for all citizens and by distributing it more equally, instead of letting it become an elitist tool of access and exclusion in the hands of a few. That is exactly what the proposals of the social banking networks aspire to do for the global financial system. They do not want to be "revolutionary," because revolutions have seldom done any good on the field of economy; rather, they want to improve, and further develop, what we already have.

Summing up, social banking and social finance are *not* about creating alternatives *against* the system, but about creating alternatives *within* the system. They are about developing the (capitalistic) system toward its "inbuilt" best. They point toward the development of public and individual consciousness, which may prove more effective in the long run than most regulative measures. In the end, the crisis has proven to be a question of culture and education, not of formal rules. It has shown that banking and finance is much more a mindset than a mechanism.

If this is the case, one remaining question is the practical applicability of these proposals.

As we experienced particularly during the crisis years 2008–2009, basically all leaders were inclined to reforms – first of all President Barack Obama, but also many European leaders like German Chancellor Angela Merkel, French President Nicolas Sarkozy and Britain's (then) Prime Minister Gordon Brown, who were all facing fierce resistance from the representatives of the mainstream system on Wall Street, in London and in Frankfurt. But there are also new opponents against a reasonable and balanced innovation from another side today: the radical "new left" movements, which tend to cry out for radical solutions "against the system."

As I have pointed out previously, both these extreme perspectives – restoring the system as it was and changing the system completely – are irrational, as they are dangerous. A "third way" is needed. The proposals of the social banking and social finance institutions may provide such a "third way".

But given the resistance of the mainstream banking sector and the "new left" movements alike, the extent to which the proposals of social banking and social finance institutions can be implemented will decisively co-depend on public opinion, that is, the understanding of things and participation in the debate by us all.

11 The More Important Challenge: Getting a Balanced and Integrative Viewpoint on Money and Finance

Following this insight, let us eventually underscore one last point. It is the question of financial education or "financial literacy" for a broader part of the population in Western countries, including particularly the United States and Europe. We have seen the outstanding importance of this question for the future already on various occasions.

As was discussed in the first pages of this volume with the "sandglass principle," many things in the international banking and finance business were (and still are) *irrational*. They are driven by psychology, imagination, or group behavior.[232]

Today, we are well advised to overcome the irrational attitudes of an "independent psychodynamic of economy and finance" by concrete social agreements and by a new relationship of money with the human measure. We need a more realistic approach to money and finance than the one that has been in place in the past decades.

Thus, besides the requests of juridical regulation and reform, which are mainly answers to the immediate needs of the economic crisis, the most important challenge in the long run consists in *reforming and broadening financial education*. Building and increasing "financial literacy" among a much bigger number of the average population, especially the current youth, will become crucial to build a better future. In which sense and to what extent?

As we saw in the initial pages of this booklet, most experts, politicians, and observers in the face of the economic crisis said, "We don't understand the banking and finance system anymore; we don't know how all this works any longer. It has become too complex, too intransparent, and too complicated to see through even for specialists." If this is the case, then what we need today are not new specialists who explain us the all too complicated laws of an all too speculative money and capital market. What we need is a new, practice-oriented "financial enlightenment" for all – an analogy to the "new technological enlightenment" brought forward by avantgardistic parts of the Silicon Valley community. The voice of the average bank customer and the voice of the civil society are needed.

What is necessary now is *not* a complete rethinking of economic theory; rather, we need a *new focus on interdisciplinary exchange* in order to broaden and enrich traditional economic theory. In order to achieve that, we need first and foremost a new understanding of the "big picture" – how things are interwoven between financial, social, environmental, and anthropological dimensions.[233] Since understanding

---

[232]Cf. H. C. Binswanger: The Growth Spiral. Money, Energy and Imagination in the Dynamics of the Market Process (Die Wachstumsspirale. Geld, Energie und Imagination in der Dynamik des Marktprozesses), Marburg 2006; and H. C. Binswanger: Forward to Mitigation. Perspectives for a Sustainable Economy (Vorwärts zur Mäßigung. Perspektiven einer nachhaltigen Wirtschaft), Hamburg 2009.

[233]Cf. my attempts in R. Benedikter: Global Systemic Shift and System Action Theory. In: The Globalism Research Centre, RMIT University Melbourne, http://rmit.info/browse; ID=cvfqzezbtdfiz, September 7, 2008; and R. Benedikter: Global System Shift. An Integral Perspective. In: The Unit for Sociocultural Research on Learning and Development (LCMI), University of Luxembourg, http://dica-lab.org/rab/contributions/abstracts/benedikter-abstract, 16 February 2010. One of the interesting attempts in this direction in the United States is the "World Systems Analysis" by Immanuel Wallerstein, Yale University, which I have already mentioned above, even if I do not share the majority of his ideas. See: http://en.wikipedia.org/wiki/Immanuel_Wallerstein.

"the big picture" is the indispensable prerequisite for acting rationally in an increasingly complex and interdependent world,[234] the question behind every action plan toward a contemporary financial literacy becomes: How can we succeed in understanding "the whole" of what surrounds us again? And how can such an understanding be achieved in a manner that young bankers and "normal people" will equally benefit from it?

Moving forward public and academic education interdisciplinary not only in economics but also in the humanities and the social sciences is critical here, as it is to build bridges between those in most cases still-divided fields of understanding. I think that combining the knowledge and synthesizing across the disciplines will be one key to finding ways toward solutions. There is a huge task of interdisciplinary "mind building" for the requests and challenges ahead.

Unfortunately, inter- and transdisciplinarity have long been neglected in academia on both sides of the pond[235]; and so it has the academic discipline of economic anthropology,[236] which could form the new interdisciplinary intersection point for the multilayered financial education needed. While there was a short boom in the 1990s, Western academia has experienced a neoconservative backslide to the old patterns of over-specialization since the start of the new millennium – in the United States and in Europe alike. Nevertheless, the United States is still much better off in this regard because the transdisciplinary principles of the classical Humboldt University model were kept here much more precizely than in most European countries. The result is that US universities on average dispose of educational ideals and practices that are in general more appropriate to the interdisciplinary challenges of a future-oriented education toward "financial maturity" than their European counterparts.

Thus to implement a dialogue about new ways of thinking, *methodologically speaking* it could be first of all necessary to revive the tradition of economic anthropology in a much more interdisciplinary manner than it is practiced so far, and to connect it to applied questions of values. "Economic anthropology" is the study of how the economy can be understood by human measures, how the human condition and economic behavior are connected, and how different cultural habits influence the development of different economic systems. This approach must be applied less in an ethnograpical manner (to which it is unfortunately restricted in many cases today), but more in the sense of social and cultural analysis in the broader sense – for example, in the tradition of Karl Polanyi[237] or Stephen

[234]Cf. M. Gorbachev: Manifesto for the Earth. Action Now for Peace, Global Justice and a Sustainable Future, Clairview Books, Forest Row 2006.

[235]Cf. N. von Stillfried: What About Transdisciplinarity? Its Past, Its Present, Its Potential ... and a Proposal. In: Metanexus Institute, Bryn Mawr, PA, June 4, 2007, http://www.metanexus.net/conference2007/abstract/Default.aspx?id=427.

[236]Economic anthropology: http://en.wikipedia.org/wiki/Economic_anthropology.

[237]K. Polanyi: The Great Transformation. The Political and Economic Origins of Our Time, Beacon Press, Boston 2001.

Gudeman,[238] also confined to social and cultural anthropology in the interpretations of Claude Meillassoux[239] or Emmanuel Terray.[240] This is because today instead of an economic ethnography,[241] we need an interdisciplinary study of economy as applied "societography."[242]

Regarding the *institutional design* of such an interdisciplinary dialogue about values in banking and finance and their connection to the needs of the human being, various forms are imaginable:

- from inserting some lectures and courses about the topic of social banking and social finance into mainstream economic study programs;
- to working on selected projects of research comparing mainstream and social approaches of banking and finance including the question, which approaches work most effectively in which environment;
- to including practice-oriented stages at social banking and social finance institutions for students of mainstream study programs;
- to launching alliances between universities and existing academic institutes specializing in the field;
- to implementing specialized centers of research and teaching (following the example of the program on "liberation technology" at the Freeman Spogli Institute for International Studies of Stanford University);

---

[238] S. Gudeman: The Anthropology of Economy: Community, Market and Culture, Wiley, New York, NY 2001; S. Gudeman: Economy's Tension. The Dialectics of Community and Market, Berghahn Books, Oxford 2008; and S. Gudeman (ed.): Economic Persuasions, Berghahn Books, Oxford 2009.

[239] C. Meillassoux: Maidens, Meal and Money: Capitalism and the Domestic Community, Cambridge University Press, Cambridge 1981.

[240] E. Terray: Marxism and "Primitive" Societies. Two Studies, Monthly Review Press, New York, NY 1972.

[241] Cf. J. G. Carrier (ed.): A Handbook of Economic Anthropology, Edward Elgar Publishers, Northampton, MA 2006. See also: The Society for Economic Anthropology SEA: https://seawiki.wikidot.com/.

[242] I believe that a sound balance between the disciplines in the perspective of an interdisciplinary holistic view is critical for the development of a contemporary societography. To the contrary, most existing approaches remain typically either too financially or too sociologically oriented. This is particularly true for a large part of the critique on modern economics brought forward by the paradigmatically "postmodern" parts of the contemporary humanities and social sciences. Many of them criticize things with which they have no direct experience, and which as a result they do not understand as practitioners. For example, books "against" the capitalistic system and its practices like the ones of Naomi Klein, Jacques Derrida, or Gilles Deleuze (to mention just a few), while contributing important viewpoints on the economic culture of our time, usually did not make any constructive contribution to a positive development. Instead, they were all too often playing the old "I am good, you are bad" game of social scientists "against" capitalism so familiar since the 1960s, especially in the European humanities. But this game makes not much sense anymore. We have to overcome the pseudo- "moral" attitude of "radical and overall" critique as soon as possible and replace it with more participatory, detail-oriented, and constructive approaches, given that morality (and especially academic morality) in our time no longer consists in just pointing the finger toward the (alleged) wrong, but in moving things concretely forward for the benefit of all.

- or by creating small, specialized new institutes on inter- and transdisciplinary research about the interweavement of social and economic aspects in contemporary society.

Some of these approaches may find backing and promotion by the increasing number of social banks and social finance institutions and foundations, since most of the latter seem to be well aware of the importance of education and science in current society. But there is also an increasing awareness among social banks of the fact that in order to improve their work, they in turn need more academic scrutiny and constructive critique, than they have received so far by established academic institutions.[243]

To conclude, social banker Sven Remer from the Institute for Social Banking Germany has some interesting observations and suggestions to contribute in this regard, which in the end might be more important for the future as the above-mentioned rescue and measure programs:

> Already during their education, most future bankers lose the touch with reality. Nobody teaches them a critical viewpoint on money and finance. Most of them learn simply how to

---

[243]Parallel to the development toward a stronger community service by financial institutions that is currently brought forward by social banking and social finance, there is indeed a strong movement toward increased community orientation of universities and academic knowledge – not least with the help of systemic networking, and the combination of sound theory with practice orientation. Taken together, these features toward a context and community embedded "new social knowledge" are sometimes labeled as "multiversity" – as one (even if of course not the only) future-oriented variant(s) of the current concept of "university." I think if social banking and "new social knowledge" join forces and become interactive, an important contribution toward the increase of a participatory financial literacy of broader parts of the society could be possible within relatively short timeframes. Cf. The Center for Studies in Higher Education at the University of California at Berkeley: Civic and Academic Engagement in the Multiversity. Institutional Trends and Initiatives. Proceedings of a University of California Symposium held June 10, 2005 at the University of California at Berkeley, University of California Press 2005. There it is stated:

"Civic engagement is moving to the forefront of higher education discussions as universities see ways not only to intensify students' learning experiences but also to forge stronger links with the communities they are meant to serve ... (The goal is to analyze) the important interface of civic and academic engagement, and to explore ways to further expand civic engagement... Universities have a special responsibility to engage the public that they serve ..." (pp. 5–7).

This would certainly be a trend at first glance not directly in line with the prediction of Anatole Kaletsky of The Times London who asserts that higher education will likely become more market-oriented in the coming years. Cf. A. Kaletsky: Capitalism 4.0. The Birth of a New Economy in the Aftermath of the Crisis. Kindle 2010, p. 10, p. 271, and pp. 281–282. I am convinced however that the trend toward a "new social knowledge" is not necessarily opposed to a greater market orientation; they may be complementary or even related trends according to the example of social banking: orientation toward the surrounding communities and contexts improves the competitiveness of higher education and thus their strength on the international market. In her core essay to this booklet, Barbara A. Holland rightly asserts:

"The traditional role of universities has been to generate and transmit knowledge through three functions: research, teaching, and service. However, the emerging role of universities is to generate a learning society through discovery, learning, and engagement. Increasingly, universities will be part of a network of learning – a fluid and changing network of different sources of expertise. Part of the reason for this global shift in the research culture is a new transdisciplinary approach

function in an already given environment, and how to be just a small wheel in a gigantic machinery they do not need to fully understand. They are trained to become specialists with no perspective on the greater picture, and on the social implications and effects of what they do. They are trained to handle monetary amounts, not human values; and they are trained to do so in a short-term perspective.

The thinking applied in most academic business programs is one-sidedly quantitative, not qualitative. That leads to an approach based on speculative abstraction right from the start. Young bankers are trained to think in millions and billions; but these are sums that are beyond of the capacity of imagination of most people, and thus they are beyond the human measure, beyond the capacity of establishing a human relationship with money and capital. For most people, $10,000 is a lot of money, but they can still understand and handle such an amount. But in most MBA studies, such an amount does not even exist.

It would be all important to bring economic education down again to a level, on which we can establish a personal relationship with what we learn, and with what we do. That could be done through case studies, through learning by doing in community environments, or in the in most cases small and average enterprises of the real economy. Of course, economy is not only the greengrocer around the corner, or the bicycle courier. Economy is also Daimler, Citibank and so on. The point is just that they are all connected. In most economic study programs though, there are only the big players that are making business which is beyond our capacity of imagination. The big financial streams are indeed even beyond the capacity of imagination of most bank leaders, as the crisis has shown.

---

to issues and the extensive social distribution of knowledge. Knowledge and data are now so diffuse that researchers are required to work interactively. In its original mode, research was pure, disciplinary, homogeneous, expert-led, supply-driven, hierarchical, peer-reviewed, and almost exclusively university-based. In this new mode, research is applied, problem-centered, transdisciplinary, heterogeneous, hybrid, demand-driven, entrepreneurial, and network embedded. This transdisciplinary research shares many of the same characteristics of more traditional research. Practitioners adhere to the norms of the scientific method, but they use different cognitive and social strategies. Existing knowledge is used, but the theoretical framework is creative, evolving, and cannot be reduced to its distinct disciplinary parts. The research team typically includes diverse perspectives on both the question that is being addressed and the possible applications for the research that is produced. In addition, research groups tend to be temporary and dissolve as the problems are solved or redefined, although communications persist over time through the use of technology. The results are diffused instantly through the network of participants, thus merging production and diffusion. Subsequent diffusion occurs as practitioners enter successive problem contexts ... – and the quality of research is judged by ... criteria including efficiency and usefulness." Barbara A. Holland (Indiana University): Scholarship and Mission in the 21st Century: The Role of Engagement. In: The Center for Studies in Higher Education of the University of California at Berkeley: Civic and Academic Engagement in the Multiversity, loc cit, pp. 7–13, here: pp. 7–9. An electronic version of this document is available at: http://cshe.berkeley.edu/events/civicacademic/.

From my point of view, although I fully agree with Holland's point, it is important to stress here though that standard academic scrutiny is and remains more important than community orientation and networked knowledge, even if these poles may be more and more complimentary to each other in the future. So I would sum up this point asserting (1) that with the development of the academic sector toward "multiversity" structures connected with greater community orientation and civic engagement, the ideas and practices of social banking and social finance will be facilitated without any doubt; (2) at the same time, this development shouldn't alter or even try to replace the existing habits and standards of academic research and teaching because these habits and standards have long proved to be effective (in fact, to be the most effective ones available). What "multiversity" features can and should do instead, is to add additional features (as described above) to the existing ones, where appropriate, for the benefit of the overall system.

That means: We have to bring finance and banking back from abstraction to reality. What are the important, but neglected values we have to apply in order to achieve that? The classical values of sustainable development, the consciousness of the finiteness of our resources, and an approach that puts the human being in the center . . .

Do we lack knowledge, or ethics, or both? The credit chains embrace the whole globe, and even as a specialist you face great difficulties to understand how exactly. That means we lack of knowledge of the greater picture, including the social dimension. But we also lack ethics, because we simply do not care about it anymore. What is of interest is just how much profit there is at the end of the day – in many cases regardless of the consequences. We have to change that, if we want to avoid the return of new crises in the future. And in order to do that, we first and foremost have to change the education of the new generations of bankers, but also of the broad population. (. . .)

Fortunately, ambitious European young bankers in the meantime have the opportunity to make an ordinary career in non-conventional banking. Simultaneously, an increasing number of mainstream banks in Europe are calling for a reform of the education of their new generations; many of them have developed a positive and constructive approach towards sustainability in the meantime. Young bankers who are educated in the environment of ethical banking receive the same theoretical and practical schooling like any mainstream MBA, but the social and ethical component is added, and individual critical thinking in the framework of a personalized vision of the "whole picture" is regarded as a core element in the study program.

The difference in the outcome manifests itself in practice: How do we as bankers care about the relationship to customers and projects? Must we enter into businesses, which we don't want, just to keep us growing? Questions such as these are most likely not being discussed in the cafeteria of Deutsche Bank.[244]

But will education programs toward economic and financial sustainability not remain just a niche? Remer:

I don't think so. It may take time, but in Europe, we already notice change, especially in the basic view and in the approach to reality and context of the financial business. What we do not need is a program centered around a notion of "pure ethical individualism." Rather, we need a new basic attitude of realism, through which you permanently question yourself as a banker, and as a social being. It is not about a technique, but about a mindset.[245]

What could be adopted by mainstream study programs in the United States and other parts of the world from the formation of social bankers in contemporary Europe? Remer says,

Besides that these study programs are still very young and in the stage of development, I think those elements, which reach beyond the purely technical dimension of banking, i.e. the focus onto the "real economy" and onto the relationship with the long-term needs of people. One basic question is the effort to define profit not exclusively, and not only in monetary terms. The most interesting question maybe is: How could we represent sustainable values in the annual total balance sheet of banks in non-monetary terms? To move away from purely monetary measurements of success would influence the thinking for sure. And it would still be economic (financial) thinking in the strict sense.[246]

---

[244] S. Remer: The Education of Young Bankers Lacks Knowledge and Morals ("Es fehlt an Wissen und Moral"). In: Die Zeit Hamburg, 10 November 2008. See also: Die Zeit online, http://www.zeit.de/2008/46/C-Interview-Remer?page=all.

[245] S. Remer: loc cit.

[246] S. Remer: loc cit.

So how concretely do new social economy study programs operate, for example, those at the Skoll Center for Social Entrepreneurship at the Said Business School of Oxford University or at the Institute for Social Banking Bochum?

The difference between these programs is in the concept of what they are trying to bring forward and where their focus is. In their differences, they impose a lesson about the basic complementarity of concepts and terms that is fundamental for social banking for the present and the near future. What is at stake here?

While the concept of "social entrepreneurship" is mainly oriented toward the individual entrepreneur who improves the human condition of the disadvantaged, and the poor, orienting himself or herself toward developing social communities in a given *ambient* by personal initiative, and in part also toward creating a variety of "micro-entrepreneurs" especially in poor communities and countries, the term "social banking" is the denotation for the systemic societal sector that allows social entrepreneurs to concretely experiment and enact their visions. "Social banking" is the systemic sector that finances social entrepreneurs even if they don't have the prerequisites demanded by mainstream banks and financiers.

The third pole in this overall game is the "social consumer": the one that consumes accordingly to the ideals of social entrepreneurship and social financing. This kind of "new" consumer is much more a conscious "user" of resources than the previous consumer of the materialistic "use and throwaway" society, so that I would prefer to call him (or her) a "social user" instead of "social consumer."

All these three poles form a circular unity: social entrepreneur, social banking (and social finance), and social user. They are embraced by the term "social economy." "Social economy" is the "joint organism" of the three (which is more of just the sum of its parts, but a greater whole). It is an economy that points toward community-, place-, and sustainability-centered sustainability.

So which of these three poles is, or should be, the center of the study programs on social banking? From my point of view, it is the social economy as a whole and its relationship with the mainstream economy.

Remer says,

> The Institute for Social Banking in Bochum, Germany, where I work, has the mission to contribute not primarily to a change, but rather to a further development of the contemporary educational paradigms of banking and finance. Its goal is that the bankers of the future should not orient themselves purely on monetary profit, but on the real needs and the values of people.
>
> In September 2006, we started the three-year Master Study Program, Social Banking and Social Finance. The resulting MBA is extra-occupational, internationally oriented and leads to the Europe-wide recognized degree of Master in Social Banking and Social Finance. The formation is different from mainstream MBAs in that it does not only include the "classical" knowledge of banking as it is standard today, but that it also carries a focus on values, the "making of meaning" (in analogy to the "making of money") and the psychology (including the spirituality) of real people.
>
> The core aspect we address is, as I said: How can we catch the "big picture?" We focus not merely on single activities in the banking and financial sector, but we encourage the students to not only investigate and understand relations, connections and links within this sector, but also between its concretely given social, cultural and political contexts.

A second essential feature of our educational model consists in the aspect that we explicitly challenge our students to engage in a creative-constructive attitude. They shall be enabled to critically question themselves and their chiefs at any time, in order to raise the level of collective consciousness, and in particular the level of "value consciousness," in their bank or their financial institution. We should never forget, that every bank, including traditional and mainstream banks, stays for "values." Every good banker knows that the core capital of his bank is the trust of its present and future customers.[247] To retain this trust and to develop it further it is unavoidable to behave ethically, in a community-oriented manner, and sustainably. The concept of economic sustainability is de facto the first goal of every banker, if she or he knows it or not, because from the view of the customer, the long term security of his or her assets is decisive. At the same time, always more citizens – like you and me – understand, that economic sustainability is not available without social and ecological sustainability.[248]

Last question: What is a social banker then? Is she or he something exceptional? Or are she and he already on their way of becoming mainstream themselves, given that more conventional banks are claiming to turn "ethical?"

Well, seen from the outside, I guess social bankers are quite similar to conventional bankers. In any case, there is no such thing like "the" social banker. People who work in the business of social banking represent a broad variety of academic, professional, cultural and social backgrounds. Many of them come from the traditional banking sector. Others come from sustainability oriented fields, like ecological agriculture, regenerative energies, alternative medicine or integral education. It is exactly this variety that is one of the most important strengths of social banks. Why? Because it guarantees not only important mainstream expertise in diverse relevant sectors, but it also hinders social banks to develop the fatal "group-think," that we observed during the crisis on the international financial markets.

Unfortunately, there are still just a few certificates and academic degrees for social bankers available. There are some single offerings of courses in some traditional Economy and Management Study Programs, which are of a certain relevance also for social banking, for example, courses on Microfinance or Socially Responsible Investment (SRI[249]). But there are still too few specific study degrees available. Accordingly, it is our goal not only to offer more courses dedicated to the field, but also to integrate the standpoint of social banking as an essential aspect into conventional academic curricula. We see the current crisis as a chance to establish the concept of "social banking" within the mainstream financial business. And even more important, we see the role of educational institutions as critical for creating a sound view on how banking, money and finance can serve people better, instead of exploiting them, and instead of leading them into financial illusions which lead to errors and personal tragedies that in many cases can't be corrected within a lifetime.[250]

---

[247] Cf. K. S. Cook and A. Gerbasi: loc cit; and K. S. Cook, R. Hardin and M. Levi: loc cit.

[248] NNA News: Interview with the Institute for Social Banking (Interview mit dem Institute for Social Banking). In: The UNESCO Decade "Education for Sustainable Development" 2005–2014 Journal (UNESCO Dekade "Bildung für Nachhaltige Entwicklung" 2005–2014 Journal), February 2006, http://www.eine-welt-netz.de/coremedia/generator/pm/de/Ausgabe__006/02__Interview/Interview_20mit_20ISB.html. Translation from German: Roland Benedikter.

[249] For more information about SRI, see: http://en.wikipedia.org/wiki/Socially_Responsible_Investment.

[250] NNA News: loc cit.

12 Ideas for a New "Financial Humanism:" The Interweaving of Three Core Solutions to the Financial and Economic Crisis in Order to Build a Better Future

Summing up, there are three solutions clusters to the economic crisis that have been brought to the debate by the worldwide networks of social banks and social finance institutions:

1. improve the overall system by agreeing about new rules and laws, favouring the "real economy" over the real estate and derivative "side economies";
2. propose alternative approaches to capital and money for investors and customers according to the principle: using money instead of having it;
3. create a different cultural attitude by fostering new educational approaches for young people and bankers oriented toward an "understanding of the greater picture," and toward the development of a new "human relationship" to money and finance.

According to social banks, these three solutions should not only be understood as a follow-up to the economic and financial crisis of 2007–2010. More importantly, they should be considered as long-term answers of how to prevent future crises. This is not least due to the fact that with regard to money and finance, the future counts always more than the present and the past.

Obviously, all three answers are closely interwoven, especially if we see the development of the current banking and finance system as a process that is embedded in the greater political and technological changes of our time. While there has been some initiative with regard to the second and third answers during the past few years, a.o. by civil society institutions such as the Worldwatch Institute, Washington DC,[251] the first solution has not been enacted so far in a mentionable manner, at least not on an international level. But there are increasing attempts by international leaders to put new rules into practice.

Among the social banks of Europe, there is great consensus in the view that all three aspects have to be addressed to an equal extent, and simultaneously. They have to be seen as an inseparable "threefold spiral" that must constantly evolve in time by inspiring progress in each of its parts and by mutually connecting ideas and proposals for innovation. If there is any path to a new "financial humanism" for our time, it most probably will be connected with the interweavement of these three answer patterns, while pointing out only one or two of them might not be leading to the desired results.

---

[251] The Worldwatch Institute Washington DC: http://www.worldwatch.org/. In January 2010, 60 scientists from around the world have published the latest Worldwatch report: State of the World 2010: Transforming Cultures. Washington DC 2010. There they assert that the "turn to sustainability" in the sense of a "new cultural attitude" is critical for the future of Western societies, and of globalization. At the same time, the researchers complain that there are "still too few approaches available for significant impact."

This is because

1. Education alone is not enough, you also have to act. Or in the words of famous German philosopher Georg W. F. Hegel (1770–1831): *Theory is the indispensable, but as such not sufficient prerequisite for practice*. Both theory and practice cannot exist without each other.
2. Some of the approaches to social banking and social finance are still not based sufficiently in academic thinking, or remain eclectic. Thus, they need to be further evolved and experimented in the international academic debate.
3. There are some good and some bad ideas around of how to improve the mainstream banking and finance system by imposing new rules and laws. Sure enough, most traditionally leftist and neomarxist answers are *not* an appropriate response, since with their in most cases premature forecasts of an alleged "death of neoliberalism"[252] or even an "end of capitalism"[253] they are much more populist illusionists rather than progressive realists. Instead, we need new humanistic approaches to capital and capitalism, rather than proposing to throw capitalism overboard in a kind of inebriated speculation without any credible and working alternatives.

13 Conclusion and Outlook

But would such a threefold solution strategy for the current banking and finance system as discussed here, if concretely implemented, not make social banking and social finance superfluous?

I don't think so. They will most likely retain characteristics and key features that will keep them unique, since most mainstream banks will not be able to offer all of their features – at least not with the necessary consistency and not in the foreseeable future.

So what are the prospects, if we remain realistic? What may be the future, if we take into consideration what we had to learn through the past years?

In Europe, the threat of bankruptcy by Greece and Spain,[254] later also the breakdown of the banking system of Ireland and the crisis of the Euro currency following the "great weather storm of the crisis,"[255] have covered some positive aspects of

---

[252]Cf. emblematically E. Hobsbawm: The Death of Neoliberalism. In: Marxism Today, November/December 1998, pp. 7–21.

[253]See for example M. Candeias, The Rosa Luxemburg Foundation Berlin: The Last Conjuncture. Organic Crisis and "Postneoliberal" Tendencies. In: Policy Papers of the Rosa Luxemburg Foundation 4/2009, http://www.rosalux.de/cms/index.php?id=19787&type=0 (retrieved March 6, 2010).

[254]Cf. G. Assenza and A. Martynau: loc cit, p. 14 ff.

[255]L. Bini Smaghi (Executive Board of the European Central Bank): The Future of the Euro. Why the Greek Crisis Will Not Ruin Europe's Monetary Union. In: Foreign Affairs, August 10, 2010.

the crisis: that alternative, social, and transparent models of dealing with money are being positively acknowledged in the public sphere like never before.

Nevertheless, we should not overlook that there remain some well-founded criticisms about social banking and social finance: That its current institutions are still too small to create change at a sufficiently broad level; that they remain in many cases niche institutions, and are as a consequence in some cases overspecialized; that they do not change the system as such but represent only "wholes" within the system.

I think there is even one more important critical argument. Without any doubt, social banks must undergo continuous, periodically renewed reforms to remain competitive in the rapidly changing financial sector environment; they cannot take their outstanding success, particularly during the crisis years, for granted. As P. Schwizer, A. Carretta, and V. Boscia have in my view rightly pointed out with regard to cooperative banks: "Since the 19th century, cooperative banks have been considered central players in economic and social development, both at microeconomic and macroeconomic levels, maintaining their traditional competitive power and strength in local markets. (But) over the past decades, the... banking market has been deeply modified by events such as globalisation, financial innovation, deregulation, disintermediation, consolidation and the intense process of political, social and economic integration. The new environment has enhanced the level of competition, influencing the volume, quality and price of financial services and squeezing banks' profitability. Cooperative banks, nonetheless, remain healthy and are gaining market share over their competitors. They are still strong in local markets .... (But) can this business model, based on concepts of mutuality, locality, ethics, solidarity and social cohesion, survive the (upcoming) new environment(s)?"[256]

These questions should be taken seriously by social banks (as every other argument, by the way). But besides these arguments, social banking and social finance in their current state may be fit already to be used as valid examples of "different" approaches to the finance business.

Accordingly, building upon their outstanding success in the crisis years of 2007–2010, social banks have set ambitious goals for the second decade of this century. Not only are their main networks like the Global Alliance of Banking on Values (GABV) intensifying their cooperation with the Clinton Global Initiative,[257] expanding their lending to green projects and underserved communities around the world to $2 billion, as announced at the Clinton Global Initiative annual meeting on September 25, 2009, in New York.[258] At the second full meeting of the Global Alliance for Banking on Values in Bangladesh in March 2010, leaders of the world's

---

[256] A. Carretta, P. Schwizer and V. Boscia (eds.): loc cit.

[257] The Clinton Global Initiative: http://www.clintonglobalinitiative.org/

[258] "We commit, over three years, to assist our members and other sustainable finance institutions to secure $250 million in additional capital (for the Clinton Global Initiative)," said Peter Blom, CEO of Dutch ethical bank, Triodos, and Chair of the Global Alliance for Banking on Values. "This capital will lead to $2 billion in new lending. At a time when the global financial system is struggling to lend, our members and other genuinely sustainable banks will benefit

most important sustainable banks joined in the commitment to take their value-based banking mainstream – and to reach out to 1 billion people by 2020:

> The Global Alliance for Banking on Values ... expects to grow further, and it expects the growth to come from expanding the network's membership significantly, supporting banks looking to adopt genuinely value-driven models, and the creation of new sustainable banks ... The members of the Global Alliance for Banking on Values have committed to touch the lives of one billion people by 2020. This is a major new pledge that could transform lives on a truly global scale, and make a substantial difference in our efforts to combat climate change ... "We believe sustainable banking – which focuses on people and the environment as well as on profit – should reach one billion people by 2020 when a number of key international targets converge," said Peter Blom, chair and co-founder of the GABV and CEO of the European sustainable bank Triodos. "We need to raise more money and invest in the sustainable bankers of the future so we can use this finance to its full potential. This commitment is an important line in the sand. We believe values-led banking can and should make a positive difference to the lives of one in six people within ten years."[259]

Of course, this goal as such is ambitious, and it must still be seen if it proves to be realistic. In any case, it must be combined with other measures to support the necessary innovation of the capitalistic system. From my view, there are four more strategic measures that must be undertaken:

First, to make the system more resilient, that is, "to build a system that (works) better: increasing the reserves financial institutions hold against a crisis, improving tools for modeling system-wide risks, creating better mechanisms for winding down the operations of failed institutions without triggering a market panic, and making better provisions for the people who are hardest hit."[260]

One measure (issued at the start of April 2010) that the European Union has proposed in this regard is a new "crisis-prevention tax on banks," specifically on risky transactions and "derivative" investments.[261] This tax "could generate annual revenues of at least 50 billion euros (US$67 billion), a European Commission study showed ... Proposals for such a tax, pushed by Sweden, which already operates a national levy on banks, could be used for bailouts in the event of another banking

---

millions of borrowers – from individual entrepreneurs in Asia, Africa and South America, to pioneering new green projects in North America and Europe." According to Fazle Hasan Abed, "if we are to tackle the global problems we face, we are going to need international action to do it. We believe (social) banks have the potential to change the architecture of the financial world, and start delivering lasting solutions for unserved and underserved communities and sectors." GABV: Global Alliance for Banking on Values Announces Commitment at the Clinton Global Initiative. International network commits to support $2 billion lending expansion. In: GABV News, http://www.gabv.org/News/press-release-09-09.htm, September 25, 2009.

[259] GABV News: Sustainable Banking Pioneers Plan to Touch a Billion Lives by 2020. In: The Global Alliance for Banking on Values, http://www.gabv.org/News/2010-03-09-SustainableBanking.htm, March 9, 2010.

[260] M. McArdle: In Defense of Failure, in: Time Magazine, The Vision Edition, March 22, 2010, p. 43.

[261] AFP: EU Bank tax could raise 50 billion Euros a year. In: The Business Times Singapore, http://www.businesstimes.com.sg/sub/latest/story/0,4574,380021,00.html, April 6, 2010.

crisis and are broadly backed by France and Germany, mirroring a new U.S. scheme. According to the study published by the European Commission .... 'the tax would force the banking sector to plan better for the future.' The report's authors say it 'could potentially induce the financial industry to internalise the social cost of a systemic crisis and thereby limit excessive risk-taking.' "[262]

Even if the outcome of this measure is ambivalent due to its core idea of additional taxation, which in the past decades has proved to be seldom a good idea, it seems to be worth a try. Sure enough, many of my colleagues and I remain skeptical about increased taxation in principle and in the overall view. In my opinion, the ideal way to finance future resilience of the system should be the gradual evolution from taxation to voluntary actions (and thus, the increased systemic insight of the banking and finance institutions in responsibility issues themselves).

Second, it makes sense to implement what the US Federal Deposit Insurance Corporation (FDIC)[263] proposed in March 2010: "The FDIC tries to convince the big pension funds of the USA to invest their money in small and medium sized local and regional banks in order to reinforce them, instead, as until today, investing their more than 2000 billion dollars of assets through financial investors in the derivative and hedge funds market."[264] A similar idea is currently proposed by parts of the US civil society: to move money from big to small and to community banks. This campaign is called the "Move Your Money" campaign.[265] Another closely related US initiative is the "Slow Money" alliance, dedicated to the idea of "nurture capital."[266] These could be interesting ideas for European countries too.

---

[262] AFP: EU Bank tax could raise 50 billion Euros a year, loc cit.

[263] The US Federal Deposit Insurance Corporation: http://www.fdic.gov/.

[264] Handelsblatt Düsseldorf: Small US banks collapse one after another (Kleine US-Banken kollabieren eine nach der anderen). In: Handelsblatt Düsseldorf, March 28, 2010. Translation from German: Roland Benedikter.

[265] See: The "Move Your Money" campaign in the United States. This campaign is a movement by civil society members that promotes the move of assets by average bank customers from big to small and to community banks. The movement has been made famous, among others, by Arianna Huffington (born 1950): http://moveyourmoney.info/. This campaign is going viral on "YouTube" as well: http://www.youtube.com/watch?v=uI1tqeuXy80&feature=rec-LGOUT-exp_fresh+div-1r-1-HM, http://www.youtube.com/watch?v=PdJUksOOpgk&feature=related, and http://www.youtube.com/watch?v=Icqrx0OimSs&feature=related (all retrieved on March 1, 2010).

[266] The US wide "Slow Money Alliance" presents some connatural features to the "Move your money campaign," see: http://www.slowmoneyalliance.org/. "Slow money" is dedicated to the idea of "nurture capital." It is, as its proponents say, about "a new nonprofit organizing (of finance) ... to bring money back down to earth. Founded by Woody Tasch, a pioneer in merging investing and philanthropy, Slow Money's mission is to build local and national networks, and develop new financial products and services, dedicated to investing in small food enterprises and local food systems; connecting investors to their local economies. Soil fertility, carrying capacity, sense of place, care of the commons, cultural, ecological and economic health and diversity, nonviolence – these are the fundamentals of nurture capital, a new financial sector supporting the emergence of a restorative economy ... Slow Money ... has attracted (so far) over 185 founding members including leaders in organic food, sustainable agriculture, philanthropy, and social investing ... (There is a) million Americans contributing to a grassroots, non-profit seed fund supporting small

Third, to change some essential mechanisms of the system in order to increase transparency. Particular attention should be given to establish new rules that will

---

food enterprises and investing 1% of their assets in local food systems . . . We do hereby affirm the following principles:

I. We must bring money back down to earth.

II. There is such a thing as money that is too fast, companies that are too big, finance that is too complex. Therefore, we must slow our money down – not all of it, of course, but enough to matter.

III. The 20th century was the era of Buy Low/Sell High and Wealth Now/Philanthropy Later – what one venture capitalist called 'the largest legal accumulation of wealth in history.' The 21st century will be the era of nurture capital, built around principles of carrying capacity, care of the commons, sense of place, and nonviolence.

IV. We must learn to . . . connect investors to the places where they live, creating vital relationships and new sources of capital for small (food) enterprises.

V. Let us celebrate the new generation of entrepreneurs, consumers, and investors who are showing the way from 'Making A Killing' to 'Making a Living.'

VI. Paul Newman said, 'I just happen to think that in life we need to be a little like the farmer who puts back into the soil what he takes out.' Recognizing the wisdom of these words, let us begin rebuilding our economy from the ground up, asking:

* What would the world be like if we invested 50% of our assets within 50 miles of where we live?
* What if there were a new generation of companies that gave away 50% of their profits?
* What if there were 50% more organic matter in our soil 50 years from now?" Principles of the Slow Money Alliance, In: http://www.slowmoneyalliance.org/ (retrieved April 5, 2010).

It is obvious that initiatives like these present affinities with social banking and social finance, since both share basic pillars of philosophy and vision. Not least as a result of the recent crisis, since 2008 "Slow Money" initiatives are emerging throughout the United States, with centers in Austin, Seattle, Boston, and New Orleans. The second Slow Money's National Gathering took place at the National Historic Landmark of Shelburne Farms, Vermont, on June 9–11, 2010; it was certainly not by chance that it was co-sponsored by the US social banks RSF Rudolf Steiner Foundation for Social Finance San Francisco and Wainwright Bank Boston. Obviously, the term "slow money" is an analogy to "slow food," meaning a more healthy and sustainable handling of money, as well as a more responsible and thought-out approach to finance in general; it is parallel in meaning to "slow food" versus "fast food." This concept is closely related to what we saw above as the slogan of social ecology Professor Hans Glauber: "Slower, Less, Better, More Beautiful."

Sure enough, being responsible and sustainable in the use of money seems to be necessarily "slower," because it takes more time to act in a thoughtful manner than to act like "lemmings marching to the sea" (David K. Korslund): you have to think more and longer before you act. Nevertheless, there is a certain contradiction in the term "slow money," since, as we have seen in chapters 7 and 8, social banking and social finance seem more inclined to increase the speed of money according to the slogan "using money instead of having it." In contrast, the term "slow money" could be understood as keeping the money by hesitating to give it to others; that is, hoarding it instead of investing it into the community.

Despite these inherent ambivalences the "Slow Money Alliance" is an initiative that in many aspects is related to the goals and the methods of social banking and social finance, while not being

ensure that the doubtful maneuvers many banks applied in presenting their total balance sheets to the public embellishing their real situation and camouflaging their real risks taken, will not be possible anymore. These actions consisted mainly of the practice of temporarily outsourcing debts (especially in the derivative sector) and in artificially reducing the overall debt on the eve of the presentation of the total balance sheets to the public, only to restore the debt to the previous level immediately thereafter.[267] The point here is that such practices are still used in the mainstream banking sector – unaltered by the crisis.

Fourth, to differentiate the system, that is, to introduce a wider range of options for customers and investors of how to place their money. Social banking and social finance are one answer within a concert of answers needed in this regard.

All these four measures are not identical, and thus they have to be enacted independently from each other and in autonomous ways.

So to conclude, what are the overall prospects?

Former Russian president and Nobel Peace Award Laureate, Mikhail Gorbachev (born 1931), has written a moving piece about what he sees as strategical decisive for a better global future: (1) peace; (2) fight against poverty, for global social justice and common wealth; and (3) the rescue of environment and ecology.[268] If these three centers of gravity may prove to be the right ones, then social banking and social finance – with its dedication to financial common wealth, social cohesion, sustainability, and possibly also to a transnational "Financepeace" in cooperation with leading politicians[269] – may indeed have a contribution to make. Perhaps not the most important one, but one that, like money itself, will be positioned in the very center of things.

And if it is plausible what Reihan Salam predicts as a potential "cultural change" in the coming years in the United States (and we can assume that similar developments are possible in Europe too): that increasing numbers of people may "return to their roots as the champions of mutual aid (and) cooperative living . . ., in which (for example) local governments take on the task of building high-tech infrastructures

---

completely identical to them. The main affinity is the goal of "bringing money down to earth," which is identical with social banking's goal to pull money away from the derivative and the real estate bubbles and bring it back into the "real economy." The main difference in my view is that social banking and social finance at their best are uncompromisingly oriented toward the future, that is, toward working with capitalism in a more sustainable way, whereas the "Slow Money Alliance" seems to present certain features that I regard as typically "green" and in part oriented toward a "return to the roots of simple and natural life." As I have pointed out previously, this is a tendency that I regard not only as regressive in its nature, but also as impossible in practice. Instead, I believe we have to go forward with the help of the opportunities and tools of our time, by making use of globalized capital in a more human, context- and community-oriented way.

[267]K. Kelly, T. McGinty and D. Fitzpatrick: Big Banks Mask Risk Levels. Quarter-End Loan Figures Sit 42% Below Peak, Then Rise as New Period Progresses; SEC Review. In: The Wall Street Journal, 8 April 2010, http://online.wsj.com/article/SB10001424052702304830104575172280848939898.html.

[268]M. Gorbachev: loc cit.

[269]Cf. chapter 4.

owned by the entire community,"[270] then something similar is imaginable for the money and finance sector. Mutual aid and cooperative living could lead to societal agreements, where local governments take on the task of building new local and regional financial infrastructures owned by the surrounding community. Rightly, this could "evolve into a new confidence that citizens working in common can change their lives, and in doing so can change the world around them."[271] Social banking and social finance could assumingly be one instrument among others for such a development toward a *specifically democratic* and inclusive approach to money and finance.[272] They will not point toward the *replacement* of existing institutions, but

---

[270]R. Salam: The Dropout Economy, in: Time Magazine, The Vision Edition, March 22, 2010, p. 41.

[271]R. Salam: loc cit.

[272]At this point, we need one last observation about the long-term impact of social banking and social finance – this time in a global *geopolitical* perspective, which may result in being even more relevant than any strictly financial and economic outlook. It's about the *growingly important interface* between sustainability in global *finance* and sustainability in global *democracy*.

The point is: It is still often underestimated how important the (implicit and explicit) ethical dimension of social banking and social finance and their "best practice" input is for the further development of capitalism under the conditions of globalization. Social banking and social finance are indeed a contribution not only to the further development, but also to the sheer continuation of capitalism as a democratic, individualistic, and freedom-centered endeavor on a global level. This is because we start to live in an period of multipolar power, which includes not only the United States, Europe, and the West, but also China and other regional and international powers, many of which are not democratic and do not cultivate freedom oriented forms of government, economy and finance. The new multipolar world gives way to a period of "competing (or contested) modernities," that is, to an age where the concepts of "modernization" and "modernity," including capitalism, are no longer defined mainly in a Western, democratic way, as they were previously. Many of the arising powers are eager to develop their own cultural models and modes of capitalism, which are in part not in accordance with Western democratic values.

As Martin Jacques, co-founder of the English think-tank "Demos" and research fellow at the London School of Economics, has pointed out, "the most likely scenario for the future is that China continues to grow stronger and ultimately emerges over the next half-century, or rather less in many respects, as the world's leading power ... China's continued development will be one of the forces that shapes the century. But China will not be just any old superpower. It has its own distinctive combination of attributes: a huge population, a sense of its identity as a civilization as well as a nation state, a long-standing influence on the nations and cultures that border it, and a diaspora that impacts not just its region but the world. China's habits of governance are not those of the Western world; its values – let us say harmony and stability, rather than liberty and justice – are not those of the West. The roles of both the state and the extended family as social mechanisms in China differ from those in modern Western societies. All of this means that the 21st century will be one of 'contested modernities.' Until around 1970, modernity was, with the exception of Japan, an exclusively Western phenomenon. But as China assumes a bigger role in global economics and politics, that is changing ... A self-confident giant with a billion-plus population, China will likely resist globalization as we know it. This exceptionalism will have powerful ramifications for the rest of the world." M. Jacques: When China Rules the World: The End of the Western World and the Birth of a New Global Order, Penguin Press 2009. Cf. M. Elliott: Into the Unknown. In: *Time Magazine*, August 10, 2009, pp. 32 ff.

toward the *addition* of complementary options, thus contributing to the pluralistic differentiation of the financial options for customers and communities (as mentioned above by trend experts like Gartner Inc.).

To put this it into perspective with our topic: China will push its own ideals and concepts of "capitalism." As core concepts of Chinese history, "integration" and "inclusion" are traditionally strongly related with "national unity" and with "stability and peace;" Western concepts like human rights or constitutional state do not play any significant role. Thus, if Martin Jacques is right, the upcoming epoch will not only be one of "competing modernities," but also one of "competing concepts of capitalism and finance" – with a presumingly strong impact toward non-democratic "paradigms." It seems likely that no concept of "capitalism" will be able to remain completely untouched by such an overall development, at least not in the middle and in the long run – because cultural "paradigms" are at least to the same extent an effect of changing socio-economic environments, as they influence or even co-"create" them.

With the raise of China as the new global superpower that increasingly uses state capitalism as a tool of global outreach, but does not include the notions of freedom, participation, individualism and democracy into it, the financial system may be at least partially threatened as an endeavor of freedom, as Ian Bremmer, president of Eurasia Group, has brilliantly underscored:

"Twenty months of economic and political turmoil have American voters ready to reject Washington and anyone connected with it. And we have company: British voters couldn't wait to sweep Gordon Brown from 10 Downing Street. A recent poll in *Le Parisien* found that nearly 60% of respondents expressed 'no confidence' in French President Nikolas Sarkozy. A poll in the magazine *Stern* gave German Chancellor Angela Merkel 32% support, and just 17% said the government could solve Germany's problems. Watch news reports from Greece, and you won't need the volume on to know what citizens think of their leaders. Nor is this simply a 'Western' trend. Thousands of protesters in Thailand occupied entire neighborhoods of Bangkok for weeks to demand early elections. Crowds dispersed only after conflicts with soldiers killed more than 40 people. Japanese Prime Minister Yukio Hatoyama's poll numbers make Gordon Brown look like Nelson Mandela.

What do all these countries have in common? They're free-market democracies in various stages of economic trouble. Where do we go to find a popular government? How about China?

Three decades of double-digit economic growth can buy a government plenty of popular goodwill. There are tens of thousands of protests in China each year, but very few of those target the Chinese Communist Party directly. Many of them appeal to the party for help with local problems.

It's impossible to know how China's government would poll with its people. The country remains a police state, and foreign pollsters aren't exactly welcome. But China is not North Korea or Cuba. Journalists and foreigners can interact with ordinary Chinese and exchange views with them both publicly and privately. The accumulated anecdotal evidence suggests that China's entrance onto the international political and economic stage serves as a point of great pride, and that many citizens credit their government with wise leadership. The bigger worry is that China's solid rebound from the global market meltdown is attracting admirers (and imitators) from across the developing world. China's state-driven form of capitalism has become a threat to the future of free markets.

Why worry? China's leaders have created that model to ensure that markets don't threaten their political power. They use state-owned oil companies to lock up the long-term energy supplies. They use other state-owned and privately owned but politically loyal companies to dominate other (global) industries. They pay for all this with help from a pair of sovereign wealth funds created from the extra cash China earns from exports to America, Europe and Japan.

If only part of the possible innovations mentioned will be put into place, instead of believing the false prophets of doom,[273] America and Europe may return strengthened from the crisis. In this sense, although I agree with D. N. Chorafas

---

This trend threatens free markets for several reasons.

First, China has welcomed foreign investment for years to gain exposure to the technological, management and marketing expertise in Western and Japanese companies. As Chinese companies find their footing, their government has less need of foreign help and an interest in promoting Chinese firms at the expense of outsiders.

Second, multinational companies now must compete throughout the developing world with powerful state-owned Chinese companies.

Third, China continues to build commercial relations with international outlaws such as Iran, Sudan and Burma, making it all but impossible to impose tough sanctions.

Finally, developing countries see anxiety in America, upheaval in Europe, paralysis in Japan, and growth and stability in China. Which is the more attractive model?

Many free-market democracies are preoccupied with yesterday's accidents and today's repairs. Too few have their eyes on trouble in the road ahead." I. Bremmer: As free-market democracies flail, China is the rare "success." In: USA Today, May 26, 2010, p. 11A. Cf. I. Bremmer: The End of the Free Market: Who Wins the War Between States and Corporations? Portfolio 2010. A similar thesis is held by A. Kaletsky: Capitalism 4.0, loc cit. Kaletsky asserts that there will be competition rather than convergence between the Chinese and Western models of politico-economic development and their underlying worldviews. Cf. A. Kaletsky: loc cit, p. 11, p. 257, pp. 304–313, pp. 315–317.

All this is especially relevant since China, as well as other former developing and under-industrialized countries, has developed into a fully industrialized nation due to annual increases of economic growth of 10–15%, thus not only bringing a remarkable amount of the world population out of poverty, but also bringing the overall global consumption of resources and climate to an exponential increase within only a couple of years. The consequentially even more necessary evolution of political systems and lifestyles toward sustainability is not limited to, but includes capital use and finance efficiency. Or as former UK prime minister Gordon Brown put it: "The big issue is that we have a globalization that has brought 4 billion people into the world economy, where 10 or 15 years ago there used to be only about a billion. So you have this enormous change that has taken place in the world economy, but we have a global financial system without an effective form of supervision (of this new situation)." G. Brown: "Sometimes It's a Crisis that Forces Change," in: Time Magazine, April 6, 2009, p. 21, http://www.time.com/time/world/article/0,8599,1887600,00.html.

It should have become clear from the pages of this booklet that some of those ideas that may be able to deal positively with the "troubles on the road ahead" and the "enormous change" of the global future at the interface of finance and democracy, that is, some of the ideas able to restore confidence into capitalism as a "good" societal force *in the democratic sense*, are social banking and social finance. This is due not least because they are as much cultural as economic forces. While a large part of the mainstream Western institutions and practices of capitalism seems to be culturally discredited by the crisis, thus contributing to the expansion of non-democratic, state-centered and authoritarian concepts of capitalism, which de facto undermine its very basic notions and thus ultimately threaten the world capitalistic system as such, social banking and social finance may promote the insight into the benefits of an even more democratic use of capital and money.

Thus, my claim is that social banking and social finance may be needed in the era of "contested modernities," in order to restore confidence to the democratic notion of capitalism by infusing ethics into it, and by pointing it out as freedom promoting and humanistic social endeavor.

[273]Cf. – as just one example among many – the prediction of US financial analyst Robert Prechter that the financial system will "melt down" by 2016. See J. Sommer: A Market Forecast That Says:

in other points, I disagree with him when he asserts that "the economic crisis and credit crunch . . . has seen the destruction of the American dream as well as of the dreams of the citizens of Britain and other Western nations."[274] I believe that these "dreams" – which in my view are not "dreams" in the strict sense, but rather deeply anchored hopes for a better future – are stronger and more enduring than the crisis and the pathologies of the "neoliberal" system since the 1990s that created it.

Could it be that St. Gallen University's Fredmund Malik's daring, if not venturous, thesis could become a reality: "This crisis could be the symptom of a change . . . The solutions may not come from the economy in the restricted sense we understood it until now, and they may not come from the governments. Rather, people might learn to help each other. I think we will experience a new humaneness. The new capital is knowledge, while money will in general lose in importance. The radical egoism of the past years will be in general socially outlawed. Instead, to facilitate meaning for people will gain in importance."[275]

As always, and as encouraging such predictions may be to many, I do not fully agree with Malik, because this statement sounds far too idealistic to me. Money will not lose its importance, at least not during our and the next generations' lifetimes. But money and the relationship with money, the handling of money, can be transformed one step after another; they can become more human. The task of the future is *not* to fight blindly against what many in the wake of the crisis (including Malik) claim to be the "wrong system." *Instead*, the task is to improve the existing system by selected smart steps, and thus to help it to further evolve. Knowledge will be as important for this task as the power of individual and collective moral intuition.

So what is my personal résumé? I do not believe that socially engaged people should be dreamers. And I have always cautioned against being too idealistic if it is about dealing with the often all too concrete "hard core" realities of money and finance. The laws and habits reigning on this field can be dealt with only by hardened souls.

Therefore, I believe that socially engaged people should have both feet planted firmly on the ground even more so than their "materialistic" counterparts on Wall Street (who seem to be so "realistic" at first glance, but, as the crisis revealed, were just playing around with artificial, in many cases, nonexistent numbers "in the clouds"). Idealists today have to be realists – otherwise, they might be lost right from the start.

As far as I can tell, quite a few idealistic and progressive people (many of them members of the rising international civil society) still haven't fully adapted to the

---

"Take Cover." In: The New York Times, July 3, 2010, http://www.nytimes.com/2010/07/04/your-money/04stra.html?pagewanted=1&_r=1 (retrieved July 3, 2010). Cf. AFP: U.S. Analyst predicts doom of financial markets (US-Analyst sagt Untergang der Finanzmärkte voraus), July 21, 2010.

[274] D. N. Chorafas: Capitalism Without Capital, loc cit.

[275] F. Malik: loc cit, Translation from German: Roland Benedikter.

"iron" requirements of the monetary business of our time, thus making it hard to change it "from within" – and I would not exclude myself here. Nevertheless, positive change seems to be possible in sight – not least because the attention to and the understanding of the international mechanisms of money and finance by a larger part of the public sphere is increasing.

This is paradoxically one of the "merits" of this last economic crisis. As it seems, many who appertain to the younger generations of today – mainly those in their high school, college, and university years – have a much deeper critical interest into the problems and chances of money and finance than any of their previous generations.[276] Many of you seem to feel today's productive ambivalence at the core of things in quite a "natural way": how much good can be done with money and finance and how much can be damaged by it.

As a result of countless talks with students and citizens, I know that many today seem to have a kind of "natural feeling" that money and finance is, in its essence, a *two-edged sword* that can be used for any purpose. But while my generation (born in the 1960s) had to acquire this insight by experience, the new generations seem to have already gained this perspective. And to my view, this is a very good reason for a positive outlook.

So what can I say at this present moment in time? What can we seriously hope for?

My answer is the following:

If it is plausible,

- that in the end it has always been and will always be "the power of ideas"[277] that decides the fate of economy, culture, and society,
- that any crisis has always two sides that are inextricably interwoven: A negative and a positive one, the negative one being loss, insecurity, and grief, the positive one being its overall outcome that in most cases functions according to the "CCC principle": "Crisis Creates Consciousness",

then there is some reasonable hope for progress.

As one wise guy said, "The future is already here – it's just not evenly distributed." (William F. Gibson)

[276] U. Reifner: Financial Literacy in Europe, Nomos Publishers, Hamburg 2006. Some rather mixed till obverse indications though are found under "Financial Literacy" at: http://en.wikipedia.org/wiki/Financial_literacy (retrieved March 11, 2010).

[277] P. Krugman: What to do. In: The New York Review of Books, Vol. 55, No. 20, December 18, 2008.

Social banking and social finance are here to distribute the future more evenly. Because we already know about how this future can take place in a positive manner[278,279]; and because this future belongs to all of us.

---

[278]As M. Sandel rightly states: Insight "... as an exercise in self-knowledge carries certain risks ... (It) teaches us, and unsettles us, by confronting us with what we already know ... There is an irony: the difficulty consists in ... (the fact) that thinking teaches you *what you already know*. It works by taking what we know from familiar unquestioned settings and making it strange. It estranges us from the familiar ... not by supplying new information, but by inviting and provoking a new way of seeing." M. Sandel: What's the right thing to do? In: http://www.justiceharvard.org/index.php?option=com_content&view=article&id=11&Itemid=8. I would conclude with saying that this is exactly what social banking and social finance do, or want to do, with the old views of mainstream banking and finance. Social banking wants to take the familiar look of banking and finance and turn it around, so that we can look at it in an alternative way. And it aspires to do that for the sake of the "overall wealth" of the social sphere of our age – and thus also for the cultural dimension (in the broad sense) of current (mainly Western, but increasingly also worldwide) "economy driven societies" as a whole.

[279]Obviously, while the principles to follow seem to be clear (and in large part indeed "already known" by many), there remain obviously a lot of questions to address with regard to the concrete everyday practices, which this booklet could only touch here and there. I hope that these questions will be further pursued by empirical research. Among the still open crucial questions on the future of social banking and social finance to address are:

1. As mentioned earlier, in-depth research is needed to determine how much of the overall shareholder capital of a social bank can be sustained over what timeframe by the core process of social banking alone (i.e., by relatively low return rates, while making donations and so on); what are the limits of the maximum amount under which conditions; and how a "mixed" model of investment would look like without losing touch with the founding principles of social banking. All these are particularly difficult and pressing questions at the moment given that social banks are growing so rapidly, and as a result might face problems when dealing with bigger amounts of capital that may force them to diversify their investment strategies. The question is: How far can such a diversification of investment go, for example by putting part of the money in mainstream investment models in order to co-finance the core business of social investment, without moving away from the principles of social banking and social finance? Or to put it in other words: How "pure" must the principles of social banking be applied to achieve the overall goals of social finance in the long run? Is there, as some state, a difference between the mid-term and the long-term perspective, corresponding to the difference – and complementarity – between tactics and strategy? And is it thus allowed, or even preferable, to use "impure" mid-term tactics to achieve the "pure" long-term goals? This recalls the principal questions examined in footnote 112.
2. We need more and better empirical and statistical research regarding the ratio of financial activity to real economic activity over the past several decades. This would indicate the degree of financialization of the real economy that has been taking place, and indicate if, and how, the growingly disembedded globalized financial business that followed the "sandglass principle" has in fact become a potential drain on society.
3. We need a more accurate and broader comparison of the returns of social funds and community development notes over the past several years in order to further empirically explore and differentiate the field of social banking and social finance.
4. Also, we need applied research toward a more flexible and enlarged concept of the time value of money. We need a concept that applies a broader, multilayered expectation of returns in the marketplace rather than to the impact of financial interest rates alone. In order to sustain such a concept, applied quantitative research is needed to determine how "side returns" such as a

14 Epilogue: Toward a "Financepeace?" The Integrative Mindset of Social Banking and Social Finance and Its Critics

During 2010, political and economic measures have been undertaken that have partly moved in the general direction indicated in this booklet, and which have improved the regulation of the financial system. Barack Obama's reform of the US financial system in July 2010 included the implementation of an early warning system to avoid further crises, better governmental control of the derivate market, and an extended transparency and liability request for hedge funds and mortgage traders. It also foresaw the creation of a financial consumer protection agency (called Consumer Financial Protection Bureau) in the framework of the US Federal Reserve bank, as well as participatory rights of shareholders in determining the income of bankers.[280] Also in July 2010, the German national parliament implemented laws that restrict parts of the derivative market and prohibit some practices of its very high-risk sector.[281] The G-20 summit (i.e., the summit of the 20 leading national economies of the world) in June 2010 in Toronto brought the (though non-committal) agreement that national debts must be reduced noticeably in a mid-term perspective. Its declared goal was also to halve yearly national budget deficits by 2013.[282] At the same time, important matters discussed in the aftermath of the crisis

---

clean and healthy environment, social cohesion, sustainability in the use of resources, a cultural climate of trust and responsibility, and a working "real economy" can be measured, and how they can be expressed through the terms and values of the international financial markets.

5. Finally, whereas mature "real economies" provide relatively little opportunity for "outperformance," which is what every professional investor is seeking, "sophisticated" Wall Street investors are disciplined by the marketplace to chase high returns that are outstanding, but not sustainable. As we have seen, this leads to all sorts of problems, including volatility, asset bubbles, and speculation (the so-called "Casino Capitalism"). It creates "fast money". Social finance is a conscious and explicit rebuttal of that practice. Social finance invests in the real economy. This is "slow money:" a totally different set of expectations, a different culture, and a different risk profile. A comparative empirical research about the different features, specific capacities, relative strengths and weaknesses, and about the performances of "fast money" versus "slow money" is needed, not least to seek possible complementary fields, where useful. This is because we cannot assume that in every case and in any circumstances "slow money" is unconditionally better than "fast money;" if this was the case without further in-depth empirical inquiry, a new ideology would have been born. Therefore, the question in the perspective of rational progress is where and under what conditions which approach works better, to what extent, and why.

280 D. Schepp: Obama Signs Financial Reform Legislation into Law. In: Daily Finance, 21 July 2010, http://www.dailyfinance.com/story/investing/obama-signs-financial-reform-legislation-into-law/19562674/ (retrieved August 20, 2010). See also T. Noyes: Reforms put Wall Street in its place. In: The Guardian London, May 21, 2010, http://www.guardian.co.uk/commentisfree/cifamerica/2010/may/21/obama-financial-reform-bill-wall-street (retrieved July 15, 2010).

281 AFP: German parliament votes for prohibition of "naked sales" (Deutscher Bundestag stimmt für Verbot von Leerverkäufen), July 2, 2010.

282 First German National Television ARD: G-20 agree upon deficit reduction (G-20 beschliessen Defizitabbau). In: ARDtext, June 27, 2010, http://www.ard-text.de/index.php?page=120, p. 120.

such as an international banking fee to create prevention funds against future financial crises and a fee on financial transactions directed foremost against high-risk speculative finance have so far failed to be implemented.[283]

Nevertheless, some of the implemented measures may be in the process of at least partially modifying the overall situation. However, the destiny of the further development of the financial sector remains uncertain. It is an open question if the reforms undertaken will in the end remain only minor modifications, or if they will be able to spark the beginnings of a change that is not only a maculature for (in essence) continuing as before, but of a "real" change in the habits and attitudes, and in the basic concepts of finance and its relationship to reality. It particularly remains to be seen if the relationship between the "real economy" and the two "waterheads" "above" and "below" it, i.e. the "derivative" and the "real estate" speculative markets, have been sustainably changed, or only partially and temporarily corrected.

In any case, the overall banking and finance system remains instable and thus endangered by new crises. There is some evidence that big banks are more endangered now than before the reforms to devolve their problems to the system, not least because 2 years after the collapse of Lehman Brothers in september 2008, some of the biggest global banks have further increased in size.[284] Despite all efforts, there is still not sufficient sustainability in sight. The facts that in the first half of 2010 alone, 86 more US banks have collapsed,[285] and that a "stress test" of European banks carried out by the European Federal reserve bank in cooperation with the Committee of European Banking Supervisors (CEBS) in July 2010 led to the failure of seven banks while producing mixed overall results, are certainly not reassuring signs for the emergence of a more balanced finance sector.[286] On the contrary, there are indications that many banks have returned to their former practices of intransparency, for example, by advising their customers as improperly as before the crisis.[287] Given that in August 2010 one of the international big players, Deutsche Bank, declared

[283]Second German National Television ZDF: Merkel fails with banking fee (Merkel blitzt mit Finanzsteuer ab). In: ZDF-Videotext, June 26, 2010, http://www.teletext.tv-on-line.cz/zdf-teletext/, p. 140. There are some signals though that the European Union could implement aspects of the financial transaction fee independently from the United States. Cf. Austrian National Broadcasting Network ORF: European Union may implement financial transaction fee alone (EU könnte Finanzsteuer im Alleingang beschliessen). In: ORF Teletext, June 28, 2010, p. 120.

[284]Handelsblatt Düsseldorf: "The big banks have become even more dangerous" ("Die großen Banken sind noch gefährlicher geworden."). In: Handelsblatt Düsseldorf, August 28, 2010, p. 1 (retrieved August 28, 2010).

[285]Austrian National Broadcasting Network ORF: USA: This year already 86 banks collapsed (USA: Dieses Jahr schon 86 Bankenpleiten). In: ORF Teletext, June 25, 2010, http://teletext.orf.at/, p. 160.

[286]Kleine Zeitung Bregenz: Seven European Banks Fail Stress Test (Sieben europäische Banken durch Stresstest durchgefallen). In: Kleine Zeitung, July 4, 2010, http://www.kleinezeitung.at/nachrichten/politik/oesterreich/2416135/sieben-europaeische-banken-durchgefallen.story (retrieved July 7, 2010).

[287]AFP: According to "Financetest," Banks Continue to Advise Their Customers Badly (Banken beraten ihre Kunden laut "Finanztest" weiter schlecht), July 20, 2010.

that it would avoid investments in renewable energies in the United States because of its "enduring sorrows" about "insufficient sustainability" (of the economic and financial background)[288], it seems improbable that things have been permanently fixed.

A similar ambivalence is currently visible in the theoretical sector, that is, in the sector of *thinking* about finance and economy in the aftermath of the crisis. On the one hand, there seems to be a relatively broad opening up of financial and economic theory for a new "interpretational pluralism" unprecedented in the past decades. Many leading thinkers around the world, not least the Nobel laureates and analysts assembled in the "Institute for New Economic Thinking" (INET) in New York, founded by disputed macro-investor George Soros, are asserting that unconventional, alternative, and "fundamentally" innovative thinking is no longer banned, but, on the contrary, is needed after the crisis, in order to provide fresh ideas and new practical inputs.[289] "It's ok to think in unconventional ways, because we need it," as *Financial Times* columnist John Kay put it.[290] Nobel Laureate Joseph E. Stiglitz observed that "the economics profession bears more than a little culpability. It provided the models that gave comfort to regulators that markets could be self-regulated, that they were efficient and self-correcting. Bad models lead to bad policy."[291] Given the problems of mainstream economic thinking to fully foresee the crisis and to identify the systemic distortion that caused it (which we have tried to condense in the model of the "sandglass principle"), a new theoretical pluralism has been introduced that can be regarded as a huge opportunity. If it is true that economic thought is "in need of a new paradigm. . ., of new ways of thinking about economics and finance from the bottom up,"[292] then the basic mindset of social banking and its viewpoints on issues of banking and finance may have their place within the concert of different voices that is currently marking the end of the one-sided dominance of neoliberal economic thinking characteristic of the past decades. The crisis has "forced change" (Gordon Brown) also in this (more theoretical) sense.

At the same time, part of the progressive financial theory seems latterly more busy to defend the basic pillars of capitalism against the uprising of radicals, rather than to seek realistic new solutions. In his history of the evolution of economic thought and his forecast on the coming years (called "Capitalism 4.0"), Anatole

---

[288]Handelsblatt Düsseldorf: Deutsche Bank dispises the USA (Deutsche Bank verschmäht die USA). In: Handelsblatt Düsseldorf, August 11, 2010, p. 1.

[289]Cf. the statements of I. Golding, Director of the James Martin 21 Century School, Oxford University, and other leading scholars in: The Institute for New Economic Thinking: The Role of the Economic Profession in the Crisis. In: The Institute for New Economic Thinking: http://ineteconomics.org.video/, 25 July 2010 (retrieved August 22, 2010).

[290]I. Kay, In: The Institute for New Economic Thinking: What Is the Institute for New Economic Thinking? In: http://ineteconomics.org.video/, July 20, 2010 (retrieved August 22, 2010).

[291]J. Stiglitz, In: The Institute for New Economic Thinking: Joseph Stiglitz in the Financial Times on the Need for New Economic Paradigms. In: http://ineteconomics.org/blog/joseph-stiglitz-need-new-economic-paradigm.html (retrieved August 22, 2010).

[292]J. Stiglitz: ibid.

Kaletsky has pointed out how the unhealthy monism of "neoliberal" ideology in the economic and financial sciences came to damage the common good, and thus ultimately the economy itself.[293] While defending capitalism resolutely against its critics, Kaletsky pleas for a new practice-orientation of economic science, including a serious rethinking of the regulatory role of the state,[294] demonized too often during the "neoliberal" years. I think that Kaletsky's plea particularly for a more pragmatic, realty-oriented economic and financial theory is valuable as it points toward strengthening and expanding the relationship between academic theory and the "real economy." However, it remains questionable if largely defensive endeavors in favor of capitalism as such may be able to provide the new impulses needed.

Finally, it seems that the crisis has proven that any analysis of the financial and economic system is *necessarily by its own nature* already an "ethical analysis" – that is, an analysis informed and influenced by "ethical" motives; as well as an analysis *about* contemporary ethics. Ethics are still widely underestimated, sometimes even belittled in the contemporary financial sciences. In contrast, Amativa Krishna Dutt and Charles K. Wilber point out: "Can economic analysis and policy formulation be free of ethical considerations? ... Ethics enters economics at the ground level, and trying to leave out ethics runs the risk of leading to bad economic analysis and bad policies... (This is because) all individuals who make decisions in the economy have ethical values, which affect their behavior and the nature of their interactions with others. (That's why) the evaluation of economic performance and policies requires a thorough analysis of ethics. This includes questions regarding the role of markets and the government, and the importance of efficiency, growth, and fairness."[295]

---

[293] A. Kaletsky: Capitalism 4.0. The Birth of a New Economy in the Aftermath of the Crisis, Bloomsbury Publishing, London 2010.

[294] This is an important issue mainly in the contemporary Anglo-American world, however less in Continental Europe where the Reagan–Thatcher belittlement of the state and the government role in economy and finance was never that accentuated as in the Anglo-American sphere. European governments played a much pronounced role in finance and economics also in the "neoliberal" constellation between the Reagan–Thatcher era (i.e., the 1980s) and the start of the crisis in 2007, for example, as welfare states or as public investors and regulators. This is one aspect that makes of Kaletsky's book an analysis mainly for capitalism in the English-speaking world, less for the realities of Europe (and for parts of the rest of the world, for example, Africa). Like most of the current English-speaking literature on the history of capitalism, on the crisis and the subsequent reforms, Kaletsky's book has the tendency to extend what may be perfectly right for the Anglo-American constellation of the past 40 years to the whole world, and to claim it to be "the" reality of contemporary capitalism as such. While I agree with many of his observations and theses, I do not think that is completely the case. Thus, also his future concept of a "capitalism 4.0" remains only partly relevant for Europe (and other parts of the world), even though it proclaims itself as a "global concept." At the same time, Kaletsky is paradoxically also right with his claim to cover "the whole world," since the Anglo-American system and practice of capitalism of the past decades indeed heavily influenced, if not dominated, the system of global capitalism.

[295] A. K. Dutt and C. K. Wilber: Economics and Ethics. An Introduction, Palgrave MacMillan, New York, NY 2010.

What thus became visible through the crisis is the renewal of a basic insight that stood at the very beginning of modern economic thought: that money and capital are something that is inseparable from ethics, that is, from the sphere of individual and collective moral intuition (e.g., German philosopher Georg Friedrich Wilhelm Hegel's "Sittlichkeit"). Or put into other words: That money and capital are ethical not by circumstances or in certain contexts, but by their very nature itself.[296] This new, old insight is a third important outcome of the crisis – its cultural heritage, so to say.

Summing up, there may be three main positive outcomes of the crisis of 2007–2010:

1. a spectrum of applied political and economic measures dedicated to improve the regulation of the international financial and economic system;
2. a reopening of financial and economic theory within the recognized academic sphere, now interested more than in the past decades in "alternative" and civil society approaches, as well as in a new pluralism of viewpoints;
3. a new recognition of the fundamental ties between economy and ethics.
   As we have pointed out in this volume, social banking and social finance may serve as motors and catalysts for all three of these trends – if they will be able to provide "best practice" examples accepted by the mainstream on how a different, more sustainable and ethical finance is feasible.

Overlooking the situation in the aftermath of the worst days of the crisis, many in civil society and in the social banking sector believe that some encouraging steps have been taken; but these may have been only first steps, and that much remains to do.[297] In particular, many think that, besides the three trends mentioned above, it will be as important to create new "mixed" initiatives between mainstream and alternative finance approaches based on a fundamentally integrative intention.

As we saw in chapter 4, there has been indeed a request in this regard from members of the European Parliament in June 2010. It was the call for a new "Financepeace" – following the example of "Greenpeace" – in the sense of the participation of civil society institutions in the regulatory reordering of the financial system.

But "Financepeace" means more than just regulation procedures and law issues – it is about the evolution of a mindset. If we want to enact common sense measures in an integrative instead of a confrontational manner, if we want them to be inclusive instead of creating new divisions and conflicts, then we have to conceive them in the sense of a "Financepeace" that means more than just a temporary public reconciliation.

---

[296] In this sense, money and capital are something "spiritual," as pointed out in Chapter 6.

[297] Obviously, this brings us back to the "deep ambivalence" of where are started. It really seems that there will be no future without deep ambivalences; and "evil be to him who evil thinks" ("honny soit qui mal y pense").

According to what we have seen in this booklet, "Financepeace" could be first of all a call to fix the distortions of the "sandglass principle". But in the broader sense, "Financepeace" would not only bring the banking and finance sector back to the real economy and to draw dry as much as necessary the "waterheads" "above" and "below" in order to stop their threatening of the real economy. It would also mean to create "peace" through symbolic actions involving the participation of broader parts of the civil society into financial policymaking,[298] and to increase the "financial literacy" of people in order to make them active parts of a reformed system.[299] Such an understanding would transcend the specific initiative of "Financepeace" launched by members of the European Parliament in June 2010.

Summing up, "Financepeace" could be a useful signal word[300] for all three timely trends mentioned:

1. to enact regulatory measures in a participatory way;
2. to implement and recognize an "interpretational pluralism" of integrative traits;
3. to recognize that ethics, economy and finance are not separated fields, but parts of one and the same procedure.

Social banking and social finance are about a "Financepeace," because they are concerned with these three dimensions. Their mindset is about establishing an ethical, "balanced" and "integrative" viewpoint. "Balanced" means not to fall into extremes in judgments. "Integrative" means not to prefer one's own ideology over others, but rather to search for the relative legitimity of every approach and then to try to connect them, as far as possible, into a "third," pragmatic standpoint that is much more tied to concrete situations and contexts and their specific, timely needs than to the alleged "timeless" truth of any ideology.

In this sense, social banking and social finance are about a mindset that tries to bridge leftist and rightist approaches in order to "read" reality, and then to change this reality to the better. The resulting mindset tries to validate community like the leftists, but at the same time believes in the value of the individual, like the neoliberals.

That may be more difficult to simply cling to an ideology; but it is appropriate to the inspiration of our time. In fact, the civil society is itself a "third way" beyond left and right – at least of how it conceives itself. What the civil society will need

---

[298] In this sense, Enlightenment today also means: enlightenment "from below," i.e., through the civil society and its applied experiences, not only "from above," i.e., through the elites – even if their exceptional role is certainly not belittled by more participation. Cf. R. Benedikter: Enlightenment. In: M. Juergensmeyer et al. (eds.): The SAGE Encyclopedia of Global Studies, SAGE, London 2011 (forthcoming), and R. Benedikter: Third Way Movements, ibid.

[299] As a result of the crisis though, many Europeans feel more than ever insecure and financially illiterate. Cf. AFP: Many Germans believe they are financially illiterate (Viele Deutsche halten sich in Finanzfragen für unwissend), July 19, 2010.

[300] If properly discerned from private uses of this word for (in some cases rather dubious) entrepreneurial purposes, like found on the internet, and in counselling advertisements.

for the coming years is a more explicit cultural matrix (in the form of an integrative cultural philosophy, or an overarching "paradigm"). That is what is still missing, and the readers of this volume are certainly most welcome to help to elaborate it – since it will be the "third way" mindset that may lead us out of the insensate polarization between left and right, which has returned to threaten the future of globalization (especially in the form of a new dialectics between the global North and South).[301]

In this sense, "Financepeace" is eventually not only about the participation of civil society in the political and economical efforts to reorder the international financial system, or about confining the influence of lobbyists on decision-making processes, or about bringing it nearer to democratic discussion and decision making with the citizen. It is – in my opinion at least to the same extent – also about creating a "peace" between the different ideologies involved in the pillars, as well as in the perspectives of the financial system.

What we have seen in this volume is one basic motive: That social banking and social finance are about a new location of capitalism in modern, as well as in modernizing, societies. This is the chance, but at the same time also the inherent difficulty – and the still elevated vulnerability – that social banking both as a mind-set and as a practice must deal with. This is the main motive throughout the history of social banking and social finance: to locate itself in a "third" position outside the left–right polarization. This position is neither Marxist nor neoliberal; it appreciates capitalism, but searches for new, more sustainable forms of it.[302] Since the time of Rudolf Steiner, Silvio Gesell and the social efforts of benefactors and the churches, social banks have always tried to express and establish such a third position. In this, social banking is an integral part of the present "third way" movements. If it is plausible, as Serge J. Van Steenkiste holds with Anatole Kaletsky, that in the coming years "experimentation and pragmatism will color public policy, economics, and business strategy, even it means uncertainty, ambiguity, and inconsistency,"[303,304] then social banking may serve as one promising approach (among others) within this experimentation.

But exactly this is also the reason why social banking may be attacked from the two sides:

1. By the remnants of the "leftists" (Marxist), and
2. by the remnants of the "rightist" (Neoliberals)

alike.

---

[301] Cf. R. Benedikter: Third Way Movements, loc cit.

[302] Or as Ernst Ulrich von Weizsäcker has convincingly pointed out, current "leftist" and "rightist" ideologies and their respective lifestyles have not necessarily to be abolished, but to be evolved. See: E. U. v. Weizsäcker et al.: Factor Five: Transforming the Global Economy, Earthscan Publishers, London 2010.

[303] S. J. Van Steenkiste: Review of A. Kaletsky, Capitalism 4.0, In: http://www.amazon.com/Capitalism-4-0-Economy-Aftermath-Crisis/dp/1586488716/ref=sr_1_1?ie=UTF8&qid=1290913152&sr=8-1.

[304] Cf. A. Kaletsky: loc cit, pp. 8–9, 26 ff., 306 ff.

We thus should be conscious of the fact that it is exactly the "intermediate" self-location of social banking and social finance that indeed offers different points of attack. But these attacks and the resulting dialectics will also increase the reception of social banking and social finance in the public sphere: the sphere that German social philosopher Jürgen Habermas called "the sphere of public reason." If this is the case, social banking may become an even more active part of the public sphere. And that in the end may be progress for everybody involved.

Social banking is in its present form certainly still less oriented toward those who "want to predict the future," but rather to those "who make it happen" (Antoine de Saint Exupéry). Nevertheless, with the foundation of new research and teaching institutes at universities around the globe, it is also becoming an academic and scientific approach in its own right.

Thus, in pondering where the future of social banking itself lies, I plea for the balanced combination of both: "predicting the future" (i.e., participating more intensely in public and scientific discourse) and "making the future happen" (i.e., continuing to build upon the goal of financially "reaching out to one sixth of the world's population by 2020"). Overall, regarding the (sometimes delicate) balance between those two centers of activity, I am with Italian philosopher Giovanni Sartori who says:

"The fact is that human beings don't move to change their attitudes and habits 'coldly,' i.e., guided exclusively by pure reason, or thought. Human beings set themselves in motion if there is some kind of lively 'warmth,' i.e., if they are moved by passion, or by fear (including the passion and fear for money, and power). And so science must consider this, and act accordingly. It must try to predict a course, a trend, but not the exact moment, when it will be possible to definitely realize it."[305]

At the same time, I agree with American-European Nobel Laureate Mario R. Capecchi who says:

"Science (is) a series of circles: the smallest circle is the one in which everyone is doing the same thing. As you move farther out, fewer people are willing to go there, but you're charting new areas. Go too far, step out of bounds, and you're in science fiction. So you have to be careful. But you want to be as close to the edge as possible."[306]

What Sartori and Capecchi are outlining may be good approaches for the future of social banking and social finance as well. Because social banking and social finance rely on dedication and passion, and they should identify the new and work toward it, but not pay too much attention to when it may be possible to "realize" it "definitely." And because social banking and social finance are reform-oriented social endeavors "at the edge" of the current financial system, they have enormous chances of doing something innovative; but at the same time, they have to be careful

---

[305] G. Sartori: The Ecological Collapse. The Politics of the Ostrich (Il collasso ecologico. La politica dello struzzo). In: Il Corriere della Sera Milan, 15 agosto 2010, p. 1, http://www.corriere.it/editoriali/10_agosto_15/sartori-collasso-ecologico_93258b4c-a83b-11df-94a2-00144f02aabe.shtml (retrieved August 15, 2010).

[306] M. R. Capecchi, In: N. Gibbs: The Nobel Warrior. In: Time Magazine, October 12, 2007, http://www.time.com/time/magazine/article/0,9171,1670524,00.html (retrieved August 21, 2010).

to not "step out of bounds," but to take one step after the next. I am confident that the discussion about what is feasible, what it means to be "charting new areas," and what is "out of bounds," which is going to dominate the coming years *within* the social banking and social finance sector, can be of benefit to the mainstream financial and economic system as well.

In the end, the overall endeavor that lies before us is certainly about finance, economics and thought in their relationship with practice; but it is without doubt also more than that. It includes the challenge to change a mindset, and to establish new social ethics. The respective efforts might be still slow, partial, and incomplete, but they have started. The financial and economic crisis of 2007–2010 has ignited and accelerated the insight that change cannot be sustainable if carried out on the surface, but that it must reach the deeper convictions to be effective. It ultimately includes that we "must change our lives."[307] Or as philosopher Peter Sloterdijk (maybe a little bit too emphatically) puts it: "...the cathartic basic thought of (the crisis and its effects) is clear: The 'old human being' must hush, before the new one can come into existence. At the beginning of everything is an ethical decision, and individual decision within one's will. This decision separates those, who believe we should continue as hitherto from those, who want to exit the old life in order to give birth to a new one. The call for the new is intrinsic in today's circumstances. The atmosphere is vibrating from its appeal. Everybody seems to hear this appeal. The state of the world itself transmits the message."[308]

Social banking and social finance are attempts to start with the decision "to give birth to the new" – among other attempts in the plurifold field of reform, transition, and innovation of our time.

Further Readings

F. De Clerck: Ethical Banking. In: L. Zsolnai, Z. Boda and L. Fekete (eds.): Ethical Prospects. Economy, Society and Environment, Springer 2009.

R. Douthwaite: The Ecology of Money, Green Books, Dartington 2008.

"Ethical Banking:" In: http://en.wikipedia.org/wiki/Ethical_banking (retrieved March 3, 2010).

"Financial Crisis of 2007–2010." In: http://en.wikipedia.org/wiki/Financial_crisis_of_2007%E2%80%932010 (retrieved March 5, 2010).

Institute for Social Banking Bochum, Germany: http://www.social-banking.org/en/news/ (retrieved December 10, 2010).

Institute for Social Banking Paper Series: http://www.social-banking.org/en/researchteaching/isb-paper-series/ (retrieved December 10, 2010).

Institute for Social Banking recommended reading list on the future of social banking and social finance: http://www.social-banking.org/fileadmin/isb/file/ISBLiteratureResources.pdf (retrieved December 10, 2010).

A. Marshall and U. Masen: Banking on Trees. In: Time Magazine, November 30, 2009, pp. 38–43.

C. Scheire and S. De Maertelaere: Banking to make a difference. A preliminary research paper on the business models of the founding member banks of the Global Alliance for Banking on

[307] P. Sloterdijk: Du musst Dein Leben ändern: Über Anthropotechnik (You must change your life: About Anthropotechnology). Frankfurt am Main 2009. Translation: Roland Benedikter.

[308] P. Sloterdijk, In: E. Karcher: loc cit. Translation: Roland Benedikter.

Values. Artevelde University College Gent, in cooperation with the Global Alliance for Banking on Values, supported by the European Social Fund, Artevelde Hogeschool Gent, June 2009.

The United Nations Decade "Education for Sustainable Development" 2005–2014: http://www.unesco.org/en/esd/ (retrieved December 1, 2010).

V. Vandelmeulebroucke, K. Beck and K. Käufer (eds.): Networking Social Finance. Edited by the International Association of Investors in the Social Economy INAISE, Brussels, June 2010, www.inaise.org.

O. Weber and S. Remer (eds.): Social Banks and the Future of Sustainable Finance. Routledge International Studies in Money and Finance, London 2011 (forthcoming).

About the Author

Roland Benedikter, Dott. lett. (Comparative Cultures and Literatures), Dr. phil. (Sociology), Dr. phil. (Education), Dr. rer. pol. (Political Sciences), born in 1965, serves as European Foundation Fellow 2009–2013, in residence at the Orfalea Center for Global and International Studies of the University of California at Santa Barbara with duties as the European Foundations' Research Professor of Sociology and as Visiting Scholar/Research Affiliate at The Europe Center, Stanford University. Since 2006, he serves as the Founding External Advisor and Founding External Examiner of the "European Integrated Masters Program (EIMP) in Social Banking and Social Finance" at the University of Plymouth, UK, which is a project of the "UNESCO Decade: Education for Sustainable Development 2005–2014," and has been awarded the Special Prize of the Continuing Education Innovation Awards 2010 by the German Federal Institute for Vocational Education Bonn. Since 2007, he serves as a lecturer on global developments and future trends at the Institute for Social Banking Bochum, Germany.

In the past 20 years, Benedikter has been a research affiliate and visiting professor at leading universities in the United States, the United Kingdom, Australia, Germany, Switzerland, Austria, Italy, Bulgaria, Turkey, and Peru. Institutions include Columbia University, New York; Georgetown University, Washington DC; Villanova University, Philadelphia, RMIT University Melbourne; Northampton University; Vienna University; Clemens Ohridski University Sofia; Mersin University; and Universidad Catholica del Peru, Lima. He is associated with the Potomac Institute for Policy Studies Arlington, Virginia, and with various other think tanks in the United States and in Europe, and is listed as an expert for social science programs for the European Union and the Italian government.

Benedikter has published 12 books and more than 80 peer-reviewed articles, including *Economy and Culture in Dialogue* (Bolzano 1996) and the sevenfold book series *Postmaterialism: The Second Generation* in Vienna's Passagen Verlag (2001–2005; Volume 1: Introduction into Contemporary Postmaterialist Thinking, Volume 2: The Human Being in the Economic Civilization, Volume 3: Labour, Volume 4: Nature and Environment, Volume 5: Capital, Volume 6: Globalization, Volume 7: Perspectives of Contemporary Postmaterialist Thinking). He has co-authored Ernst Ulrich von Weizsäcker's "Report to the Club of Rome" 2003: "Limits to Privatization. How to Avoid Too Much of a Good Thing" (English 2005, German

R. Benedikter, *Social Banking and Social Finance*, SpringerBriefs in Business,
DOI 10.1007/978-1-4419-7774-8, © Roland Benedikter 2011

2006, Chinese 2007). His writings have been translated into German, Italian, French, Spanish, Russian, Chinese, Bulgarian, Hungarian, Slovenian, Turkish, and Macedonian.

Authorized homepages: http://en.wikipedia.org/wiki/Roland_Benedikter and http://europe.stanford.edu/people/rolandbenedikter/.

Contact: rben@stanford.edu and r.benedikter@orfaleacenter.ucsb.edu.

Critical Acclaim for This Publication

"This volume provides a description of social banking and social finance, their background in the history of ideas and their importance within the current globalized economy. It is not only an excellent didactical introduction, but also an entertaining and at the same time scientifically sound and differentiated explanation, which to my knowledge is so far unparalleled in English-speaking academia. I believe that the insights of this volume can have a progressive impact on the thinking about money and finance of the new generations, as well as the broader public in the United States and in Europe. I therefore consider this volume to be one step (among the many necessary) toward a realistic and sober rethinking of capitalism. Even if it is just a brief text and thus a small step, it is an important one. Because, as German philosopher Friedrich Nietzsche said, every long voyage starts with a brief first step. And this step, as compressed, simple and surprising as it may sometimes seem, may prove to be inspiring for those which come afterwards. I think that Benedikter's volume is a valid response to the profound challenges arisen with the economic and financial crisis of 2007–2010. The solutions and perspectives it proposes are useful tools to help us to avoid further crises."

Professor Dr. Hans Christoph Binswanger, Chair Emeritus of National Economics, University St. Gallen, Switzerland, and former director of the Swiss Research Association on National Economics, Zürich

"The recent crisis has shown that the time for more differentiated and just approaches to money and finance is ripe. I hope that with this outstanding didactical introduction oriented not primarily toward specialists, but to students and teachers, as well as to the broad public, the discussion about how we can move forward in making better use of money and finance will gain further momentum. This volume is an important contribution to broadening the financial literacy of our time."

Professor Dr. Udo Reifner, Department for Economics and Social Science, Hamburg University

"This is a clear and intense text. It has the advantage of summoning up some of the most important questions of current economics and finance in a short, easily understandable and well-structured way. The reader is on the one hand provided insight into the main issues of today's debate about the future of capitalism. On the other hand, she and he are informed about the ongoing (r)evolution in the banking and finance sector. The present change goes beyond the traditional reductionisms of the mainstream banking and finance sector. It starts to demonstrate how the creation of economic value on the one hand and a sustainable social and environmental development on the other hand can be integrated into one and the same approach. The international educational sector has to be grateful for this volume."

Professor Dr. Leonardo Becchetti, Department of Economics, Università Roma II "Tor Vergata," Italy

"One of the first soundly scientific publications of its kind in English, this volume provides a complete overview over the contemporary field of social banking and social finance. Written in a short and easily understandable manner, it explains the history, the philosophy, the current state, and the perspectives of social banking and social finance in the United States and in Europe. This volume is an indispensable first entry for everybody who wants to know how we can deal with money in a better, sustainable way."

Professor Dr. Ernst Ulrich von Weizsäcker, dean emeritus, Bren School of Environmental Science and Management, University of California at Santa Barbara, former policy director of the United Nations, Centre for Science and Technology for Development New York City, member of the Club of Rome, ordinary commissioner of the World Commission on the Social Dimensions of Globalization

"Without need of prior knowledge, this volume is the ideal introduction to social banking and social finance for students and teachers. As a result of the economic crisis of 2007–2010, the request for a better handling of money and finance has increased on a global level. Social banking and social finance are answers that while not everybody must agree with them, they are worth to be known by everybody who wants to join the discussion on a well founded basis."

Professor Hanns-Fred Rathenow, director of the Institute of Social Sciences and Education in History and Politics, head of the Center for Global Education and International Cooperation, The Technical University of Berlin

"Social banking is a field of civil society engagement that has surfaced to international attention during the most recent financial crisis. This volume is an excellent introduction from a contemporary viewpoint. It departs from outlining the main traits of the economic crisis of 2007–2010, but its insights and teachings are not limited to it. This volume uses the crisis just as a starting point to explain how the financial system can move forward toward a more rational constellation of balance and inclusion. It is as unique as it is valuable."

Professor Dr. James Giordano, The Oxford Uehiro Centre for Practical Ethics, Oxford University, director of Academic Programs of The Potomac Institute for Policy Studies Arlington, Virginia

"I appreciate particularly the interdisciplinary and multilayered approach of this volume. It is one of the first English publications that transcends the limits of reducing social banking and social finance to 'developmental aid' for the so-called 'developing world,' or to simply identify it with approaches like 'helping the poor', like it has been done too often in the past. Instead, as this volume shows, social banking and social finance are more: They are about rationally and soberly *innovating* the system of capitalism, but without *revolutionizing* it. That is because social banks consider capitalism as a basic social good of modernity, that in the aftermath of the crisis has to be transformed into a 'better' capitalism which serves the greater society instead of benefiting just a few. The whole argumentation of this volume is about creating a broader range of options for the average bank customer in the United States and Europe and to make the use of capital more 'humane,' by serving the specific needs of the 'real economy' instead of abstract speculation. This volume, although short and concise, gives a quite realistic picture of the situation and its perspectives. The author finds the right balance between simplification, precision, and vision."

Professor Dr. Michael Opielka, Department of Social Welfare and Social Politics, The University of Applied Sciences Jena, Germany